Understanding the economy
Second edition

Andrew Dunnett

By the same author

Understanding the market

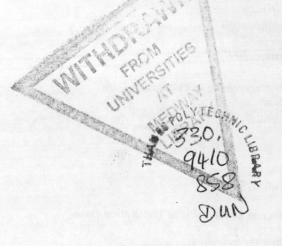

Longman
London and New York

Longman Group UK Limited
Longman House
Burnt Mill, Harlow
Essex CM20 2JE, England
and Associated companies throughout the world

*Published in the United States of America
by Longman Inc., New York*

First published 1982
Second impression 1984
Second edition 1987
Fourth impression 1991

British Library Cataloguing in Publication Data
Dunnett, Andrew
 Understanding the economy – 2nd ed.
 1. Great Britain – Economic conditions –
 1945–
 I. Title
 330.941′0858   HC256.6
ISBN 0-582-44652-X

Library of Congress Cataloguing in Publication Data
Dunnett, Andrew, 1948–
 Understanding the economy.

 Includes index
 1. Economics. 2. Great Britain – Economic conditions –
1945–   . I. Title.
HB171.5.D84   1987   330   86–7197
ISBN 0-582-44652-X

Set in 10/11pt Times Roman Linotron 202

Printed in Malaysia
by Chee Leong Press Sdn. Bhd.,
Ipoh, Perak Darul Ridzuan

Contents

Chapter 5 The determinants of aggregate demand – monetarist interpretation

Chapter 6 Cost inflation

Chapter 7 International aspects of inflation

Chapter 8 Exchange rates, competitiveness and trade flows

Chapter 9 The labour market: unemployment

Preface

This book is directed towards first year students doing economics either as a single discipline or as part of a broader social science degree (such as business studies); at those students taking professional examinations (for example, in accountancy); and at students of A-level economics. My experience with students such as these over several years made me increasingly convinced that no suitable text existed, and indeed none has subsequently appeared. The problem with existing texts is that they are either too long-winded and weighty so that students miss the wood for the trees or too lightweight and descriptive with no strong analytical foundation. The applied texts which have appeared in recent years, though useful as supplementary texts, have no unifying structure running through them.

This book differs first in approach. It is non-mathematical since experience with my students has taught me that the effort involved in understanding the mathematics often stands in the way of an appreciation of the *economic* analysis. However, I take issue with those of my colleagues who equate the use of mathematical techniques with analytical rigour. The two never have been equivalent and I believe that this text is highly analytical, rather than descriptive, even though the mathematical techniques it uses are of the most rudimentary kind.

Second, the methodological approach of this book differs from that of existing texts, which tend to be naively empiricist, assuming that we can either prove or disprove a particular theory simply by looking at the data. Moreover, these texts tend to be complacent, in as much as they give the impression that economists understand the way the economy works – whereas, in fact, we do not. I have tried to integrate within this text a more sophisticated methodological position which should allow students to realize that economic theories are no more than *theories*. I have also tried to give students an appreciation of how these theories and ideas came to be developed, so that they can place them in their historical and political perspective.

Though I have pointed out the shortcomings of empiricism, I have, however, tried to encourage students to confront their theories and prejudices with empirical data and to this end the book contains a fair amount of statistical material – enough, I hope, to whet the reader's appetite to seek out more for himself.

In addition to the difference in approach, the coverage of this book differs markedly from existing texts.

I place considerable emphasis on the open nature of the economy. This reflects my view that a book about the workings of a macroeconomy where one-third of output is exported (as it is in Britain) should not be the same as a book about an economy where less than 10 per cent is exported (as it is in the USA). Hence, I discuss the determination of the exchange rate and purchasing power parities in depth, and devote a chapter to international aspects of inflation.

There is a whole chapter devoted to economic growth and the post-war problems of the UK economy. I have spent some time discussing the current debates on, for example, Bacon and Eltis's contention that the public sector is too large, the de-industrialization debate, and the Cambridge Economic Policy Group's case for import controls.

I have also included a section on the Limits to Growth (which is only rarely included in macrotexts) and the recent work of Hirsch on the social limits to growth, which I think is quite important in establishing a perspective.

A whole chapter is devoted to an explanation of the relationship between the government's budget position, its borrowing requirement and the impact that this therefore has on the growth of the money supply and interest rates. This leads to a discussion of the merits of higher (or lower) public spending.

I have included a section on forecasting models. To some extent, this replaces the discussion of IS/LM analysis often found in macrotexts and is certainly easier to understand and probably of greater practical significance.

The labour market is discussed in rather more detail than one would normally expect to find in macrotexts. This reflects my view that it is a key area not just because of the inflationary forces therein but also because it is in the analysis of the labour market that the crucial differences between monetarists and Keynesians can best be seen.

Two related themes run through the book, helping to form a unified structure from the individual chapters. The first of these themes is to do with how prices are determined and therefore how inflation is caused (and by implication how it can be controlled). The second theme is the debate between the Keynesians and the monetarists and all that this entails, both in its economic and political aspects.

The over-riding consideration in deciding upon the form that the book should take was the desire to give students a framework within which to analyse important contemporary policy issues. Whether I have been successful in this is something which the reader must judge for himself.

I would like to thank those of my colleagues who have given me help and support during that time at Ealing when this book was in preparation; in particular, John Crowley, Philip Wyatt, Carol Rees and David Glen. My thanks are due also to my wife, Jenefer, who typed the first draft of the book and to Gillian Hodges, who typed the final draft. My students did not help at all and yet somehow the whole exercise would have been pointless without them.

Preface to the second edition

The basic philosophy of the second edition remains the same as the first. Recent economic events and developments in the discipline itself have only tended to reinforce my view about the importance and relevance of the material covered. There are however two wholly new chapters in the second edition.

The first of these chapters is an extended treatment of the labour market. Perhaps the most contentious and important debate in economics at the present time centres around the proposition (supported by Mrs Thatcher's Conservative Government) that the level of unemployment cannot be reduced significantly by expansionary policies. This proposition rests upon a particular interpretation of the labour market which is explained and appraised in greater detail than was done in the first edition. The role which rational expectations plays in the monetarist platform is also explained.

The second of the new chapters provides an extended coverage of the exchange rate, trade flows and competitiveness. There have been massive swings in exchange rates since 1980 and this new chapter is designed to help the reader interpret the significance of these for domestic output and employment and to appraise the case for a more positive policy towards the exchange rate. Moreover, for any small open economy such as the UK it is now widely believed by macroeconomists that the trade sector 'drives the whole model'. Many foresee a situation in the latter half of the 1980s in which the UK economy again becomes balance-of-payments constrained, a condition for which neither depreciation nor protectionism provides an effective remedy.

The section on the run-down of the manufacturing sector has been much extended. More extensive use has been made of empirical material in other chapters. In addition, each chapter is now followed by questions designed both to test the reader's understanding of what he has read and to extend this understanding. Teachers can use these questions in whatever way they see fit but I would suggest they form the basis for class discussion, since it was in this context that many of them were originally used as part of my teaching at Ealing. It should be pointed out that many of the questions do not necessarily have a 'right' or a 'wrong' answer. Therein lies their potential as a stimulus to class discussion.

As before my thanks are due to friends and colleagues at Ealing College of Higher Education and at the National Institute for Economic and Social Research where I spent the year 1985–86. Special thanks to those who helped make NIESR nicer.

Acknowledgements

We are grateful to the following for permission to reproduce copyright material:

Bank of England for table 5.1; The Economist Newspaper Ltd for tables 2.1, 2.2; the Controller of Her Majesty's Stationery Office for figs 10.1, 10.2, 13.1 and tables 3.2, 3.3, 6.1, 9.1, 10.5, 10.6, 10.7, 10.8; Lloyds Bank plc for table 10.4; Manchester University Press for table 6.2; National Institute of Economic and Social Research for tables 13.4, 13.5; Organisation for Economic Co-operation and Development for fig 3.1.

Chapter 1
Models of the economy

1.1 A simple model of the macroeconomy

The purpose of this chapter is to present the reader with a number of models of the workings of the economy. For illustrative purposes, we shall first choose to talk about a desert island economy – one which is not subject to any outside influences. Suppose that there are just three people living on this island – doubtless the sole survivors from the shipwreck which left them stranded on this remote shore – and suppose further that each of these three individuals specializes in producing that in which he is most skilled. Individual A specializes in producing food, B specializes in making clothes and C specializes in making and repairing the crude dwellings in which they live. None of these three individuals is therefore self-sufficient, since each requires food, clothing and shelter to live, but by specializing and exchanging their surpluses, each of them is able to enjoy higher levels of consumption of food, clothing and shelter than if each person produced everything for himself. This island economy therefore possesses some of the features of a real world economy – people on the island act as individual economic units and there is specialization and exchange. There is one important feature which we have not mentioned, however. In the real world, exchange takes place by means of transactions involving the use of an acceptable medium of exchange, usually money. In the absence of any such medium of exchange, the alternative is to engage in barter transactions, that is, to swap goods for goods rather than goods for money. Let us make the rather unlikely assumption that on our desert island there is an acceptable medium of exchange and that therefore the inhabitants decide to engage in monetary transactions rather than in barter. Let us assume that the medium of exchange they choose is coins, no doubt salvaged from the shipwreck, and that the value of coins they managed to salvage totals £10. This therefore represents the money supply in our desert-island economy.

Let us further assume that the following chain of events takes place over a given period of time, say one month. Individual A, who initially owns the £10, uses it to buy clothes from B. B, in turn, uses his income of £10 to pay C to repair his hut, and C, in turn, spends his income in buying food which A has produced. These transactions are illustrated diagrammatically in Fig. 1.1. We could therefore say that, in the month in question, total expenditure in our island economy was £30. This is equal to the total income of the three individuals and it is also equal to the value of the goods and services produced in the economy. Thus we could say, total expenditure = total income = value of total output of goods and services.

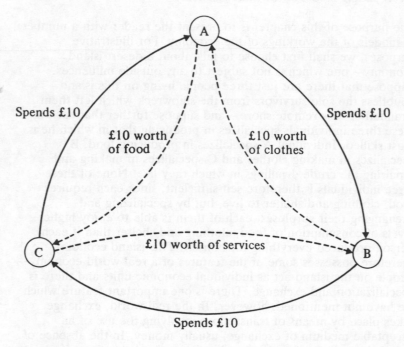

Fig. 1.1

What is true for our desert island economy is not necessarily true for our real world economy, but the equality between expenditure, income and output should be regarded by the student at this stage as something which is generally true.

It is important to note that total expenditure at £30 per month is financed by a money supply of only £10. The relationship between the flow of expenditure and the stock of money is given by the velocity of circulation of money. In our example this velocity is three times per month, that is, each pound changes hands three times in every month. In a year, therefore, money can be expected to change hands 3 × 12 = 36 times, and we would therefore say that the velocity of circulation is thirty-six times per year.

If the events of this one month are repeated throughout the rest of the year, total expenditure will be 12 × £30 or £360 per year and this will be equal to total income and the annual value of output (or total product as it is usually known). If we consider our three individuals as comprising the whole of the national economy then we can say that, national expenditure = national income = national product = £360 per year.

Per capita income is therefore £120 per year, but this unfortunately tells us nothing about the standard of living of our three individuals. That is, we cannot say from this information how much food, clothing and shelter the inhabitants are able to consume. We know the value of total output but we do not know what volume of goods and services this represents. To emphasize this point, consider what would happen on our desert island if the stock of money were doubled to £20. If we assume that the velocity of circulation remained unchanged at 36 times per year, then the value of national product would be £720 per year. This may represent a real increase in the value of goods and services produced and sold, or it may simply reflect a fall in the value of money, such that the purchasing power of each pound is only half what it was previously. Thus we should be careful to distinguish between increases in the real value of national output and increases in the money value of national output.

In many ways our desert island economy is not a particularly realistic model of a real economy. It has no contact with other islands, so there is no foreign trade. There is also no government on the island so there is no such thing as taxation or public spending. A more subtle point, however, is that the standard of living of the inhabitants may well be much higher than our estimates of national product would have us believe. That is because if a statistician were preparing national income accounts for our island he would include only those goods and services which were the subject of money transactions. He would thus exclude all the food which A produced and consumed himself, all the clothes which B produced and consumed himself, and the value of all the work which C did on his own shelter. If all of the individuals on the island were self-sufficient and did not indulge in money trade with their fellows then conventional methods of measuring national output would value it at zero. This failure to take account of 'home production' (that is, the production of goods for one's own consumption) also occurs in real economies, but it is likely to be a more serious shortcoming in the national accounts of our desert island.

3

1.2 A model of production and consumption

Our second model of the macroeconomy contains not three individuals but two *sectors*, a household sector (H) and a firm sector (F). In order to simplify matters initially, we will make the following assumptions:

 (i) The economy is 'closed', that is, there are no imports or exports in our model.
 (ii) Households spend all their income. They spend it, of course, on the output of the firm sector.
(iii) The firm sector is able to sell all that it produces. That is, firms do not build up stocks or run down stocks.
(iv) The firm sector is ultimately owned by the household sector, because all the paid up share capital of firms is held by households.

The model, which is illustrated in Fig. 1.2, has a consumption side to it and a production side. The right-hand side illustrates the consumption aspect, where we have assumed that the flow of

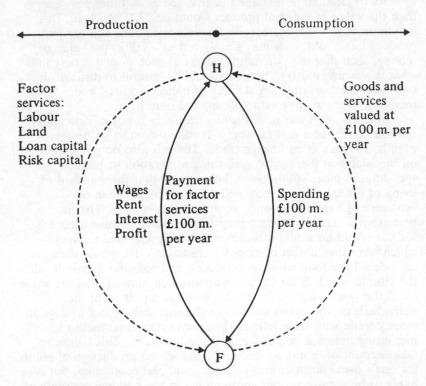

Fig. 1.2

expenditure by households on purchasing goods and services produced by the firm sector is, say, £100 m. per year. Thus there is a flow of spending represented by the solid line and a corresponding flow of goods and services represented by the dotted line. This much is familiar to us from our previous desert island example.

The left-hand side of the model illustrates its production aspect. In our example, the value of goods and services produced and sold by the firm sector is £100 m. per year. To produce this, firms must hire factors of production – labour, capital, land and so on – the value of which is also £100 m. This is because of assumption (iv) that we made, that the income of the firm sector (£100 m. per year) is all distributed in the form of wages, rent, interest and profit. Wages and salaries are payment for labour services. Rent is a payment to the owners of land. Interest payments are a return to loan capital and profits represent the return to risk capital. The firm sector, then, uses factor inputs valued at £100 m. to produce output valued at £100 m. At the end of the day it is left with nothing (that is, we assume that the firm does not retain any profits, it distributes them all to shareholders).

In our desert island economy, we noted that total spending, total income and the value of total output were all equal. Here, too, we see that total spending, total income and the value of goods and services produced are all £100 m. per year. This model illustrates the way in which spending flows around the economy in a circular fashion from households to firms as payment for goods and services and back again to households as payment for factor services. No matter where we measure this flow, the size of the flow will be the same.

1.3 Equilibrium in the circular flow of income

Provided the four assumptions that we made in section 1.2 are satisfied, the circular flow of income will settle down at a particular level and stay there indefinitely. As long as nothing happens to disturb it, the circular flow of income will remain in a state of equilibrium or balance – in our example it will be £100 m. per year.

This follows naturally from the assumptions we made. Households spend all their income (£100 m.) on buying goods and services produced by the firm sector. Thus the value of goods and services which the firm sector produces and sells is also £100 m. per year. To produce this output firms hire £100 m. worth of factor services and the income of the household sector is thus £100 m. per year, which they in turn spend on buying goods and services and so on. This will continue indefinitely unless something happens to disturb the equilibrium.

What could happen to alter the size of the circular flow of income? Consider the first assumption that we made in section 1.2, that there are no imports or exports in our model. Suppose we now relax this assumption. If households spent part of their income, say £10 m., on buying imported goods, then expenditure on domestically produced goods would fall to £90 m. Firms find their sales have fallen to £90 m. and since there is no point in producing goods which cannot be sold, they will cut production to £90 m. worth per year. Because they are producing less, they need fewer factors of production – in fact they only need £90 m. worth of factors to produce £90 m. worth of goods. Thus household income falls to £90 m. Figure 1.3 illustrates this.

Provided households do not buy any more imports, their expenditure on domestically produced goods and services in the next time period will be £90 m. Thus firms will continue to produce £90 m. worth of output and hire £90 m. worth of factors to do so. In short, the size of the circular flow of income will settle

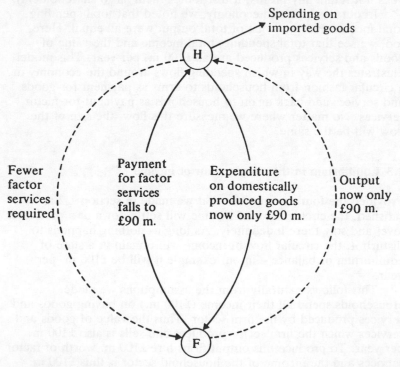

Fig. 1.3

down at a new lower level of £90 m. per year. This has occurred because expenditure has *leaked out* of the domestic economy. As a result output and income also fall. As we shall see later, the level of employment will also be affected by this fall in output. Because they are producing fewer goods, firms will need less labour than they did previously. Therefore, the level of employment falls and, other things being equal, unemployment rises.

We have seen how spending on imports represents a leakage from the circular flow. By a similar argument, exports increase the overall level of spending in the economy and raise output, incomes and employment. Suppose firms receive additional export orders of £20 m. They will therefore raise their output from £90 m. per year to £110 m. per year. This will mean they have to hire more factors, and factor incomes therefore increase to £110 m. In the next time period, firms will be able to sell £110 m. worth of goods to domestic customers, even though no more export sales are achieved. Thus the size of the circular flow of income increases to £110 m. and stays there, as a result of the *injection* of additional spending into the economy in the form of export demand.

Spending can be injected into the economy, or can leak out of the economy in other ways. If people save part of their income, rather than spend it, then domestic expenditure will be reduced and, other things being equal, output will fall, leading to a fall in income and employment. Thus saving too represents a leakage from the circular flow. Firms too can save by not distributing all their profits. Thus undistributed corporate profits also represent a leakage of spending from the circular flow.

Finally, the government influences the size of the circular flow of income by its expenditure and taxation policies. If it increases income tax, for example, then households' disposable income, or take-home pay, will fall and this causes them to reduce their spending. Thus an increase in the amount of income tax taken by the government represents a leakage or withdrawal of spending from the circular flow in the same way as increased saving or expenditure on imported goods.

The same will be true for all other forms of taxation. An increase in corporation tax on companies' profits, for example, will reduce the amount of profits that firms can distribute to their shareholders, whose income will therefore fall.

Government expenditure, on the other hand, represents an injection into the circular flow. Increased expenditure on defence, road building, pensions, unemployment benefit or student grants all have the same effect in terms of our model. They inject additional spending into the circular flow which raises output, incomes and employment. Additional defence spending, for example, results in increased sales for factories making tanks, riot shields, army boots and so on. These factories will increase their output and in doing so may take on more labour.

Summary

We have seen how the level of expenditure – or aggregate demand – in an economy is influenced by the volume of injections and withdrawals. In the model that we have presented an increase in demand leads to an increase in output and (possibly) to an increase in employment. This will not always be the case, of course. In an economy which is already operating at full capacity, a further increase in demand cannot result in an increase in output. This is a point to which we shall return.

1.4 The model of the circular flow – axiom or paradigm?

One important question should be raised at this stage. Do the models we have presented so far constitute axioms or paradigms? That is, do they represent sets of ideas about the way in which the economy operates, which are self-evidently true and which therefore everyone agrees on (axioms) or do they represent the views of a particular school of thought, views which are disputed by other schools (paradigms)?

The model of section 1.1 is undoubtedly axiomatic since the ideas which it sets forth are true by definition. Although the ideas of sections 1.2 and 1.3 appear to be a logical extension of these ideas, we have in fact introduced what amounts to a particular *interpretation* of the way the macroeconomy works, an interpretation which is accepted by some groups, but disputed by others. As we shall see later on, these ideas which we could call the Keynesian paradigm would not necessarily be accepted by the so-called monetarist school. The key element in the paradigm is the emphasis on the level of *demand* as being the factor which determines output and employment. Not all economists would be happy with the emphasis accorded to the level of demand in this model, preferring to concentrate more on the so-called supply side of the economy. We shall return to this point in subsequent chapters.

Questions

1. State whether the following are injections or withdrawals from the circular flow of income:
    (a) spending on imported goods;
    (b) saving part of one's income;

(c) government spending on defence;
(d) an increase in taxation;
(e) an increase in export sales;
(f) building a Channel Tunnel.

Does it make any difference to your answer if the Channel Tunnel is financed by the Government as opposed to private companies?

2. Does an increase in aggregate demand always lead to an increase in output? If not, why not?

3. Other things being equal, what effect will a cut in taxes have on the level of unemployment?

4. If people buy Toyota cars (assembled in Japan) rather than British Leyland cars what effect will this have on the British economy?

5. State what effect the following will have on aggregate demand in the British economy other things being equal (state increase/decrease/no change and explain why). Also state what the effect will be on output.

(a) a cut in income tax;
(b) a Japanese electronics company builds a factory in Wales;
(c) hire purchase regulations are eased;
(d) central government spending on higher education is cut;
(e) retirement pensions are increased;
(f) a military force is sent to recapture the Falklands;
(g) increased expenditure on policing inner-city areas.

Chapter 2
The balance of payments and the determination of the exchange rate

In Chapter 1 we assumed that our desert island was completely isolated from outside influences, whereas the British economy, which is the real subject of our study, is in reality subject to many such external influences. We are a relatively small country operating in a big world. Thus, the world economic climate affects the British economy, but the state of the British economy has little impact on the rest of the world. It is important to understand the world economic environment within which the British economy operates and moreover to understand the nature of the links that we have with the rest of the world. These links, of course, are primarily in the form of trade between Britain and the rest of the world, but in addition to flows of goods and services across international frontiers, there are also flows of capital (that is, money) for which there is no corresponding good or service rendered. The international payments system forms the backdrop against which the action takes place. The purpose of this chapter is to describe that backdrop.

The essential feature which distinguishes international trade from inter-regional trade is that with the former different currencies are involved. It will be instructive to see how the value of one currency in terms of another is determined.

2.1 The equilibrium exchange rate

We can analyse the behaviour of foreign exchange markets in the following way. Let us look at the market for pounds. Every working day transactions take place on foreign exchange markets at prices which ensure that the market is cleared. Since for every transaction there must be a buyer and a seller, the function of the foreign exchange dealers is to adjust prices in such a way that the number of pounds which people wish to buy at the prevailing market price is exactly equal to the number which (different) people wish to sell at that price. Normally, as with any other commodity, the lower the price the more pounds people can be persuaded to buy. Thus, to find a buyer for his sterling the broker

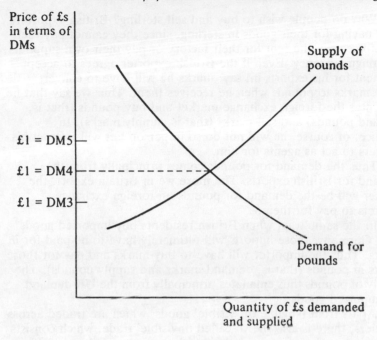

Price of £s in terms of DMs

Supply of pounds

£1 = DM5

£1 = DM4

£1 = DM3

Demand for pounds

Quantity of £s demanded and supplied

Fig. 2.1

has only to drop his price – though hopefully not below his buying price, otherwise he will make a loss.

In Fig. 2.1 the vertical axis measures the sterling exchange rate, or the price of pounds in terms of other currencies. We have chosen the Deutschmark as our yardstick, though we could have chosen the dollar, the franc, the yen or any other currency. The horizontal axis has an implicit time dimension. It measures the number of pounds demanded and supplied *per unit time* – per day, if you like. We have chosen to draw conventional demand and supply curves,[1] indicating that the higher the sterling exchange rate the more sterling people wish to sell, and conversely, the cheaper sterling becomes the more people will wish to buy. This behaviour is essential to ensure a stable market, though there are occasions in which contrary behaviour is observed. For example, in speculative situations, a fall in the value of the pound may induce people to sell more, not less, sterling since they fear a further decline in the exchange rate and hence a capital loss to the holders of sterling. For the moment we shall regard such behaviour as merely short-run aberrations to the more logical pattern, though, as we shall see later, such aberrant behaviour may be rather common in the real world.

Why do people wish to buy and sell sterling? British exporters want paying for their goods in sterling, since they cannot pay their workforce, pay the rent for their factory or pay their own suppliers in foreign currency. Even if the British exporter agrees to accept payment for his exports in, say, marks he will have to convert these marks to pounds when he receives them. Thus we say that he will enter the foreign exchange market and buy pounds (that is, demand pounds) and sell marks (that is, supply marks). In practice, of course, he will not do so in person but will instruct his bankers to act as agents for him.

Thus the demand for pounds comes principally from the demand for British exports. The more we in Britain export, the greater will be the demand for pounds on foreign exchange markets to pay for them.

In the same way, when British residents buy imported goods from Germany, those imports will ultimately have to be paid for in marks. Thus the importer will have to buy marks and pay for those marks in pounds (that is, demand marks and supply pounds). The supply of pounds thus emanates principally from the UK demand for imported goods.

Apart from tangible or 'visible' goods, which are traded across frontiers, there is also the so-called 'invisible' trade, which consists of services such as insurance, banking, tourism and shipping. This invisible trade has exactly the same effect on the demand and supply of pounds as visible trade and is, in fact, very important for the British economy since historically we have had a surplus on invisibles (that is, we export more than we import).

There is a third set of items which affect the demand and supply of pounds – the so-called capital account transactions. If, for example, a German resident wishes to purchase shares in ICI (a British company), he will have to buy those shares in pounds, thus augmenting the demand for pounds on the foreign exchange market. This transaction thus has the same effect on the market for pounds as a British export. However, when the German resident receives his dividend on the shares he has purchased, which he will get in pounds, he will convert these into marks (that is, he will supply pounds to the foreign exchange markets) and thus the receipt of these dividends has the same effect as a foreign import into Britain.

The balance of payments accounts record all the transactions involving the purchase or sale of sterling during a certain period (say, the previous month, quarter or year). It can be subdivided as follows:

Visibles + invisibles = Current account balance = Balance of trade

Balance of payments = Balance of trade + Balance on capital account.

2.2 Fixed and flexible exchange rates

With the demand and supply schedules depicted in Fig. 2.1, the equilibrium exchange rate (that is, the rate at which the demand and supply of pounds is equal) would be £1 = DM4. Consider what would happen if the demand for pounds increased as shown by a shift in the demand curve to D' as in Fig. 2.2. (The reasons why such a shift might occur will be discussed later.) The equilibrium exchange rate will increase to DM5 = £1 and, provided the exchange rate is perfectly free to vary, the market exchange rate will in fact appreciate to this level. In practice, however, the exchange rate is not free to vary in this way because governments, for a variety of reasons, have an interest in manipulating the exchange rate. It is convenient to describe two different exchange rate regimes – fixed exchange rates and flexible (or floating) exchange rates. These are, in effect, polar cases and the sort of policy pursued in practice will be somewhere in

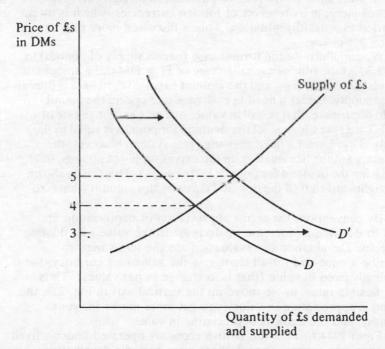

Fig. 2.2

between these two extremes. As the names imply, a flexible exchange rate policy is one in which the exchange rate is determined from day to day by the forces of demand and supply. No attempt is made by the monetary authorities to intervene in foreign exchange markets and the prevailing exchange rate is always the equilibrium one (that is, the one which equates the market demand for pounds with the market supply of pounds). At the other extreme is the fixed exchange rate policy whereby the monetary authorities are committed to maintaining a particular 'par value' or parity. On any particular day, of course, it would be most unlikely if this official 'par value' were the same as the equilibrium exchange rate. At the official exchange rate there will either be too many pounds offered for sale in relation to the number that people wish to buy, or too few; that is, there will either be an excess supply of pounds or an excess demand. In the former case the Bank of England has to buy up the excess supply of pounds that nobody else is willing to purchase at the prevailing price, and it will have to pay for them in foreign currencies. In the latter case, when there is an excess demand, the Bank of England will supply the extra pounds needed, which it will normally do quite readily since it will receive payment in foreign currencies. It can thus increase its reserves of foreign currencies, which is often regarded as a healthy situation. This is discussed more fully in section 2.3 below.

We can illustrate the former case (excess supply of pounds) in Fig. 2.3. At the official exchange rate of £1 = DM4, the amount of pounds demanded is q_D and the amount supplied q_S. There is thus an excess supply. Under a flexible exchange rate system the pound would depreciate, that is, fall in value, to a new exchange rate of DM3.5 = £1, at which level the demand for pounds is equal to the supply at q_E. Under a fixed exchange rate system, however, the monetary authorities will buy up the excess supply of pounds, thus increasing the demand for pounds by $(q_S - q_D)$. This can be shown by a rightward shift of the demand curve by this amount (that is to D').

By convention, the terms appreciation or depreciation are used to describe an increase or decrease in the value of a floating currency. Devaluation or revaluation are the terms used to describe a once-and-for-all change in the value of a currency that is nominally fixed in value (that is, a change in par values). Thus with flexible rates, as we move up the vertical axis in Fig. 2.3, the pound is appreciating in value (you get more marks for your pounds), and the mark is depreciating in value.

From 1944 to 1972 the British economy operated under a fixed exchange rate regime, though there were periodic devaluations. Since 1972 the exchange rate has been allowed to float. What this

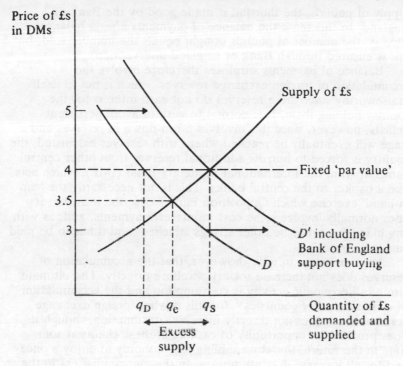

Fig. 2.3

means in practice is not that the Bank of England no longer intervenes on foreign exchange markets to buy and sell pounds as it sees fit, but that the Bank of England has officially abandoned its commitment to any particular exchange rate. In fact there is still continuous intervention in foreign exchange markets by the Bank of England, but the purpose of this intervention is no longer to preserve any particular parity. It may wish, for example, to modify the speed at which the exchange rate moves either up or down, or it may wish to buy up currencies when they are being offered at cheap rates.

2.3 The accumulation of reserves

To operate a fixed exchange rate policy it is necessary to hold stocks of foreign currencies which can be used to buy up one's own currency when the occasion demands. A balance of payments deficit is financed in this way; that is, when the demand for pounds on capital and current account taken together falls short of the

15

supply of pounds, the shortfall is made good by the Bank of England. In this sense the balance of payments *always* balances (that is, the number of pounds bought equals the number sold, but this is ensured through Bank of England intervention).

Balance of payments surpluses therefore involve the accumulation of foreign exchange reserves, which is not in itself praiseworthy since these reserves do not earn interest for the country holding them. It is normal to wish to avoid persistent deficits, however, since this involves a run-down in reserves and a stage will eventually be reached when, with reserves exhausted, the country is forced to borrow additional reserves from other central banks or from the International Monetary Fund (IMF), which acts like a banker to the central banks. This is not necessarily the 'cap-in-hand' exercise which Opposition Parties describe it as, but it does normally involve some cost in interest payments, and, as with any loan, there may be other strings attached, and it has to be paid back.

It is important to note, however, that the accumulation of reserves does not increase society's welfare directly. The ultimate aim of all economic activity is consumption and the accumulation of claims on other countries – for this is what foreign exchange reserves are – does not directly increase consumption, though it does provide the opportunity of cashing in these claims at some time in the future, thereby enabling the economy to enjoy a once-and-for-all increase in consumption. In the mercantilist era in the seventeenth century the wealth of an economy was judged by the amount of gold it had accumulated, and thus the accumulation of such wealth was the ultimate objective towards which the nation strived. Although the vestiges of the mercantilist tradition still survive, this view is now regarded as incorrect. The amount of gold possessed by the *individual* may indeed measure his wealth, but what is true for the individual is not true for society. The wealth of a society is measured in terms of its productive capacity, its ability to produce a stream of consumption goods and services for the benefit of its citizens. Many countries, particularly developing countries, have chosen policies designed to promote a rapid expansion of productive capacity and this has usually involved borrowing heavily abroad. In other words, they have allowed other countries to build up huge claims on their economies. This is not necessarily a case of 'living beyond one's means' however; rather, it may represent an effective stratagem for development.

2.4 Exchange rates and purchasing power parities

The market exchange rate, as we have seen, is determined by the demand for and supply of a currency on foreign exchange markets, manipulated to a greater or lesser extent by central banks. Ultimately, however, we would argue that the exchange rate between two currencies must reflect the internal purchasing power of those currencies, or what is known as the purchasing power parity. Suppose the exchange rate between pounds sterling and French francs is, for example, £1 = 8Fr. There must be some relationship between what can be bought in the shops in France for 8Fr and what can be bought in the shops in Britain for £1. Take a particular commodity, such as a jar of coffee, which costs, say, £1 to buy in Britain. The cost of this same item in France will not be exactly 8Fr, but it can be argued that it cannot diverge too much from that price. If the price of coffee in France was substantially less than 8Fr (say 5Fr) and it were possible for jars of coffee to be traded without restrictions between France and Britain, then it would be profitable to buy up coffee in France and export it for sale in Britain. The effect of this would be to increase French exports and increase British imports, thus increasing the demand for francs and the supply of pounds on foreign exchange markets. *Ceteris paribus*, this would lead to an appreciation in the value of the franc and a depreciation in the value of the pound, assuming that exchange rates were perfectly free to vary. If coffee were the only thing that was traded between Britain and France the franc would appreciate against the pound to £1 = 5Fr. In the real world where thousands of commodities are traded, or could be traded, between Britain and France, the exchange rate must, in the long run, reflect the difference in the price of a typical bundle of goods in France and a similar bundle of goods in Britain. Thus there will be a tendency for exchange rates to reflect purchasing power parities.

In reality, however, market exchange rates will not be equal to purchasing power parities. There are five main reasons for this. First, not all goods and services are capable of being exported and imported. Physical goods such as cars, television sets, food and so on can be traded internationally, but things such as houses, the services of the local garage or the window cleaner cannot. Thus market exchange rates only reflect internal purchasing power to the extent that an individual's income is spent on goods which are, or could be, traded internationally.

Second, few countries allow completely free trade in all those goods and services which are, or could be, traded. For a variety of reasons governments may impose trading restrictions – quotas or levies – on imports. To the extent that this reduces international trade it also reduces the extent to which market exchange rates will reflect the internal purchasing power of a currency.

Third, the market prices of goods and services are affected by sales taxes. If, for example, France imposes a higher rate of sales tax on coffee than Britain does, then the price of coffee in the shops in France will remain higher than in Britain.

Fourth, even though exchange rates may be nominally floating, they are seldom completely free to vary. If we take the other extreme, where exchange rates are rigidly fixed, then the export of coffee from France to Britain, which we described in our previous example, will not tend to make the franc appreciate. Instead it will cause a run down of foreign exchange reserves at the Bank of England to pay for the imports from France.

Fifth, and this is perhaps the most surprising reason of all, there are large differences in the profit margins which companies are able to make in the various national markets in which they sell. For example, when cars were sold in Belgium in 1980 retailers typically had a profit margin of only 10 per cent whereas the mark-up in Britain was nearer 30 per cent. Moreover, the system of exclusive dealerships in Britain enabled car companies to restrict competition and prevent price cutting. This produced a situation in which the price of a car in Britain was almost 30 per cent higher than an identical model sold on the Belgium market, even after due allowance is made for the difference in sales taxes. In other words, when the Belgium franc price is converted into sterling

Table 2.1 New Car Prices, mid-1980

Model	New car prices (including tax) Belgium (£)	Britain (£)
Jaguar XJ6	10 407	15 339
Mercedes Benz 200	5 918	7 823
Princess 2000HL	3 690	5 170
BMW 316	4 025	5 100
Maxi 1750HL	3 168	4 671
Austin Allegro 1.1	2 204	3 220
Mini Clubman	2 152	3 135
VW Polo	2 115	3 115
Vauxhall Chevette	2 061	3 088
Renault 5	2 260	2 960
Ford Fiesta	2 240	2 925

Source: *The Economist*, 3 May 1980, p. 75

Table 2.2 New car prices in the EEC

	Allegro 1.1 2-door (£)	Mini 850 City (£)
Denmark	4124	2995
Ireland	3363	2608
Britain	3220	2499
France	2751	2040
Holland	2652	1944
Belgium	2204	1677
Luxembourg	2204	1677
Italy	2417	n.a.
Germany	n.a.	n.a.

Source: *The Economist*, 3 May 1980, p. 75

using the official exchange rate we see that there are large
differences in the prices of identical cars. Table 2.1 illustrates the
situation that existed in 1980 and Table 2.2 shows that these price
differentials were widespread throughout the EEC – a free trade
area. The discrepancy in car prices between Britain and Europe
received widespread public attention in the 1980s but little
narrowing of differentials occurred.

Classical economists argued that the price of identical goods
sold in different markets would in the long run be equalized by the
forces of competition. They called this the 'law of one price'.
These tables provide startling evidence that, in the short run at
least, the law does not hold. They also provide valuable evidence
about how firms set prices. Clearly it is more profitable for firms to
sell on some markets than on others, and what this implies is that
companies do not base their prices on production costs; rather the
price they charge is based on 'what the market will bear'; that is,
they charge relatively high prices where demand is inelastic and
lower prices where demand is more elastic.

Of course, while these price differences exist there is an
incentive for enterprising individuals or companies to buy up cars
on cheap markets for resale on expensive ones, a practice which
the car companies not unnaturally try to prevent. Inasmuch as this
does occur, there will be a tendency for the law of one price to
reassert itself, either through an equalizing of profit margins or
through movements in exchange rates. This in turn will have an

impact on rates of inflation in the countries concerned, a point to which we return in Chapter 7.

2.5 Policies to correct payments imbalances

The balance of payments, as we have seen, always balances, but this is only achieved through the intervention of the central bank, either buying or selling currency as it sees fit. Without these official transactions, however, if there is a continual tendency for the supply of pounds to outstrip the demand for them, then we can talk of a payments imbalance – in this case of a balance of payments deficit. Such payments imbalances, if they are chronic, give cause for concern and some policy must be taken to redress the imbalance. We shall confine ourselves to a discussion of the problems caused by balance of payments deficits, though it is worth noting that those countries who experience chronic surpluses appear to find it equally difficult to remove them.

A balance of payments deficit – that is, an excess supply of pounds on foreign exchange markets – can be tackled in a variety of ways. The main types of policy are set out below. It should be noted that all of the policies mentioned will probably be effective in eliminating a balance of payments deficit provided they are applied sufficiently strictly, but that all of them involve undesirable side-effects. It is because of the seriousness of these side-effects that some policies are either not rigorously applied, or are not applied at all. The policy maker may feel that attaining a balance of payments equilibrium is a less important objective than, say, reducing inflation, reducing unemployment or promoting economic growth. In this case, policies which reduce a balance of payments deficit, but also have the effect of increasing unemployment, may be eschewed. In macroeconomics there is often a conflict between objectives, and we shall discuss this more fully in Chapter 11.

Raising interest rates

By bringing about an increase in interest rates, the Bank of England can attract foreign capital into the country. The world capital market is often said to be competitive, which means that the international investor will place his money wherever it can find the highest return. Thus, if British interest rates rise relative to those in other countries, this will increase the demand for the bonds and bills offered for sale by the public and private institutions in Britain. In order to purchase these bonds, foreigners will first have to acquire sterling. Thus the sale of a bond is just like an export since it adds to the demand for pounds.

Restrictions on capital movements; incomplete convertibility

If a citizen of a particular country is free to buy and sell that country's currency for whatever purposes and in whatever amount, then that currency is said to be *freely convertible*. In practice, most countries place restrictions, either temporary or permanent, on their citizens' freedom to do so, since this is one way of relieving balance of payments difficulties. Typically, there may be restrictions on the freedom to export capital, or on the citizen's right to sell currency when he goes abroad on his holiday. In 1967, for example, the government introduced restrictions on the amount of sterling (then £50) which British tourists could take abroad with them.

In Britain some form of exchange control was practised right up until 1979, when it was abandoned by the then Conservative government, who believed that the workings of the market in foreign exchange should be unfettered. The immediate effect was to render redundant those civil servants working in the Exchange Equalization Account for the Bank of England, whose job it had formerly been to monitor and control movements of foreign exchange. Whether the removal of controls led to greater fluctuations in the exchange rate than would otherwise have occurred is difficult to say.

Reducing domestic demand

By increasing income taxes the government can reduce the post-tax incomes of those in employment. Similarly, the incomes of other members of society can be held down by reducing spending – or reducing the growth of spending – on pensions, social security benefits and so on. In so far as a proportion of people's incomes will be spent on imported goods, a fall in incomes will necessarily bring about a fall in spending on imported goods. Reducing domestic demand – what is known as *domestic deflation* – has been one of the most important instruments used by governments to reduce balance of payments deficits.

The major drawback with this policy is that, although it may be effective in reducing spending on imports, it also reduces spending on domestically produced goods and services, and this may have deleterious effects on some of the other objectives of macroeconomic policy, particularly the level of unemployment, as we shall see later.

Quotas, import tariffs and export subsidies

An import quota is a restriction placed on the amount (measured either in value terms or in physical units) of a particular

21

commodity which importers are allowed to bring into the country. Clearly, the smaller the quota, the less will be imported, and the greater will be the beneficial effect on the balance of payments. An import tariff is a tax on imported goods, which may be levied on all imported goods or on just a few specific items. This has the effect of making imports more expensive relative to domestically produced goods, and domestic consumers will therefore tend to buy less imported goods. An export subsidy, which again can either be specific or general, is any measure such as a tax concession or a preferential loan granted to exporters which is designed to make exporting more profitable and hence encourage the growth of exports.

It should be noted that if all countries adopted these policies, then the policies would be self-defeating and international trade would be reduced. Because of this, it is often claimed that such defensive policies are 'anti-social' in some global sense. Moreover, it is argued, they invite retaliatory action from other countries and run counter to agreements freely entered into, such as the General Agreement on Tariffs and Trade, and the regulations of the European Common Market and are therefore, in some sense, illegal.

Some authors, notably those of the Cambridge Economic Policy Group, point out however that any country with a balance of payments deficit must take steps to reduce imports and boost exports. Whether this is done by domestic deflation or by import tariffs makes little difference to the foreign exporter hoping to sell his products in Britain. Either way, the amount of imported goods that the British economy can absorb while maintaining a balance of trade equilibrium will be reduced.

Changing the exchange rate

The effect of devaluation on the balance of trade is more difficult to predict, being the subject of some debate both on the theoretical level and on the empirical level. We shall present two models of how a devaluation could, in theory, improve the balance of trade.

Model One: devaluation makes exports cheaper

It could be argued that the fall in the external value of the currency would immediately result in a rise in the price of imported goods (causing domestic consumers to buy fewer imports) and a fall in the price of British goods (causing a growth of British exports), the two effects combining to produce an improvement in the balance of trade. Things are not quite so simple, however. The price of what we buy from abroad relative to the price of what we sell abroad is known as the *terms of trade* and the devaluation clearly worsens the terms of trade. Thus to pay for the same volume of imports we now have to export more than previously since relative prices have moved against us.

The extent to which a devaluation will improve the balance of trade depends, among other things, on the degree to which the demand for imports and the demand for exports are sensitive to price; in other words, on the price elasticity of demand for imports and the price elasticity of demand for exports. Consider the import side. The price elasticity of demand for imports is defined as:

$$\frac{\% \text{ change in quantity of imports bought}}{\% \text{ change in price of imports}}$$

If this elasticity is just unity (strictly speaking minus one) then it implies that a 10 per cent devaluation, which results in a 10 per cent rise in the price of imported goods, will result in a 10 per cent fall in demand for imports. Thus expenditure, in pounds, on imported goods remains unchanged; that is, the supply of pounds to the foreign exchange market is unaltered. Similarly, in order for a devaluation to reduce the supply of pounds to the foreign exchange market, the demand for imports would have to be elastic (that is, elasticity greater in absolute value than one).

Clearly, therefore, we cannot argue that a devaluation will inevitably reduce a balance of trade deficit. The degree of responsiveness of both the demand for imports and exports to price changes is the crucial determining factor and it has been argued that these elasticities are low in the short run so that the immediate effect of a devaluation is to worsen rather than improve the trade balance. Only when consumers, both at home and abroad, adjust themselves to the changed set of relative prices, and this will occur only slowly, does the balance of trade start to improve. This produces a phenomenon known as the 'J curve' effect, illustrated in Fig. 2.4. It is generally reckoned that it takes one to two years before the beneficial effects of a devaluation are felt. Certainly, the sterling devaluation of 1967 did not produce a surplus on the balance of trade until 1969.

Model Two: devaluation makes exporting more profitable

As we saw in section 2.4, the sorts of goods which constitute the most important part of foreign trade, namely manufactured goods, are often sold on markets where the price is administered or manipulated by the seller rather than being determined by the interaction of demand and supply as it would be on a competitive market. Following a devaluation, an exporter therefore has a choice of cutting the price, in foreign currency terms, of his

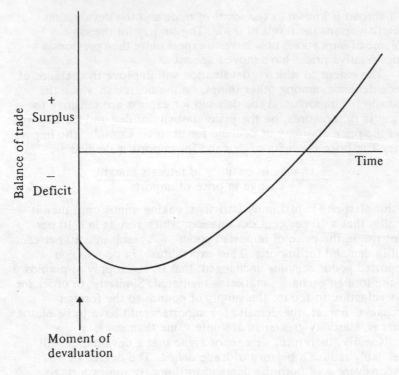

Fig. 2.4

exports, or keeping the same price, in which case exporting
becomes more profitable to him. An example will help to illustrate
the point.

Let us imagine that a BL Mini Metro sells at £3000 in Britain
and that in Germany the same car sells at DM15 000. BL choose
this price, taking into account the price at which comparable cars
from rival manufacturers sell on the German market. They
probably want to ensure that it is priced 'competitively'; that is,
that its price is comparable with the price of cars with which it
competes for sales. Now, with an exchange rate of £1 = DM5, the
export revenue accruing to BL is exactly $\frac{15\ 000}{5}$ = £3000 per car and
thus they would be indifferent whether they sold the car on the
domestic market or on the overseas market. In practice they might
prefer to sell on the home market since the cost of home sales
would probably be lower.

Now suppose the pound is devalued to £1 = DM4 (again
choosing easy numbers to illustrate the principle involved). BL

may choose to keep the DM price of the car at DM15 000 as before, since this is their favoured selling price taking into account all those factors which their marketing managers tell them are important. At the new exchange rate, export revenues are now

$$\frac{15\ 000}{4} = £3750 \text{ per car, making overseas sales much more}$$

profitable than domestic sales, even taking into account the slightly higher cost of selling overseas. Thus the profit-seeking company will direct its energies to increasing exports, which it hopes to do not by cutting prices but by increasing expenditure on advertising and so on.

On the import side, the effect of the devaluation will be to make exporting to Britain less profitable. To continue with our example, the price of Volkswagen cars sold in Britain will have been chosen taking into account the price of its competitors' products. If the price of Volkswagen cars on the British market goes too high, then sales will dwindle; therefore a devaluation of the pound will probably not result in any change in the price of Volkswagen cars sold on the British market, or at least the price may not rise by the full amount of the devaluation. The number of marks received by the German exporter for each car sold in Britain will, however, fall. Thus exporting to Britain becomes less profitable, and other things being equal this will reduce the flow of imports into Britain.

In practice, the effect of a devaluation on the balance of trade will occur both through the process of model one and model two – model two being more applicable to those goods sold on oligopolistic markets (where the seller has some discretion in price setting) and model one being more applicable to those goods sold on competitive markets (where the seller has little discretion as regards his selling price). It should be noted, however, that in both cases the beneficial effects of the devaluation on the balance of trade may take quite some time to manifest themselves.

Moreover, the beneficial effects depend on the devaluation actually bringing about a change in relative prices – that is, the price of British goods relative to foreign goods. This may not occur because, in addition to being affected by the exchange rate, relative prices will also depend upon relative inflation rates – that is, the rate of domestic price inflation in Britain relative to the rate of price inflation overseas.

Let us say, for example, that it takes eighteen months for the beneficial effects of a devaluation on the balance of trade to occur. If, during this period, the rate of domestic inflation is higher than the rate of inflation overseas, this will reduce the extent to which the devaluation actually succeeds in changing relative prices. If the two effects are of equal weight, the devaluation of the exchange rate being exactly cancelled out by the higher rate of domestic inflation relative to that overseas, then at the end of the eighteen-month period nothing will have happened in real terms. The exchange rate will have fallen, but domestic prices and money incomes will have increased more rapidly than overseas, so that the amount of foreign currency that can be purchased with the average person's income will be unchanged. We could say that the *real* value of the currency was unchanged.

2.6 The UK balance of payments

The principal source of balance of payments statistics is the *United Kingdom Balance of Payments*, known as the 'Pink Book'. Figure 2.5 is based on data from the 1985 edition. The top half of Fig. 2.5 relates to the current account. As can be seen, the invisibles balance showed a surplus throughout the period, which is normal for the UK economy. The visibles balance showed a deficit, except for the early 1980s when there was a substantial surplus.

The sum of the visibles balance plus the invisibles balance

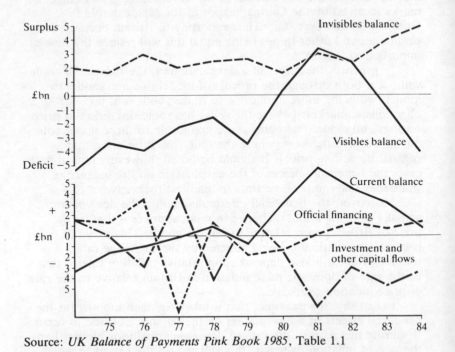

Source: *UK Balance of Payments Pink Book 1985*, Table 1.1

Fig. 2.5

gives the current account balance shown in the lower half of the figure. The graph shows that in the later half of the 1970s deficits on visible trade were more or less offset by surpluses on invisible trade so that the current account was approximately in balance. In the early 1980s however both invisible and visible trade were in surplus so that the current account balance showed a large surplus.

Figure 2.5 also shows capital flows. These became substantially negative after 1980 – that is, there was a net outflow of investment from the UK economy which coincides, perhaps not coincidentally, with the ending of foreign exchange controls in 1979–80. These net investment flows comprise more or less the whole of the capital account balance. If one were to add the capital account balance to the current account balance the resulting figure could be described as the *balance of payments deficit or surplus*. As has already been mentioned, the balance of payments must sum to zero so that this deficit or surplus must be covered by official financing. This official financing is also shown in Fig. 2.5. A positive sign indicates that the Bank of England was selling pounds and acquiring foreign exchange. A negative sign indicates that the Bank is using reserves of foreign currencies to buy up pounds on the foreign exchange market.

Table 2.3 UK Balance of Payments 1984 (£m.)

	Visible balance	−4101
plus	Invisible balance	5036
equals	Current balance	935
plus	balance of investment and other capital transactions	−3291
equals	'balance of payments deficit'	−2356
of which	official financing	1316
	balancing item	1040

Source: *UK Balance of Payments Pink Book 1985*, Table 1.1

A summary of the balance of payments for 1984 is shown in Table 2.3. There are of course errors and omissions in the recording of balance of payments data so that the accounts will not in practice sum to zero. A balancing item, shown in Table 2.3, is therefore introduced to ensure equality (in an accounting sense) between debits and credits in the accounts. This balancing item is purely notional and does not relate to any transactions which have actually taken place. Were it not for this balancing item, of course, official financing would exactly equal the balance of payments deficit or surplus.

Notes

1. The reader who is not thoroughly familiar with demand and supply analysis and the concept of elasticity is recommended to read through Appendix A before proceeding.

Questions

1. Is the distinction between the Balance of Payments and the Balance of Trade the same as the distinction between visible and invisible trade? If not explain what the distinction is.

2. Delete whichever is incorrect:
'An increase in foreign sales of Austin Rover cars will increase/decrease/leave unchanged the demand for pounds and increase/decrease/leave unchanged the supply of pounds. This will tend to make the value of the pound float up/down.'

3.

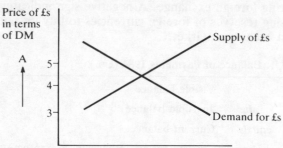

Fig 2.6   Quantity of £s demanded and supplied

(a) In Fig. 2.6 a movement along the price axis in the direction A represents a depreciation/appreciation in the value of the pound. Delete as appropriate. Under what circumstances would one use the terms devaluation/revaluation as opposed to depreciation/appreciation?
(b) The equilibrium exchange rate is approximately ...
(c) Under a fixed exchange rate system if the official exchange rate was £1 = DM 4.0 this would mean there was an excess demand/excess supply of pounds at the official rate. What would happen as a result of this?

4. Assuming the United Kingdom is a net exporter of oil how would one analyse (in terms of the model in Fig. 2.6) an increase in the price of oil? (Assume the demand for oil is inelastic.)
Assume now that the United Kingdom is a net importer of oil. What would be the effect of a rise in the price of oil? Assume now that the price elasticity of demand for oil is unity (i.e. a 10 per cent price increase causes the quantity demanded to fall by 10 per cent).

5. State what the effect of the following would be on the demand for pounds and the supply of pounds. Indicate whether the effect will be shown on the Current Account or the Capital Account of the Balance of Payments.

   (a) The Austin Metro sells well in France.
   (b) A successful sales campaign in Britain for Vauxhall Cavalier cars.
   (c) The London Borough of Ealing decides to raise money by offering bonds for sale to the public, some of which are sold overseas.
   (d) British troops stationed in Germany get a pay increase.

6. The basic differences between a fixed exchange rate and a floating exchange rate is:

   (a) under a fixed exchange rate regime the rate at which one currency exchanges for another never changes;
   (b) under a floating exchange rate regime central banks never intervene in the foreign exchange market so they don't need to hold stocks of foreign currencies;
   (c) under a fixed exchange rate the value of a currency is directly fixed to gold;
   (d) only under a fixed exchange rate regime are there declared par values;
   (e) in a floating (or flexible) exchange rate regime the actual rate of exchange varies within a narrow band whereas under a fixed exchange rate regime the rate of exchange does not vary at all.

7. Assume a BL Maestro sells for £5000 in the UK and 72 000 Fr in France. On which market does BL make most profit per car sold, if the current exchange rate is £1 = 12 Fr?
If the £ appreciates in value *vis-à-vis* the franc but BL keeps its French price at 72 000 Fr which of the following is true:

   (a) Exporting becomes less profitable to BL than previously.
   (b) Exporting becomes more profitable to BL than previously.

8. Which of the following policies would *ceteris paribus* 'improve' the trade balance (i.e. reduce the size of a trade deficit)?

   (a) Raising interest rates.
   (b) Reducing employees' National Insurance Contribution.
   (c) Increasing student grants.
   (d) Staging the World Cup in England.
   (e) Placing restrictions on convertibility.

9. The following Balance of Payments accounts records the autonomous transactions for a particular year:

Visible exports	+100
Visible imports	−100
Invisible exports	+20
Invisible imports	−20
Net capital flows	−10

29

(a) What was the trade balance?
(b) What does the negative sign on net capital flows indicate?
(c) What accommodating transactions was it necessary for the central bank to make?

Chapter 3
Inflation: a preview

3.1 The facts

Having established some sort of perspective by our discussion in
Chapter 2 of the international context within which national
economic events take place, we are now in a position to begin our
analysis of what some regard as the most intractable economic
problem facing governments – the problem of inflation.

Figure 3.1 shows OECD statistics on the rate of price inflation
in selected countries for the period 1973–78. The reason for
choosing this period is that it illustrates the international dimension
of the inflation phenomenon, a theme we study in detail in
Chapter 7. Statistics collected for different countries are not strictly
comparable, since different countries use different bases for the
collection and compilation of their statistics. The Retail Price
Index in the United Kingdom, for example, may be based on a
different bundle of goods from that used in France. For our
purposes this is not very important, however, since what we are
interested in is the *fluctuations* in the rate of inflation that these
countries have experienced in the 1970s. A few moments' perusal
of these statistics reveals the following features.

First, there is a broad similarity in the inflationary profile of
the various countries in the 1970s. Typically, inflation rates were
relatively low up until about mid 1973. There was then a rapid
acceleration in inflation rates for the next two years, after which
the rate fell back, only to rise again in some countries, but to a
lower peak, before falling again. Second, some countries have
experienced higher peaks than others and some countries have
encountered their peaks earlier than others. In Germany and the
Netherlands, for example, the peaks are of very modest
proportion, whereas in Japan and Britain the peaks are much
higher.

Any 'explanation' of the causes of inflation that the economist
offers should be capable of explaining these facts and others, which
we shall discuss below. These statistics relate to the inflationary
experience of OECD countries in the 1970s, but at different
periods in the past, and in other countries, the inflationary history

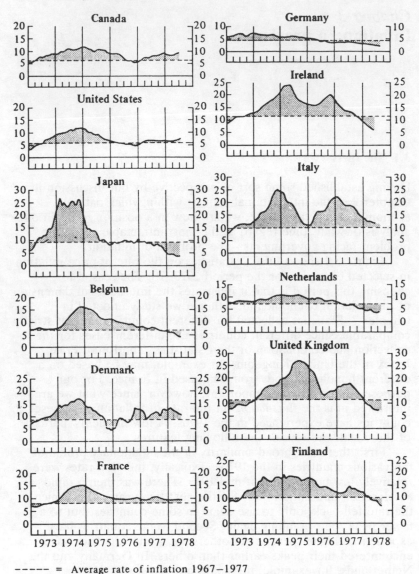

----- = Average rate of inflation 1967–1977

——— = Actual rate of inflation (percentage change over 12 months, all goods and services) The shaded areas thus represent the improvement or deterioration in comparison with 1967.

Source: *OECD Main Economic Indicators Sept. 1978, p. 148*

Fig. 3.1

has been very different. For example, in several South American countries rates of inflation of 500 per cent per annum are commonplace, and in Germany in 1922–23 the rate of inflation was many times greater than this; in fact, prices rose so fast that money became unacceptable as a means of payment and people reverted to barter transactions. Clearly, these inflations are of a different order of magnitude to the inflations experienced in the OECD countries in the 1970s. Nevertheless, there may be important consequences to be learnt from them, and we shall discuss them more fully below.

It seems reasonable to liken the inflation experienced by the OECD countries in the 1970s to some sort of international disease, capable of being transmitted across frontiers. Some countries, however, would appear to have a certain degree of immunity to the disease. It would appear then that we can begin our analysis of the inflationary process either in the context of the international economy or in the context of the national economy; that is, we can begin by studying 'world inflation' or 'domestic inflation'. As we shall see, it makes little difference to our analysis which of these two we take as our initial focus of attention, since it is the interaction between the two to which we must eventually turn. Moreover, the types of explanation which economists offer for the existence of inflation are the same whether the focus is the domestic or the world economy.

Many macroeconomics textbooks begin to explain the causes of inflation in the context of a 'closed economy'; that is, one which does not indulge in foreign trade. Although this is quite unrealistic, particularly for a country such as the United Kingdom where more than a quarter of total spending goes on imported goods, it is a necessary simplifying assumption which has to be made until a picture of the inflationary process can be built up. It should be clear that the world economy is itself a 'closed economy' (since there is as yet no inter-planetary trade!) and that in the following analysis, when we discuss the inflationary process within the context of a closed economy, this is equally applicable to the 'closed' national economy and the world economy.

3.2 An analogy with microeconomics

Consider the market for widgets (a hypothetical commodity much loved of economists). If widgets are not subject to price control then the market price of widgets – the equilibrium price – will be determined by demand and supply, in the same way that the price of pounds was determined in Chapter 2. The equilibrium price of widgets will rise if either the demand curve for widgets shifts to the right, or the supply curve shifts to the left (or both). Now consider widgets to be a 'composite commodity' – the bundle of goods and services which the average household buys each month (the same average household in fact that is used to compile the index of retail prices). We can then re-label the vertical axis in Fig. 3.2 as the Retail Price Index or the *price level*. Movements up the vertical axis therefore represent an increase in the average price level or 'inflation'. By analogy, therefore, rises in the price level can be caused by shifts in the aggregate demand schedule (the equivalent of the demand curve) or the aggregate supply schedule (the equivalent of the supply curve). That is, inflation can be caused by demand factors or supply factors.

3.3 Shifts in aggregate supply

Consider for a moment the supply schedule. In microeconomics, the supply curve shows the maximum amount that suppliers are willing to supply at any particular price. Apart from price itself, the main determinant of this is the cost of supplying any particular amount, since revenue and cost together determine the profitability of any particular sale. The lower the profitability of any sale, the

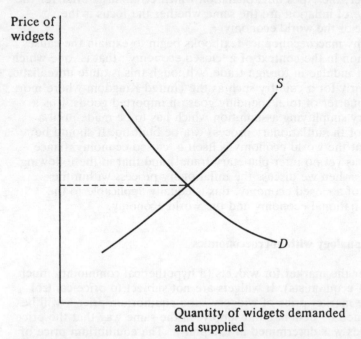

Fig. 3.2

less willing will sellers be to make that sale. An increase in production costs will, other things being equal, decrease profitability. Thus an increase in the costs of production will lead to a leftward shift of the supply curve, and to an increase in equilibrium price.

Similarly, in macroeconomics, inflation can be regarded as being *cost induced* when it results from a leftward shift of our (notional) aggregate supply schedule, reflecting an increase in production costs, as in Fig. 3.3.

Before proceeding with our analysis we should note two important features about Fig. 3.3. First, what we are measuring on the horizontal axis is our widget-based, composite commodity, *real output*. The output of the economy, consisting as it does of millions of different goods and services, has perforce to be measured in terms of the money value of those goods and services; that is, the market price at which they change hands. The problem with this is that the real value of money is falling – it is as if we are using as our measure of length a yardstick which is continually shrinking. We could never get an objective measure of the length of any object if we did it this way. If, however, we knew that our yardstick was shrinking by 10 per cent a year we would know that a measurement taken in 1978 could be compared with one taken in

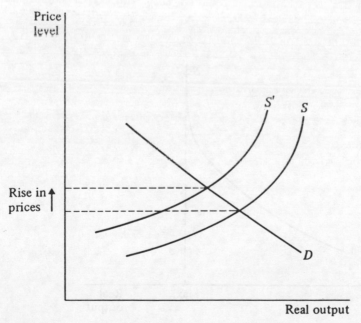

Fig. 3.3

1977 by multiplying the 1978 figure by $\frac{100}{110}$. Similarly, if we knew that the value of money was shrinking by 10 per cent per year we could multiply the money value of output in 1978 by $\frac{100}{110}$ before comparing it with the value of output in 1977. By *deflating* the value of output in this way, we could therefore assess the extent to which *real* output had changed.

The second point to note in Fig. 3.3 is that the slope of the supply schedule becomes steeper as real output increases – using our elasticity concept we could say that the supply curve becomes more inelastic – that is, less responsive to changes in price. The economic rationale for this is as follows. At any particular point in time the state of technology can be taken as fixed and the factor endowments (labour, capital and land) can also be assumed to be fixed. As output increases, more and more of these factors will be drawn into the production process until eventually there will be no idle factors of production – no 'spare capacity' – in the economy. At that point in time, with all the factors fully employed, the economy will be producing as much as it is capable of producing with the given state of technology. Real output cannot be

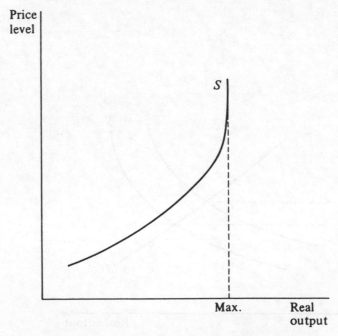

Fig. 3.4

increased beyond this level, and we can therefore amend our figure to that shown in Fig. 3.4.

What sort of cost increases could be responsible for a shift in the supply schedule such as that shown in Fig. 3.3? In the context of the world economy they could be autonomous increases in the cost of essential raw materials brought about through producers' cartels flexing their economic and political muscle (the rise in the price of oil being the most obvious example of this). Or, in other cases, the increase in costs may be attributable to natural causes, such as late frosts ruining the coffee bean harvest.

In the context of the domestic economy, the cost increases can take the form of increased wage costs brought about by a situation in which groups of workers compete against each other for larger shares of the national cake – so-called wage-push inflation.

3.4 Shifts in aggregate demand

Thus, autonomous increases in costs can cause inflation both in the context of the world economy and in the context of the domestic economy. This, however, is only half the picture. The pressure of demand is also important. Just as the price of widgets can rise as a result of a shift in the demand for widgets, so an increase in the aggregate *price level* can be caused by an increase in aggregate demand. Imagine for a moment that widgets are an essential raw material used in production (widgets have this happy knack of being anything the author deems them to be) and that the annual supply of widgets is fixed. If the demand for widgets increases (because new uses are discovered for them or because people are buying more of the finished product which widgets help create), then the price of widgets will rise because buyers are competing amongst each other to secure larger proportions of the available supply. Similarly, if we now redefine widgets to be our composite commodity, an increase in the price of this composite commodity – that is, a rise in the price level – can be caused by an increase in aggregate demand. In other words buyers are competing for the available supply and are thus driving up the price.

The factors that can give rise to an increase in aggregate demand, both in the context of the world economy and the domestic economy, are complex and varied. One thing is certain, however – which is, that the level of demand is influenced by the activities of governments and of monetary authorities.

Before we can go on to discuss factors which affect demand, a further complexity should be noted. Inflation caused initially by demand pressure can be viewed, paradoxically, as cost-push inflation if the focus of our analysis switches from the world economy to the national economy. Consider our example of widgets as an essential raw material used in production. A rise in the world price of widgets can be caused by the establishment of a producer cartel, or it can be caused by an increase in the worldwide demand for widgets. From the focus of the national economy, however, the effect is the same – a rise in the price of imported widgets which increases the production cost of all goods with some widget content. In terms of the national economy, this would be termed cost inflation, even though the rise in the price of widgets could have been triggered off by an increase in the world-wide demand for widgets, and hence, at the international level, the roots of the inflation lay in demand pressure.

3.5 Demand versus cost inflation

By this stage the reader may well be wondering why we have taken such pains to make the analytical distinction between cost-induced and demand-induced inflation. Is it possible to distinguish the two in the real world? Is this not just two different ways of describing the same phenomenon? Is it possible to have pure cost-push inflation – that is, cost-induced inflation which is not accompanied by an increase in aggregate demand?

To shed some light on these questions, consider the following example of a hypothetical economy in which just three commodities are traded – shirts, bread and haircuts.

The prices at which they are sold are p_S, p_B and p_H and the amount bought (and therefore the amount sold) x_S, x_B, and x_H respectively. $p_S x_S$ is thus total spending on shirts, and total expenditure in the economy (aggregate demand) is thus equal to expenditure on shirts plus expenditure on bread plus expenditure on haircuts:

that is, aggregate demand $= p_S x_S + p_B x_B + p_H x_H$ [3.1]

Now this equation is true by definition (thus strictly speaking it should be termed an identity). Therefore, the right-hand side must *always* equal the left-hand side. Bearing this in mind, consider what would happen if, as a result of militant action on the part of the Shirtworkers Union, wage rates rose in that industry. Note that here we are considering wage increases which result not from *demand* pressure in the labour market but from *autonomous* increases in wage costs, that is, increases in wages which are independent of the state of demand in the labour market. Will this spark off pure cost-push inflation?

There are several possible scenarios. The increased wages could all be offset by increases in labour productivity, such that *wage costs* did not rise. Or the increase in wage costs could all be paid out of profits, such that shirt prices were unaffected. If we assume that neither of these two things happen, however, then the result will be that shirt prices rise.

Suppose that, in an effort to control inflation, the government introduces policies which increase the amount of tax revenue taken out of the system and it therefore succeeds in keeping the level of aggregate demand at its pre-existing level. An increase in the price of shirts in a situation in which aggregate demand is held fixed must result in one or more of the following chain of events since there are only three possible ways to make equation [3.1] balance, either:

(a) x_S, the amount of shirts purchased, falls by exactly the same amount as the price rose, thus leaving $p_S x_S$ (total expenditure on shirts) unchanged, or

(b) x_S does not fall, but x_B and x_H (spending on other commodities) do fall, or

(c) p_B and p_H fall.

Consider each of these in turn.

(a) This is the case where the shirtworkers are 'pricing themselves out of the market'. Demand for their product falls in direct proportion to the increase in its price (that is, the price elasticity of demand = 1). The demand for shirt workers' labour will, therefore, fall as the demand for the product which they produce falls. This, we could tentatively say, would lead to unemployment amongst shirt workers.

(b) In this case, the demand in other sectors of the economy falls, creating depressed labour markets and possibly unemployment in those sectors. The shirt workers have benefited at the expense of workers in other industries. They have 'grabbed a larger share of the national cake' for themselves.

(c) This case represents a change in relative prices, shirts becoming more expensive relative to other commodities. The overall price level has remained unchanged, however.

The most likely outcome of the shirt workers' action is some combination of (a) and (b). This represents a fall in the volume of production, accompanied by a rise in unemployment.

We could, therefore, describe this as a *deflationary* situation. Paradoxically, however, what we have here is both a fall in output and employment (deflation) coupled with a rise in the price level (inflation). Thus by restricting the level of aggregate demand in a situation in which autonomous cost increases are occurring, the government has produced the worst possible outcome.

That is why post-war governments have – until recently – preferred to act in an accommodating fashion, allowing the level of aggregate demand to rise so that the same volume of goods can be bought at the new higher prices. By allowing demand to rise they prevent the fall in sales – and therefore the fall in output and employment – that would otherwise have occurred. If the government acts in this accommodating fashion it is evidence that, even though it may be capable of restricting demand, it is unwilling to do so, preferring the evil of inflation to what it regards as the greater social evil of unemployment.

Such a policy may encourage inflation in the longer term, however, for by their action the shirt workers now appear to have gained increases in wages without suffering any fall in employment. This will have a demonstration effect on workers in other industries. Thus, the bread makers and the hairdressers will also push for wage increases which, if granted, will result in increases in the price of bread and haircuts. Inflation, therefore, proceeds and, as it does so, people develop expectations that the government will continue to act in an accomodating fashion by allowing demand to rise. If a new government comes into office committed to reducing inflation at any cost, it will not succeed in doing so by acting on the demand side of the economy as long as these autonomous increases in wage costs continue to occur. In other words, if the cause of inflation is cost-push factors, inflation cannot be reduced by controlling aggregate demand. This is why it is so important to know what the cause of inflation is. One cannot control it until its cause is known.

3.6 Measuring the rate of inflation

Suppose that we continue to consider an economy in which only three goods are traded – shirts, bread and haircuts – and that over a particular twelve-month period the price of shirts rose by 10 per cent, the price of bread rose by 10 per cent and the price of haircuts by 20 per cent. What is the overall rate of inflation over the period? Clearly it would be incorrect to simply average the inflation rates (to give a figure of 15 per cent) or to give equal weight to each commodity (to give a figure of 13.3 per cent). What we need is a set of weights which reflect the importance of each item in people's overall spending. The weights we use will be the proportion of the average household's expenditure devoted to each commodity. These are shown in Table 3.1.

Thus, the rate of inflation works out to be:

$$(10\% \times 0.3) + (10\% \times 0.5) + (20\% \times 0.2) = 12\%.$$

This is the principle on which price indexes are worked out in practice. In Britain, the best known of these indexes is the General Index of Retail Prices, commonly called the Retail Price Index (RPI). The weights used in this index are based on an annual

Table 3.1

	Increase in prices over 12-month period (%)	Weights Proportion of the average households spending devoted to each commodity
Shirts	10	0.3
Bread	10	0.5
Haircuts	20	0.2
		1.0

sample survey of spending habits, the Family Expenditure Survey.
Table 3.2 shows the weights used in 1985. Note that these
weights relate to the average household. Low income households
will tend to spend a larger proportion of their income on
'essentials' like food and a smaller proportion on 'luxuries' like
restaurant meals. Detailed information on spending patterns is
available from the Family Expenditure Survey. This information is
used when compiling the price index for a low income, average
and high-income household. Table 3.3 shows the weights for
various income levels and types of households for 1985.

It is particularly important to note that the RPI is not an index
of essentials or of basic requirements needed to live. If this were
the intention then certain 'luxury' items, like alcohol, tobacco and
hairdressing, would be excluded from the index but this would
involve the statisticians in the impossible task of deciding what is
'essential' and what is a 'luxury' good. Rather, the index seeks to
cover all those goods and services purchased by the typical
household.

Table 3.2 General index of Retail Prices

Weights to be used in 1985

Food	190
Bread	10
Flour	1
Other cereals	4
Biscuits	5
Cakes, buns, pastries, etc	5
Beef	13
Lamb	5
Pork	5
Bacon	6
Ham (cooked)	2
Other meat and meat products	17
Fish	6
Butter	3
Margarine	2
Lard and other cooking fats	1
Cheese	5
Eggs	4
Milk, fresh	16
Milk, canned, dried, etc	3
Tea	4

Housing	153
Rent	31
Owner-occupiers, mortgage interest payments	31
Owner-occupiers, dwelling insurance premiums and ground rent	5
Rates and water charges	45
Charges for repairs, maintenance, etc.	9
Materials for home repairs, decorations, etc	17

Fuel and light	65
Coal	6
Smokeless fuels	2
Gas	24
Electricity	29
Oil and other fuel and light	4

Durable household goods	65
Furniture	13
Radio, television, etc.	11
Other household appliances	16
Floor coverings	6

Transport and vehicles	156
Purchase of motor vehicles	55
Maintenance of motor vehicles	15
Petrol and oil	50
Motor licences	9
Motor insurance	10
Cycles and other vehicles	3
Rail transport	6
Road transport	8

Miscellaneous goods	77
Books	4
Newspapers and periodicals	13
Writing paper and other stationers' goods	5
Medicine surgical, etc goods	5
Toiletries	9
Soap and detergents	6
Soda and polishes	3
Other household goods	2
Travel and sports goods, leather goods, jewellery, etc	17
Photographic and optical goods	4

Coffee, cocoa, proprietary drinks	4	Soft furnishings	7	Toys	4
Soft drinks	4	Chinaware, glassware, etc	2	Plants, flowers, horticultural goods, etc	5
Sugar	2	Hardware, ironmongery, etc.	10		
Jam, marmalade and syrup	1	**Clothing and footwear**	**75**	**Services**	**62**
Potatoes	7	Men's outer clothing	11	Postage	2
Other vegetables, fresh, canned and frozen	12	Men's underclothing	4	Telephones and telemessages	16
Fruit, fresh, dried and canned	11	Women's outer clothing	4	Television licences, TV set and video rentals	12
Sweets and chocolates	13	Women's underclothing	3	Other entertainment	11
Ice cream	2	Children's outer clothing	9	Domestic help	4
Other foods	11	Children's underclothing	1	Hairdressing	7
Food for animals	6	Hose	3	Boot and shoe repairing	1
Alcoholic drink	**75**	Gloves, haberdashery, hats, etc	3	Laundering	1
Beer	44	Clothing materials	1	Miscellaneous services	8
Spirits, wines, etc.	31	Men's footwear	5	**Meals bought and consumed outside the home**	**45**
Tobacco	**37**	Women's footwear	7		
Cigarettes	34	Children's footwear	4	**Total, all items**	**1000**
Tobacco	3				

Note: Index households are all households *other than* (a) those the head of which had a recorded gross income of at least £350 a week in the second half of 1983 and the first half of 1984 and (b) those in which at least three-quarters of the total income was derived from national insurance retirement or similar pensions and/or supplementary benefits paid in supplementation or instead of such pensions.

Source: *Department of Employment Gazette*, March 1985.

Table 3.3 Patterns of household expenditure, by household composition and income level

| | Percentage of expenditure allocated to: | | | | | | | | | |
	Housing	Fuel, light and power	Food	Alcohol and tobacco	Clothing and footwear	Household and other goods	Transport and vehicles	Services and miscellaneous	Total of all groups
All UK households	**15.84**	**6.20**	**20.69**	**7.65**	**7.31**	**15.44**	**14.99**	**11.88**	**100**
Household composition									
One adult:									
Low income pensioner	12.39	16.14	30.72	5.40	4.89	13.78	2.90	13.78	100
Other retired	30.56	19.82	18.59	3.67	4.96	11.78	7.32	13.30	100
Non-retired	19.92	7.07	17.43	9.01	5.44	14.04	14.29	12.80	100
One adult, one child	13.16	8.99	22.95	6.89	11.72	13.84	10.76	11.69	100
One adult, two or more children	10.58	9.51	26.74	6.34	10.48	14.13	8.68	13.54	100
One man one woman:									
Low income pensioner	13.19	11.55	30.10	8.19	6.52	14.38	6.44	9.63	100
Other retired	20.54	7.71	20.42	5.90	5.61	15.68	12.48	11.66	100
Non-retired	17.60	5.39	18.41	7.75	6.50	15.49	16.39	12.47	100
Two men or two women	15.71	6.13	18.90	8.20	7.54	12.19	17.72	13.61	100

One man, one woman with:									
One child	15.53	6.03	20.71	7.27	7.64	16.97	15.31	10.54	**100**
Two children	15.23	5.75	21.19	6.40	7.80	16.92	14.28	12.43	**100**
Three children	13.48	5.93	23.86	7.09	8.41	15.07	13.95	12.21	**100**
Two adults, four or more children	12.61	6.93	27.98	6.51	8.31	16.36	11.56	9.74	**100**
Three adults	13.97	5.04	18.79	8.80	7.03	16.74	19.26	10.37	**100**
Three adults, one or more children	13.59	4.82	21.88	9.14	8.66	14.76	16.13	11.02	**100**
Four or more adults	10.77	4.42	19.94	10.70	8.56	13.72	20.52	11.37	**100**
Four or more adults, one or more children	9.42	5.05	23.01	11.06	9.62	13.98	15.70	12.16	**100**
Income level:									
Households with gross household income in the:									
Lowest 20 per cent	14.20	13.04	28.71	8.22	5.76	13.10	6.59	10.38	**100**
Middle 60 per cent	16.36	6.59	21.96	8.00	7.17	14.96	14.26	10.70	**100**
Highest 20 per cent	15.34	4.31	17.26	7.00	7.80	16.70	17.66	13.93	**100**

Source: *Department of Employment Gazette* December 1985

Questions

1. Which of the following could *ceteris paribus* be responsible for causing an increase in the price of houses in Ealing, a suburb of West London. Carefully explain the nature of the causal mechanism in each case, stating whether the mechanism is of the demand-pull or cost-push type.

   (a) A cut in tax relief on mortgage interest payments.
   (b) An increase in the cost of bricks.
   (c) A fall in house prices in Acton (which borders on Ealing).
   (d) An increase in the money supply.
   (e) An increase in wages paid to BBC employees, many of whom live in Ealing.

2. Which of the following statements are correct?

   (a) An increase in Value Added Tax (VAT) is deflationary because it reduces aggregate demand.
   (b) An increase in VAT is inflationary because it increases prices.
   (c) An increase in VAT is reflationary because it increases aggregate demand.
   (d) An increase in VAT is reflationary because it reduces aggregate demand.

3. Which of the following statements are correct?

   (a) Cost increases invariably lead to price increases.
   (b) An increase in wages will definitely give rise to cost-push inflationary forces.
   (c) An increase in wages will *ceteris paribus* increase aggregate demand.
   (d) A reflationary policy need not be inflationary.

   (i) (a) and (c) only   (ii) (b) and (c) only   (iii) (c) and (d) only   (iv) I think there must be a misprint.

4. In 1974 oil prices rose rapidly. In 1986 they fell. Were cost-push or demand-pull factors responsible for these movements?

5. 'In Monravia inflation was 30 per cent in 1983 and in that year an incomes policy was introduced with the result that a year later inflation had fallen to 15 per cent.' What is wrong with this statement?

6. In Bogravia people buy only imported wine, cheese (which is home produced) and theatre tickets. The proportion of income spent on these three items is as follows:

   wine 30 per cent
   cheese 60 per cent
   theatre tickets 10 per cent

   Between January 1986 and January 1987 the price of imports rose by 30 per cent, cheese by 45 per cent and theatre tickets by 10 per cent. What was the rate of inflation over the 12-month period?

   (a) 35%   (b) 37%   (c) 15%   (d) 47%   (e) too difficult without a calculator.

Chapter 4
The determinants of aggregate demand –
Keynesian interpretations

4.1 Preview

In Chapter 3 we saw how the causes of inflation can be interpreted either in terms of demand factors or in terms of cost factors. In this chapter and in Chapter 5, we shall look at the factors which determine the level of aggregate demand. In Chapter 6 we look in more detail at wage-push inflation. Our analysis in these three chapters is essentially that which relates to a 'closed economy' – one that does not have trading relationships with the rest of the world. This unrealistic assumption will be relaxed in Chapter 7, where we consider the phenomenon of inflation in the context of an open economy such as the United Kingdom's.

As the reader is no doubt aware, there is no consensus of opinion amongst economists as to how the determinants of the level of aggregate demand should best be analysed. This lack of consensus is evident in many other areas, but this issue is one of the main battle areas between the two major opposing schools of thought. Since this issue is so crucial, we have devoted some space to an elaboration of the key points of difference between the two schools; and we have attempted to put the Keynesian views into perspective by examining some of the pre-Keynesian ideas about the workings of the macroeconomy.

4.2 Demand inflation

The idea of inflation being caused by too great a flow of spending in the economy is normally associated with the name of J. M. Keynes, though it is useful to note that Keynes's classic work, *The General Theory of Employment, Interest and Money* (1936), also incorporates a cost-push analysis of inflation. Keynes is the single most important influence on contemporary thinking about the way the macroeconomy works. The level of aggregate demand, in this view, is the most important determining variable in the economic system. When we talk of the level of aggregate demand, it should be made clear that we are talking about the size of the flow of spending. Thus, it might be more accurate to talk of the *rate* of aggregate demand, so emphasizing that it is a flow and not a stock.

Consider what happens as the level of aggregate demand rises in an economy which is currently suffering a recession. Individual firms will find that the demand for their product is increasing. Future sales prospects look brighter and the firm decides to step up its production, as it now feels confident that it can sell more than it was doing previously. In order to produce more it may need to take on more labour, or to pay its existing workers to work overtime. It may feel so confident about future sales prospects that it decides to increase its productive capacity by installing extra machines.

The spending which each individual firm is undertaking in paying men to work overtime, employing additional labour, and buying new machinery, has a reinforcing effect on aggregate demand, which rises still further. The further increase in aggregate demand confirms the optimistic expectations of future sales prospects, and more expansion of production and employment is undertaken.

There will come a time, however, when the response of the economy to increases in aggregate demand starts to become sluggish. Firms will want to increase production, but they will find it difficult to do so as they encounter difficulties in hiring extra labour. To overcome this they may offer higher wage rates in an attempt to attract workers from other firms and other industries. These rival firms are forced to retaliate by paying higher wages in order to retain their existing workforce. Additional difficulties may be encountered. Firms wanting to expand production by installing new machines may find that there is now a long waiting-list for new capital equipment. The capital goods industries will be facing similar problems to the firms they supply, with rising wage costs eroding profitability. However, with full order books and customers waiting for delivery, firms can afford to increase prices without affecting sales, and this they do as a means of restoring profitability. Thus, prices in the economy begin to rise.

In this view, then, the level of demand in the economy determines the volume of production and investment. It determines the level of employment (and unemployment) and, when the economy is operating at full capacity, it determines the rate of inflation.

4.3 The determinants of aggregate demand – injections and withdrawals

What then determines the level of this crucial variable, the level of aggregate demand? As we have seen before, there are a number of conflicting opinions amongst economists on this question. In this chapter we put forward the explanation offered by the Keynesian school of economists, and in Chapter 5 we look at the main opposition group, the monetarist school. It should be apparent, however, that most economists would profess to have some sympathies with both groups, so that the versions we shall present of 'Keynesian' and 'monetarist' ideas should be seen as 'ideal types'.

We saw in section 1.3 that crucial to the Keynesian view of the workings of the macroeconomy is the concept of macroeconomic equilibrium. Spending is assumed to flow around the economy in a circular fashion – from households to firms as payment for goods and services, and back to households again as payment for the factor services, labour, capital, etc. which were used to produce the goods and services. The economy was said to be in equilibrium if the volume of the circular flow settles down at some particular level and stays there. Equilibrium will be maintained as long as the spending which 'leaks out' of the system in the form of savings, spending on imports and tax payments, is exactly matched by an equal volume of injections – investment, government spending and export sales.

When people spend their income on buying domestically produced goods they are creating income for the firms who make those goods. The firms use that income to pay their workforce, their suppliers, their shareholders, etc. who thus receive income, which they in turn spend. Now consider what would happen if, instead of spending all their income on domestically produced goods, they spent part of it on imports. This spending does not create income for domestic firms, who therefore suffer a fall in income. Payments to their shareholders, their workforce, etc. will therefore be reduced. Since these groups will have suffered a fall in income, they in turn will reduce their spending, and so on. In theory this process would continue and a new equilibrium would be reached at a lower level of national income since, in each successive spending-round, the size of the fall in spending will become less and less.

Suppose on average people spend 80p out of their last £1 of income. Let us suppose that income drops by £1 as a result of the initiating rise in imports. Consumption therefore falls by 80p, and this means domestic incomes will be reduced by 80p. In the next round, consumption will fall by 64p (80 per cent of 80p), implying a similar fall in domestic incomes. In the following round consumption falls again, as does income, but this time by 51.2p (80 per cent of 64p), and so on. This process continues through successive rounds until the fall in consumption and income becomes infinitely small, at which point the level of income will have reached its new equilibrium.

The overall drop in national income (that is, the change in the equilibrium level) which is brought about by the initial withdrawal will, however, be larger than the size of the initial withdrawal. This is the so-called *multiplier* effect. A change in the volume of injections or withdrawals will produce a larger change in aggregate demand once the changes have fully worked through the system.

The reader may remember that, in the introduction to this chapter, we stated that we would be analysing the determinants of aggregate demand in the context of a closed economy. The presence of imports and exports would appear to be incompatible with this assumption. We can reconcile this paradox however.

In terms of the Keynesian model, the impact on aggregate demand of, say, a rise in withdrawals is the same whether this withdrawal takes the form of a rise in savings, an increase in spending on imported goods or an increase in taxes levied by governments.

Thus, spending on imports is just one particular type of 'leakage' from the system, and is analytically indistinguishable from other types of leakage.

4.4 The manipulation of aggregate demand: the budget

The level of aggregate demand in the economy can be manipulated by the government. If it increases income tax this will reduce people's disposable income (or 'take-home' pay) and therefore reduce their ability to spend. This will lead to a fall in spending. On the other hand, if the government increases its spending (say, on education or roads or pensions) then this will increase incomes (of teachers, road-builders and pensioners) and therefore lead to an increase in spending.

The overall level of government spending relative to its revenue from taxation is known as its budget stance.

If government spending exceeds government tax revenue, this is said to be a budget deficit. There is thus a net addition to aggregate demand since the government takes out of the economy (in the form of taxation) less than it puts back (in the form of government spending). Such a budget is sometimes described as reflationary, which simply means that it adds to aggregate demand.

When government spending equals total tax revenue, this is said to be a balanced budget, and when tax revenues exceed government spending the budget is in surplus. A budget surplus is described as deflationary in the sense that it reduces aggregate demand.

4.5 A methodological note: an alternative view of the macroeconomy

We noted at the beginning of Chapter 4 the extent to which

Keynesian ideas transformed the way we view the workings of the macroeconomy. The concept of injections and withdrawals, of equilibrium in the circular flow, of the multiplier – all these ideas we owe to Keynes.

A word of warning, however. One should guard against the temptation of regarding Keynes as some sort of Messiah sent to show men – and particularly the pre-Keynesian or classical economists – the error of their ways. Although Keynes is often presented in this light, there is a two-fold danger in so doing. First, it encourages us to believe that the classical economists were fools, and thus prevents us from trying to understand their view of the world. Second, it encourages the belief that Keynesian economics is correct, whilst the economics which preceded it was incorrect. That is, it leads us to accept uncritically that the Keynesian view of the world is, in some sense, 'true'. This is a very dangerous epistemological position.

What Keynes did was to present a way of analysing the workings of the macroeconomy. He provided a *theory* about the way the economy worked. Since his death in 1946, this has proved to be an enormously useful way of looking at the economy, and of controlling it.

But this success should not obscure from us the fact that the economy will forever remain to us a 'black box', the workings of which we can never see. The 'black box' sends out signals – prices are rising, unemployment is falling and so on – but we can never really know what causes these things to happen. All we can do is to construct models whose purpose is to simulate the behaviour of the real economy. The suitability of the models will be judged by the extent to which they appear to be able to accurately simulate what has happened in the real world, and what will happen in the future. If the simulations are realistic then we can say that the real world must be like our model. The causal relationships existing within the black box must be like the causal relationships of our theory.

In order to illustrate more clearly the point that Keynesian theory is nothing more than a *theory* about the way the world works, and in order to put Keynes's ideas into some sort of perspective, it may be useful to investigate briefly some aspects of the classical system which the Keynesian revolution overthrew.

4.6 The classical view

For the classical economists, the study of the macroeconomy relied heavily on the so-called theory of value: demand and supply analysis. This is clearly seen in their analysis of the behaviour of savings, investment and the rate of interest.

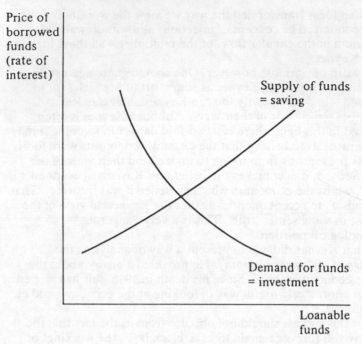

Price of
borrowed
funds
(rate of
interest)

Supply of funds
= saving

Demand for funds
= investment

Loanable
funds

Fig. 4.1

The rate of interest is the price of borrowed funds. For the classical economists it was natural to argue that this price would be determined by the interaction of the supply of these funds and the demand for them.

The supply of loanable funds must come from income not consumed or savings. Similarly, the demand for funds comes from persons and businesses wishing to undertake investment in some project. In the classical system, the flow of savings is always matched by an exactly equal flow of investment, and this equality is ensured by movements in the interest rate. Therefore, provided the government balances its budget (government spending = government tax revenues) and that some mechanism ensures that the flow of imports is matched by an approximately equal flow of exports, then there can never be a situation in which there is a net withdrawal of spending from the circular flow, or a net injection of spending into the circular flow. The spending which 'leaks-out' of the economy in the form of savings is always injected back into the economy in the form of an exactly equal volume of investment.

In our discussion of the Keynesian system, we saw how an increase in savings (a leakage of spending) will lead to a fall in aggregate demand. In the classical system, this does not happen

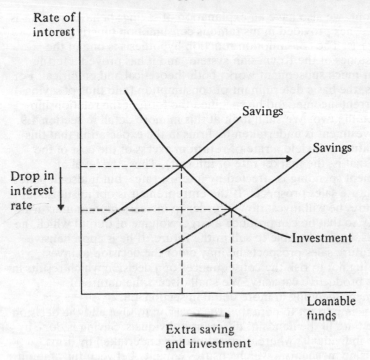

Fig. 4.2

because a fall in the volume of savings will cause interest rates to fall and thus encourage extra investment.

In Fig. 4.2, the increase in savings is shown by a shift in the savings function, reflecting a change in attitudes towards saving. This causes a movement along the investment schedule, as interest rates drop.

This analysis of the workings of the macroeconomy has a kind of faultless logic. Keynes attacked it however, not because it was logically inconsistent, but because it was unrealistic. Savings behaviour, he argued, will not be much influenced by the rate of interest, and the decision to invest will depend upon other factors in addition to the rate of interest.

4.7 The Keynesian view – the behaviour of savings and investment

Savings are the residual element of income which is left over when consumption plans are satisfied. As such, the decision to save and the decision to consume were, for Keynes, two aspects of the same thing. Thus, if we have a satisfactory explanation of consumption behaviour, we also have an explanation of savings behaviour. This is what Keynes provided in his famous consumption function hypothesis. The consumption function hypothesis is one of the cornerstones of the Keynesian system, and it has proved a fertile area for much subsequent work, both theoretical and empirical. For Keynes, the basic determinant of consumption (and thus of savings) was current income, and he specified the form of the relationship between the two. We shall look at this in more detail in section 4.9.

Investment is undertaken by firms in the expectation that this expenditure will yield a rate of return in excess of the cost of the funds (that is, the market rate of interest). Thus, the level of investment spending is affected by interest rates, but it also depends upon future sales prospects. If the entrepreneur is optimistic about the future, he will invest now in order to increase his manufacturing capacity so that he can produce a larger volume of output which, he believes, he will be able to sell in the future. If he is apprehensive about future sales prospects he may defer the decision to invest, preferring not to risk the consequences of a decision which results in surplus productive capacity. We shall discuss the nature of investment spending in more detail in section 4.8.

It is important to note that the decision to save and the decision to invest are in the hands of different individuals. Saving is done by private individuals, whereas investment is undertaken by firms. There is no mechanism which ensures equality between the amount of saving which individuals plan to do and the amount of investment which firms plan to undertake.

If individuals decide to save more this releases resources from consumption. These resources may be taken up and used by firms to add to the stock of capital goods (that is, used for investment purposes). In this case, both savings and investment increase.

But what if investment does not increase, following a rise in savings? In this case aggregate demand will fall and the resources released from producing consumer goods will lie idle, causing the economy to go into recession. Clearly, then, the levels of savings and investment are vital elements in determining the overall level of activity in the economy, and we shall devote the next two sections (4.8 and 4.9) to a detailed examination of the determinants of these two variables.

4.8 Investment

4.8.1 Fixed capital formation

Up to now we have been using the term 'investment' without explaining exactly what is meant by it. There are in fact several different meanings of the word 'investment' and the rather cavalier attitude regarding the usage of the word amongst economists is no doubt partly responsible for the confusion surrounding it.

Both consumption and investment expenditure are components of aggregate demand. They are both spending, which creates income for someone else. The distinction between consumption spending and investment spending is in practice not very clear cut, owing a good deal to accounting conventions rather than to any analytical distinctions. Nevertheless, the convention is to treat them as though they were different types of spending.

To understand the meaning of the concept of investment in macroeconomics, it will be helpful to think of a closed economy (that is, one in which there are no imports or exports) and in which there is no government sector (that is, there is no government spending or taxation). In such an economy, we say there are just two sectors – the household sector and the firm sector. Although most individuals participate in both sectors, the two sectors are *analytically* distinct. The household sector consumes goods and services produced by the firm sector. Households derive their income by selling factor services to firms, and the firms pay the households in the form of wages and salaries, interest, dividends and rent. The households themselves are the ultimate owners of all the factors of production (labour, capital and land) because the firms themselves are ultimately owned by households. The firms merely buy in factors of production (raw materials, labour services, capital services and so on) and convert these inputs into an output which is valued more highly than the inputs (assuming the firm makes a profit). The excess of total revenues over total costs – the firm's profit – then accrues to the owners of the firm, the household sector.

The value of the total output of such an economy – or national product – can be calculated by the sum of the values added by each firm. This avoids the double-counting which would otherwise occur when firms buy factors of production from other firms. From the point of view of the economy as a whole, the contribution to total output made by an individual firm is equal to the value of its sales less the cost of factors of production bought in from other firms – in other words, its value added. The sum of all the values added is equal to the value of national product.

Now, the goods and services produced in an economy in a given year must be either consumed during that year or else they must be added to the stock of physical assets (we shall subsequently amend this statement in section 4.8.3). Thus, we can write that the value of national product (Y) must be equal to the sum of consumption expenditure (C) plus investment expenditure (I) (where the term 'investment expenditure' should be taken to mean an addition to the stock of capital goods).

$$Y = C + I \qquad\qquad [4.1]$$

It is in this restricted sense that the term 'investment' should be interpreted in macroeconomics. Investment is any act of expenditure which adds to the capital stock of the economy. If an individual purchases shares, or antiques, or a country cottage, this does not constitute investment from a macroeconomic point of view. It merely represents a change of ownership, and the stock of capital possessed by society remains unchanged.

Moreover, investment stands in direct contrast to consumption. Investment represents forgone consumption. The act of investment is one in which the purchaser abstains from current consumption in order to increase the economy's productive potential, and hence the possibilities for future consumption.

4.8.2 Gross and net investment

We should be careful to distinguish between gross investment and net investment. In the process of production, part of the capital stock is used up because machines wear out and so on, and investment purchasing may merely serve to replace the capital used up in the process of production. This would then be termed replacement investment and it does not increase the size of the capital stock. The capital stock only increases if gross investment (that is, total investment) exceeds the amount required to replace the capital used up; that is, the size of the capital stock only increases if there is a positive amount of net investment, in addition to replacement investment.

4.8.3. Inventory investment

Up to now we have been talking about investment as an addition to the stock of capital, and this fixed capital formation does, in fact, make up the vast bulk of investment expenditures. A small part of what is classified as investment expenditure, however, takes the form of inventory investment – the building up of stocks of finished goods or raw materials. This may be a voluntary act or it may be the unintended consequence of an unexpected fall in sales, which then leaves the producer with more unsold goods than he planned to hold.

That this should be treated as investment can be seen when we recall our earlier statement that all the goods and services produced in an economy in a given year must be either consumed during that year or added to the stock of capital goods in the economy. We can now see that this statement is not quite correct. All the goods and services produced in a given year must be either consumed or they must add to the stock of fixed capital or, there is the third possibility, that they remain unsold. This third category represents inventory investment. From a macroeconomic viewpoint, it makes no difference whether the increase in stocks is of raw materials bought in from other firms, or work-in-progress, or finished goods. In every case it represents output of the firm sector which has not yet been consumed or added to the stock of fixed capital.

4.8.4 The treatment of investment in the national accounts

This then is the concept of investment in macroeconomics. In practice, however, in the national accounts, the classification of expenditure into the investment category and other categories is somewhat arbitrary.

First, because of the way in which the national accounts are prepared, investment is only capable of being undertaken by the firm sector. Thus, if a firm purchases a new car for one of its salesmen, or a new typewriter for one of the secretaries, this is regarded as investment expenditure. If a private individual purchases the same items, this is regarded as consumption expenditure. The underlying motive for these purchases is the same in both cases – the acquisition of a capital asset which will yield a stream of useful services throughout the life of that asset. The only difference between the two cases is that, in the former, the acquisition of these assets is supposed to increase the economy's capacity to produce marketable goods and services, whereas in the latter case, even though the individual's capacity for self gratification may be increased by the acquisition of these assets, the individual is not able to sell the increased satisfaction he derives.

The distinction between the firm sector and the household sector is, of course, blurred when one considers the self-employed. Here the individual may choose, for tax reasons, to change his status from that of a private individual to that of a company, and thus any acquisition of capital assets he undertakes which are relevant to his livelihood would be reclassified accordingly.

Nothing that has been said should be construed as implying that there is no clear analytical distinction between investment expenditure and consumption. Such an analytical distinction does exist, but it is difficult to apply in practice. Much expenditure, of course, could be construed as both consumption and investment. Perhaps the best example of this is expenditure on education, particularly higher education. It is enjoyed for its own sake, and thus represents consumption, but it also raises the earning power of the educated individual. Since the individual has to forgo earnings and thus consumption while he is acquiring the education, we can thus legitimately talk about the individual investing in education. This dual role of educational spending has been recognized for many years by economists. It is impossible to classify it as either consumption expenditure or investment expenditure since it is clearly both.

4.8.5 *The determinants of investment*

Having spent some time discussing the nature of investment, we now turn to an analysis of investment behaviour, taken here to mean expenditure on fixed capital formation.

A feature possessed by most items of capital equipment is that they have a purchase price in excess of the value of the output they can produce in any one year. Let us say, for example, that a machine whose purchase price is £3000 can produce goods valued at £1000 in each year of its life. If this is generally true for all machines in the economy, we say that the capital output ratio is 3 : 1.

Now consider a situation in which a manufacturer is currently employing all his productive capacity to meet the demand for his product. Suppose further that on the basis of the forecasts he anticipates an increase in the demand for his product next year which will enable him to sell an additional £1000 worth of output. In order to meet this demand, he will have to invest £3000 this year. This, of course, is in addition to any investment expenditure he would have to undertake to replace capital used up in the process of production – that is, the £3000 represents net investment. We can therefore say that net investment this year will be three times the anticipated rise in sales next year.

Now, the question remains, on what does the manufacturer base his expectations of future sales prospects? The simplest explanation is to say that he will base his forecasts on what has happened in the most recent past – if sales this year have been rising he will anticipate a similar rise next year.

Thus, we can formulate what is known as the simple accelerator model of investment behaviour:

$$I_t = \alpha\,(Y_t - Y_{t-1}) = \alpha\,\Delta\,Y_t \qquad\qquad [4.2]$$

where I_t stands for net investment this year, $(Y_t - Y_{t-1})$ stands for the growth in sales this year (that is, the difference between the level of sales this year and the level last year), and α stands for the accelerator coefficient, in this case 3. (Δ is the Greek letter delta which is used to mean 'change in'.)

Keynes based his analysis of the determinants of aggregate investment around an accelerator model such as this. The key factor to note is that the model suggests that investment spending will be very volatile, since small changes in output (Y) produce much larger changes in net investment (I).

It is easy to see from equation [4.2] that if there is no growth in

output ($\triangle Y = 0$) then net investment will also be zero.
Furthermore, if the economy experiences a downturn, so that
output this year is less than output last year (that is, $\triangle Y$ is
negative), then net investment will be negative. What this means is
that gross investment will be insufficient to replace the capital used
up in the process of production. In other words, the capital stock is
being run down.

Accelerator models are only moderately successful in predicting
investment behaviour in practice. As Keynes acknowledged, the
rate of interest also affects investment and, by extending our
example, we can see how the cost of funds will affect the
profitability of an investment project and hence determine whether
or not it is undertaken.

Suppose the machine in our example has a life of four years,
after which time it is scrapped. The total value of its output, it
would appear, is £4000 and, since this exceeds the purchase price of
£3000, the investment yields a profit of £1000 and therefore must be
worth undertaking. This argument is fallacious, however, since if
the £3000 had been deposited in a bank for four years it would have
earned interest over this period. The real profitability of the project
should therefore take account of the interest cost of the funds tied
up in the project.

To properly appraise the profitability of the project we should
calculate its Net Present Value (NPV). Let us simplify the real
world somewhat and assume that the time profile of the investment
is like that shown in Fig. 4.3.

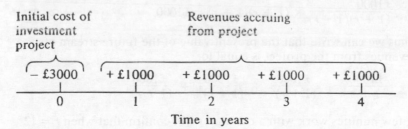

Fig. 4.3

The initial cost of the investment accrues at the beginning of
year one. The revenues which the investment generates will, in
practice, accrue continuously throughout the next four years, but for
simplicity we assume that they occur in four discrete lumps, the first
at the end of year one and the last at the end of year four.

Because these revenues occur in the future they should be
discounted, that is, they should be valued less highly than if they
had occurred earlier. Take for example the revenue of £1000

occurring at the end of year one. If the revenue had accrued at the beginning of year one instead of at the end, then it could have been reinvested (by lending it to a bank, for example); and by the end of the twelve-month period the compound interest it would have earned would have increased its value to:

$$\text{£}1000 \times (1 + r)$$

where r is the rate of interest that such funds can typically earn.

Therefore, the *present value* of £1000 accruing in twelve months' time must be:

$$\frac{\text{£}1000}{1 + r}$$

This is intuitively obvious, since $\frac{\text{£}1000}{1 + r}$ invested in a bank for twelve months will be worth:

$$\frac{\text{£}1000}{1 + r} \times (1 + r) = \text{£}1000 \text{ in twelve months' time.}$$

Similarly, the present value of the £1000 which accrues at the end of year two must be:

$$\frac{\text{£}1000}{(1 + r)(1 + r)} = \frac{\text{£}1000}{(1 + r)^2}$$

since the value of this sum of money if invested for two years would be:

$$\frac{\text{£}1000}{(1 + r)(1 + r)} \times (1 + r)(1 + r) = \text{£}1000.$$

Thus we can write that the present value of the future stream of revenues from the project is equal to:

$$\frac{\text{£}1000}{1 + r} + \frac{\text{£}1000}{(1 + r)^2} + \frac{\text{£}1000}{(1 + r)^3} + \frac{\text{£}1000}{(1 + r)^4}$$

A few minutes work with a calculator will confirm that when $r = 12$ per cent this is approximately equal to £3037, so that the NPV is £37 (that is, the discounted stream of future revenues minus the initial capital cost). However, when the rate of interest rises to 13 per cent the NPV falls to minus £25.

Now any investment project which has a positive NPV will be worth undertaking since, in effect, it gives the firm a greater return than it could get by simply lending its money to the bank. As the rate of interest rises, however, the NPV becomes negative and the firm will no longer undertake investment in the project. Thus, a rise in the rate of interest will reduce the volume of investment in new plant and machinery undertaken.

We can restate this conclusion in a slightly different way. It is easy to see that, in our example, there must be some rate of discount, somewhere between 12 and 13 per cent, that makes the NPV exactly equal to zero. This rate of discount is called the Internal Rate of Return (IRR) of the project. Now, as long as the internal rate of return exceeds the external rate of return (or the cost of funds in the market generally), the investment will be worth undertaking. On the other hand, if the IRR is less than the market rate of interest, the investment will not be undertaken.

At any point in time there will be some marginal investment projects whose IRR just exceeds the market rate of interest. As the market rate of interest rises, these projects will become unprofitable and will be shelved. Thus, aggregate investment in fixed capital formation falls as interest rates rise.

4.9 Savings behaviour

4.9.1. The consumption function

For Keynes, as we saw, the basic determinant of consumption (and thus also of the level of savings) was current income. Consumption spending, he argued, would rise as income rose. For most individuals, he argued, consumption spending rises as income rises, though in general the rise in consumption is not as great as the rise in income. In other words, people tend to save part of their increased income. A particularly simple form of functional relationship which is consistent with these assumptions is:

$$C = a + bY \qquad [4.3]$$

where C is consumption spending
   Y is income
   and a and b are the parameters of the equation. To be consistent with Keynes's assumptions, a should be a positive number and b should be a positive fraction.

Although the assumptions Keynes made seem naïve (particularly the assumption that people save part of their increased income!) a simple model of consumption behaviour of this form provides a starting point for the more sophisticated models of consumer behaviour which have developed out of it.

It is not our intention here to discuss those subsequent models. We shall merely look at some of the more important implications of the consumption function hypothesis.

4.9.2 The marginal propensity to consume: the multiplier

In the consumption function equation, b is the Marginal Propensity to Consume (MPC). It measures the proportion of any increased income which is consumed. The remaining fraction $(1 - b)$ is saved, hence $(1 - b)$ is known as the Marginal Propensity to Save (MPS).

To illustrate this, consider a simple numerical example where

$$a = 100$$
$$b = 0.8$$

If $Y = 600$ then

$$C = 100 + 0.8(600) = 580$$

Now if income rises to 700 then

$$C = 100 + 0.8(700) = 660$$

Thus spending rises by 80 when income rises by 100, implying an MPC of 0.8. Saving increases by $100 - 80 = 20$ as a result of the increase in income of 100, implying an MPS of 0.2. Since MPS $= 1 - b = 1 - 0.8$, this is seen to be correct.

The MPC is a crucial parameter in the Keynesian system since it is one of the determinants of the value of the multiplier. The multiplier, which we introduced in section 4.3, measures the impact on aggregate demand of any change in the volume of injections or withdrawals. It may be helpful to re-read that section at this point before proceeding.

Consider a closed economy as in section 4.3, where the MPC is equal to 0.8. What will be the effect in such an economy of a rise in the volume of injections of, say, £100? The immediate effect is, of course, to increase incomes by £100, which will cause an increase in spending of $0.8 \times £100 = £80$. In the next round, with incomes up a further £80, spending will rise by a further £64 and so on. Figure 4.4 illustrates the position after ten rounds. The total increase in income after ten rounds is equal to about £447. If we carried on for a very large number of successive rounds, the total increase in income would, in fact, be equal to £500. The size of the multiplier effect in this case would be equal to the ratio of the change in equilibrium income (£500) to the initiating change in the volume of injections (£100). That is, the value of the multiplier would be 5.

Clearly, however, it would take a large number of successive rounds for the full multiplier effect to work itself out. For the moment, however, it will be convenient to imagine that these successive spending rounds take place instantaneously. This will enable us to compare the original equilibrium position (that is, before the initiating rise in injections) with the final equilibrium position (that is, after the full multiplier effect has worked itself out). This is known, incidentally, as comparative statics analysis, since we are comparing two static equilibria without concerning

Rise in income

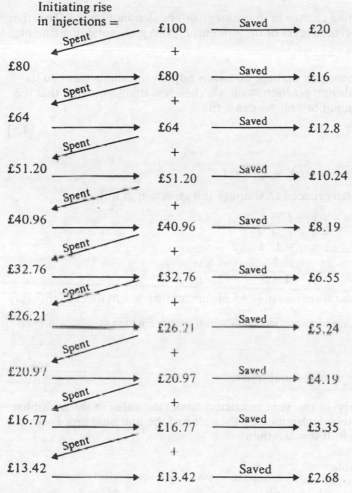

Initiating rise in injections =

	Spent ←	£100	Saved → £20
£80		+	
	Spent →	£80	Saved → £16
£64		+	
	Spent →	£64	Saved → £12.8
£51.20		+	
	Spent →	£51.20	Saved → £10.24
£40.96		+	
	Spent →	£40.96	Saved → £8.19
£32.76		+	
	Spent →	£32.76	Saved → £6.55
£26.21		+	
	Spent →	£26.21	Saved → £5.24
£20.97		+	
	Spent →	£20.97	Saved → £4.19
£16.77		+	
	Spent →	£16.77	Saved → £3.35
£13.42		+	
	→	£13.42	Saved → £2.68

Fig. 4.4

ourselves with the 'dynamic' problem of how long it takes the economy to move from one equilibrium position to another.

Provided we are prepared to work within the comparative statics framework, we can prove the above result quite simply. In a closed economy with no government sector, total spending is equal to the sum of consumption and investment expenditures

$$E = C + I \qquad [4.4]$$

Our consumption function, as before, is:

$$C = a + bY \qquad\qquad\qquad \text{[4.3 repeated]}$$

The initiating change in investment will be denoted by $\triangle I$. Together with the original level of investment, I_o, this gives total investment:

$$I = I_o + \triangle I$$

Now if we assume that the economy adjusts instantaneously to its new equilibrium position, which is the same thing as saying that it is always in equilibrium, we can write

$$Y \overset{e}{=} E \qquad\qquad\qquad\qquad\qquad\qquad \text{[4.5]}$$

and thus

$$Y \overset{e}{=} E = a + bY + I_o + \triangle I$$

We can then proceed to simplify this equation as follows.

$$Y \overset{e}{=} a + bY + I_o + \triangle I$$
$$Y - bY \overset{e}{=} a + I_o + \triangle I$$
$$Y(1 - b) \overset{e}{=} a + I_o + \triangle I$$
$$Y \overset{e}{=} \frac{a}{1-b} + \frac{1}{1-b} I_o + \frac{1}{1-b} \triangle I \qquad \text{[4.6]}$$

Thus we see from equation [4.6] that an increase in investment, $\triangle I$, will cause an increase in equilibrium income which is $\dfrac{1}{1-b}$ times as great.

That is, $\dfrac{1}{1-b}$ is the multiplier.

Clearly, in this very restricted model the value of the multiplier is completely determined by the value of the marginal propensity to consume, b. If $b = 0.8$ then

$$\text{multiplier} = \frac{1}{1 - 0.8} = 5$$

which proves the result we saw earlier.

Before concluding this section, we should re-state two caveats lest the reader is misled into thinking that the real world can be analysed in such simple terms.

The first is that we have been dealing with a closed economy model, with no government sector, and in such a model there is only one type of leakage, namely savings. In the real world, spending leaks out of the system in other forms, principally in the form of spending on imported goods and in taxation. The value of the multiplier will be affected by these additional leakages.

The second problem is that we have been using comparative statics analysis which has enabled us to predict the economy's long run response to a rise in injections *once all the changes have worked their way through the economy*. We have assumed that this process takes place instantaneously and have therefore ignored problems concerning the economy's speed of response.

4.10 National income accounting

By this stage, readers will have acquired sufficient understanding of macroeconomic concepts to tackle the problems of national income accounting. There are two basic problems involved in accounting, namely, *what* to measure and *how* to measure it. Unfortunately, because of the difficulties involved in the question of how to measure, the much more important question of what to measure is sometimes ignored. Worse still, the two questions are often confused, as the following will show.

The principal source of national income statistics in the United Kingdom is the 'Blue Book' published annually. Although the official title of this publication is now simply *UK National Accounts* it was until comparatively recently – 1984 in fact – known officially as *National Income and Expenditure*. This was a particularly misleading title, as is the phrase 'national income accounting', since we are not primarily interested in national income or in national expenditure at all. Rather, we are interested in national *product*. The confusion is compounded because there are three separate ways of estimating national product – the income method, the expenditure method and the output method. It should be made quite clear, however, that national product estimated by the expenditure method is not the same thing as national expenditure, although superficially they do appear to be the same.

The situation is complicated by the fact that the national accounts may be constructed in such a way that they appear to show that in every year

national income = national expenditure

though as we shall see this is never true unless the balance of payments (excluding official financing) is exactly zero, which it never is. The supposed equality has no more significance than the fact that at the bottom of a company's balance sheet debits exactly equal credits, that is to say, no significance at all.

Under the very restrictive assumptions of the desert island model in Chapter 1, output, income and expenditure were all equal. Since such assumptions do not hold in the real world, the three measures will not, however, be equal and national accounts statisticians may attempt to estimate all three measures separately. In practice, however, it is usually sufficient to consider just two – on the one hand, income and output and, on the other, expenditure. In terms of the demand and supply analysis we introduced in Chapter 3, we have a dichotomy as follows:

	Aggregate demand	**Aggregate supply**
Other names	Total expenditure	Total output
	Total absorption	Total product
National accounts nomenclature	National expenditure	National product
		National income
Symbol	E	Y

As we have said, in general, expenditure will not be equal to income/output though the accounts appear to show that they are. The relationship between the two is as follows:–

$$C + I + G = E \qquad\qquad [4.7]$$

Total expenditure is equal to the sum of consumers' spending, investment spending and government spending. Note that all three categories of expenditure include spending on imported goods. This, therefore, gives us no indication of the output of the economy since much of the spending could be on imports, produced outside the country. Moreover, this measure fails to include all of the output which is exported. To arrive at a measure for output, therefore, we have to subtract from the above all of the spending which goes on imported goods and add on the value of goods exported. Thus

$$C + I + G + (X - M) = Y \qquad\qquad [4.8]$$

where Y stands for income and output and $(X - M)$ is net exports. Income and output are identical because the value of goods produced and sold must be equal to the income received from selling those goods. This explains why it is correct to use the terms national income and national product synonymously. It is not correct however, to use the terms national expenditure and national product synonymously, that is, to assume that

$$E = Y$$

This was an equilibrium condition, which we imposed on our model in section 4.9.2 to find the equilibrium level of national income – that is, the level of national income at which expenditure and income would be equal.

4.10.1 *The accounts*

Having been warned about some of the more common pitfalls, the

Table 4.1 Gross National Product by category of expenditure 1980 and 1984 (£m.)

Line no.		1980	1984
1	Consumers' expenditure	136 995	194 673
2	General government final consumption	48 906	69 655
3	Gross domestic fixed capital formation	41 588	55 319
4	Value of physical increase in stocks and work-in-progress	−2 875	−177
5	Total domestic expenditure at market prices	224 614	319 470
6	*plus* exports of goods and services	63 115	91 736
7	*less* imports of goods and services	−57 718	−91 852
8	Gross domestic product at market prices	230 011	319 354
9	Net property income from abroad	−219	3 304
10	Gross national product at market prices	229 792	322 658
	Factor cost adjustment		
11	*less* taxes on expenditure	−36 355	−52 578
12	*plus* subsidies	5 590	7 797
13	Gross national product at factor cost	199 027	277 877
14	*less* capital consumption	−27 900	−38 371
15	National income (i.e. net national product)	171 127	239 506

Source: *United Kingdom National Accounts 1985*, Table 1.2

reader is now in a position to inspect the accounts for himself. Table 4.1 presents the basic accounts for 1980 and 1984. Up to line 8 the accounts correspond more or less to eqn [4.8] above. Note that two types of investment are distinguished – fixed capital formation (line 3) and inventory investment (line 4) (see section 4.8.3). In both 1980 and 1984 inventory investment was negative, indicating a running down of stocks, an unusual occurrence. Note also that in these accounts line 2 includes only current spending by government, its capital spending being included in line 3.

Gross Domestic Product (GDP) (line 8) represents the value of all the goods and services produced domestically. Part of the income resulting from this production is sent abroad, to foreign shareholders and so on, but British residents also receive income from abroad by virtue of the shares which they hold in foreign companies. The net flow resulting from this, shown as Net Property Income from abroad (line 9) is added to GDP to give Gross National Product (GNP). Net Property Income from abroad is normally positive but in 1980 it was a small negative amount, probably as a result of foreign oil companies repatriating profits from North Sea operations.

There then follows a factor cost adjustment. Up to this point in the accounts we have valued output at the prices which purchasers actually pay – 'market prices'. This may give a misleading impression of the true value of those goods and services, however, since the market prices will be affected by sales taxes (VAT, excise duty, etc.) and by subsidies. Moreover, the income actually received by the producers of this output will exclude the sales tax, which they have to pass on directly to the government, but will include the subsidies. Hence, we subtract sales taxes and add back subsidies to arrive at our figure for GNI or GNP at factor cost (line 13).

Finally, we make an allowance for that part of the capital stock used up in the process of production (line 14). This figure, a sort of depreciation allowance, is a very rough estimate since it is impossible to measure it directly. Thus, we arrive (line 15) at our measure of national income or Net National Product (NNP).

4.10.2 Current price and constant price estimates

It can be seen from Table 4.1 that NNP was approximately 40 per cent larger in 1984 than it was in 1980. This does not mean, of course, that people became 40 per cent better off in real terms since most of the increase was due to the fall in the value of the monetary yardstick by which income is measured; that is, most of the increase was due to inflation. These figures are known as *current price* estimates which means that the 1980 figures are measured in 1980 prices, the 1984 figures in 1984 prices and so on.

Figures which do take account of the falling value of money are known as *constant price* estimates. These are derived by applying an appropriate price deflator to the current price estimates. The compilation of such price deflators or price indexes was discussed in section 3.6. Table 4.2 gives a set of constant price estimates. The line numbers in Table 4.2 correspond to those in Table 4.1.

Whether constant price or current price figures should be used in any particular application depends entirely on what those figures are intended to show. Current price figures cannot show meaningful changes in the value of variables over time since any real increase is swamped by the effect of inflation. Hence constant price estimates should be used to measure, for example, the growth in consumer spending between 1980 and 1984, If, however, one wished to know

Table 4.2 Expenditure and output at 1980 prices (£m.)

Line no.		1980	1984
1	Consumers' expenditure	136 995	145 455
2	General government final consumption	48 906	50 689
3	Gross domestic fixed capital formation	41 588	45 391
4	Value of physical increase in stocks and work-in-progress	−2 875	68
5	Total domestic expenditure at market prices	224 614	241 603
6	*plus* exports of goods and services	63 115	68 528
7	*less* imports of goods and services	−57 718	−67 831
8	Gross domestic product at market prices	230 011	242 300
9	Net property from abroad	−219	2 440
10	Gross national product at market prices	229 792	244 740
	Factor cost adjustment		
11 and 12	*less* taxes on expenditure, *plus* subsidies	−30 765	−32 847
13	Gross national product at factor cost	199 027	211 893
14	*less* capital consumption	−27 900	−31 042
15	Net national product at factor cost (i.e. national income)	171 127	180 851

Source: *United Kingdom National Accounts 1985*, Table 1.5

the change in consumer spending as a proportion of GNP between 1980 and 1984 then current price estimates should be used in preference to constant price estimates.

Constant price estimates become more unreliable the further one moves away from the base year, and the unwise use of such data can lead to incorrect conclusions. For example, it appears from Table 4.2 that in 1984 the balance of trade was in surplus, exports (line 6) exceeding imports (line 7), whereas the true picture was that the balance of trade showed a slight deficit in 1984, as we can see from Table 4.1.

4.10.3 *The accuracy of the estimates*

It should be emphasized that the figures we are dealing with are *estimates* of the magnitudes we are trying to measure. As such, the figures are subject to a margin of error, the overall size of which is difficult to assess. First, we know that the figures are subject to subsequent revision. For example, as Table 4.3 shows, the estimate of GNP for 1979 shown in the 1980 Blue Book was some £7.6 bn. less than the estimate shown in the 1985 Blue Book. Although the error here is fairly small, being of the order of 4 per cent, it is very large in comparison to Britain's recorded growth rates which, in the last ten years, have varied between approximately 3 per cent and minus 3 per cent.

Table 4.3 Current price estimates of GNP in 1979 (£ m.)

as recorded in Blue Book for 1980	189 991
as recorded in Blue Book for 1981	193 175
as recorded in Blue Book for 1982	194 260
as recorded in Blue Book for 1983	195 395
as recorded in Blue Book for 1984	197 432
as recorded in Blue Book for 1985	197 566

Second, one suspects that the size of the 'cash economy' is substantial. This cash economy is comprised of all those services paid for in cash or kind which are never recorded and hence escape the attention of both the Inland Revenue and the national income statistician. However, the omission of these cash transactions from the national accounts constitutes a serious error only if they are growing or shrinking in importance over time. From the attention that it has received in the media in recent years one would gain the impression that the black economy is almost certainly growing. This is a difficult proposition to prove or disprove, of course, since by its nature the size of the black economy cannot be measured directly. We may be able to provide some objective assessment of the proposition, however, when we recall that GNP can be measured in three ways – the expenditure method, the income method and (less importantly) the output method. If the size of the black economy really is growing then we would expect to find that the expenditure-based measure of GDP would grow faster than the income-based measure since people would be spending income that they had illegally failed to report to the Inland Revenue. When we look at official estimates of the three measures shown in Table 4.4 however we find, surprisingly, that the expenditure based measure of GDP has been growing *less* rapidly than the income-based measure. It is difficult to reconcile this with the proposition that the size of the black economy is growing in importance.

Table 4.4 Index numbers of Gross Domestic Product at constant factor cost (1980 = 100)

	1978	1979	1980	1981	1982	1983	1984
Expenditure-based measure	100	102.2	100	98.7	100.2	103.6	105.1
Income-based measure	99.5	102.2	100	98.3	100.9	104.2	107.1
Output-based measure	99.8	103.0	100	98.3	100.1	103.1	106.2

Source: *UK National Accounts 1985*, Table 1.15.

4.11 Summary

In this chapter we have presented a Keynesian analysis of the workings of the macroeconomy. As we said in section 1.4, this analysis is partly axiomatic and partly paradigmatic. The axiomatic part is reflected in the way that the national accounts are drawn up. The relationships which they display between the variables are true by definition. Thus one cannot dispute that

$$Y = C + I + G + X - M \qquad \text{[4.8 repeated]}$$

since this equation does not represent the view of any particular school of thought. One can still discuss whether it is sensible or useful to measure any or all of these variables but one cannot dispute the relationship between them since it is axiomatic, true by definition.

However, part of the analysis of this chapter should be viewed as paradigm rather than axiom. It represents a particular view or interpretation of the way the macroeconomy works, a view which is not accepted by other schools of thought. In particular, the *importance* which Keynesians attach to the level of demand is a feature of the Keynesian paradigm. Monetarists, as we shall see, concentrate less on demand and more on supply side factors. Moreover, the Keynesian view of the determinants of aggregate demand, with its emphasis on injections and withdrawals, would not be accepted by the monetarist school whose views we examine in the next chapter.

Questions

1. What impact will the following have on aggregate demand, *ceteris paribus* (up/down/no change).

   (a) An increase in public spending on new roads.
   (b) The issue of a new high-yield security which encourages people to save more.
   (c) The publication of a CBI survey which reports favourable business prospects for the next six months.

2. Here are six statements about the probable effect on the economy of an increase in demand. Consider whether each of them could be correct and under what circumstances they could be correct.

   (a) The increase in demand will cause a subsequent increase in spending on imported goods. Therefore domestic firms won't benefit at all.
   (b) The increase in demand will result in increased incomes which in turn will mean that people will save more. So domestic firms still don't benefit.
   (c) The increase in demand will mean that firms can sell more. They will therefore increase their production and take on more workers.
   (d) The increase in demand will mean that firms can sell more. They are therefore likely to run down their stocks of finished goods. Production will not increase.
   (e) If the increase in demand results in higher incomes people will have to pay more income tax. So they won't be able to spend any more than they did previously.
   (f) If demand goes up, firms will take advantage of the situation to put up prices.

3. *Ceteris paribus*, what impact will the following have on aggregate demand?

   (a) The Government reduces its expenditure on Trident missiles by £10 m.
   (b) Student grants are increased by a total of £10 m.
   (c) The Government spends £10 m. more on pensions financing it by increasing taxes on the higher paid by the same amount. Which of the three above will have the biggest impact on Aggregate Demand?

4. 'If savings go up the increased flow of loanable funds will result in a fall in interest rates. This will encourage extra investment. So savings always equals investment.' What is wrong with this statement?

5. Which of the following explains why investment may not increase if the rate of interest falls. Because:

   (a) most firms have their own funds anyway so they have no need to borrow;

(b) investment is interest inelastic;
(c) the cost of funds is less important to firms than future sales prospects;
(d) people save less when the rate of interest falls and therefore funds may not be available.

6. State which of the following constitutes investment from a macroeconomic point of view.

(a) A company builds a new factory.
(b) A private individual buys Krugerands.
(c) A jeweller buys gold.
(d) A company buys a new car for one of its sales persons.
(e) An individual buys a new car to get to work.
(f) A company buys a second-hand car for one of its sales persons.

7. In recessions net investment often becomes negative.

(a) What does this mean?
(b) Why does it occur?

8. You are given the following figures on national output (GNP) and Gross Domestic Fixed Capital Formation (Investment). Assume that replacement investment is equal to 10 in each time period and that the behaviour of new investment can be approximated by an accelerator model

$$I_t = \alpha \, \Delta Y$$

Where $\Delta Y = Y_t - Y_{t-1}$ i.e. income (or output) in this period minus income last period, and α is the accelerator coefficient.

Period	1	2	3	4	5	6	7
GNP	100	100	110	120	130	127	127
Investment	10	10	40	40	40	?	?

(a) What is the value of the accelerator coefficient?
(b) What will be investment in periods 6 and 7?

9. Suppose that an economy is initially in equilibrium at a level of national income of £600 m. per year. Suppose then that an additional export order of £10 m. is received.

(a) What is the initial impact of the economy?
(b) Assuming that on average people spend only 80 per cent of their last pound's worth of income, to what level will income have risen after 3 rounds?
(c) If, on average, people spent 90 per cent of their extra income (rather than 80 per cent) would the increase in national income brought about by the exports be more or less than previously?

10. Which of the following will have the largest expansionary effect on Aggregate Demand and which will have the smallest?

(a) A reduction in employee's National Insurance Contribution

amounting to a total reduction in the government's tax take of £10 m.
(b) An increase in retirement pensions involving the government in additional expenditure of £10 m.
(c) A reduction in taxation for the higher paid amounting to a total reduction in the tax take of £10 m.

11. Use a simple model to show that if people tend to save 20p out of any extra £1 they earn then the value of the multiplier will be 5.

12. GNP is the value of all the goods and services produced in the economy in a given year. How does this differ from NNP (Net National Product)?

13. Would an increase in any of the following result in an increase in measured GNP?

(a) Wives' housekeeping allowances.
(b) Children's pocket money.
(c) Student grants.
(d) Retirement pensions.
(e) Lecturers' salaries.

14. Given the following information prepare a set of National Accounts showing:

(a) Total domestic expenditure.
(b) GDP at market prices.
(c) GNP at market prices.
(d) GNP at factor cost.
(e) National Income (i.e. net national product).

The figures have been jumbled up to make it more difficult for you. All figures are in £ bn.

Exports   56.
Net property income from abroad   1.
Taxes on expenditure   30.
Government spending   38.
Value of physical increases in stocks and work in progress   3.
Consumers' expenditure   116.
Subsidies   4.
Imports   54.
Capital consumption   22.
Gross domestic fixed capital formation   34.

15. (You need a calculator for this exercise.)
The RPI since 1977 looks like this (based on 1980 = 100)

1977	1978	1979	1980	1981	1982	1983	1984
65	73	83	100	112	120	126	132

(a) What would be the price in 1984 of a bundle of goods which cost £10 in 1980?

(b) What was the rate of inflation in 1981?
(c) What was the rate of inflation in 1982?
(d) What was the rate of inflation in 1983?
     GNP (in current prices) since 1977 looks like this (all figures in £ bn.)

1977	1978	1979	1980	1981	1982	1983	1984
146	167	198	230	255	278	303	323

Using the RPI given above as a deflator, prepare a series for GNP at constant prices.

(e) By how much in real terms did GNP in 1981 exceed GNP in 1980?
(f) By how much in real terms did GNP in 1983 exceed GNP in 1979?

(Source: *UK National Accounts*, 1985 edition)

16. In each of the following cases state whether you should use:

(i) current price estimates;
(ii) constant price estimates;
(iii) either can be used.

(a) Assessing what proportion of total expenditure goes on government spending.
(b) Working out the rate of growth of output.
(c) Determining what the trade balance is.
(d) Working out the rate of growth of government spending.

17. Why do constant price estimates become more unreliable the further you move away from the base year?

75

Chapter 5
The determinants of aggregate demand –
monetarist interpretation

We saw in Chapter 4 how, in the Keynesian model, aggregate demand is determined by the volume of injections and withdrawals. The government, if it wished to expand the economy, would run a budget deficit (government spending exceeding tax revenue); and if it wished to reduce aggregate demand it would budget for a surplus (tax revenue exceeding government spending). We said nothing about how a budget deficit should be financed, and it is to this issue that we now turn.

5.1 Financing public spending

Public expenditure can be financed in one of three ways. First, the government can raise taxes, either direct taxes on income, or indirect taxes on expenditure. Secondly, the government can borrow money from the public by the issue of Treasury Bills, which are short term loans redeemable after three months, Treasury Bonds, which are longer term loans, National Savings schemes, Premium Bonds and so on. If neither of these two alternatives are acceptable, for reasons which we shall discuss below, then the government may resort to a third alternative which is to finance spending through a process which involves an increase in the money supply. This third alternative is what is sometimes called 'printing money' though it is a misleading expression since, as we shall see, the monetary expansion involved does not necessarily take the form of an increase in notes in circulation.

In any particular year, the amount by which the government's tax revenue falls short of its spending requirements is known as its borrowing requirement – the so-called Public Sector Borrowing Requirement (PSBR). If its borrowing requirement is positive in any particular year it will be increasing the size of the National Debt, which is the total amount of government debt outstanding at any particular time, and includes both current borrowing and debt accumulated from previous years. Normally the government succeeds in meeting most of its borrowing requirement by borrowing from the public by the issue of Treasury Bills, etc. In some circumstances, however, it may be unable to persuade people to buy government securities without offering very high rates of interest, which it may be unwilling to do, and in this case it may resort to the third alternative we have mentioned, which involves an increase in the money supply.

5.2 Definition of the money supply: the cash base and credit money

Money, it is said, makes the world go round, though this is disputed. Those of a more romantic nature attribute this role to love. Both money and love share the common characteristic that neither is easy to define but there the similarity ends. Money is said to possess three functions. It is a medium of exchange, a unit of account and a store of value. In the past all sorts of different things have been used as money, including precious metals, salt (the word *salary* comes from a Latin word meaning salt) and cattle (the word *pecuniary* comes from the Latin word for cattle). Clearly, good money substances perform the three functions listed above and, in addition, are easily portable, divisable, durable – and, of course, scarce.

The definition of the money supply that we shall adopt is somewhat arbitrary. There are a variety of different definitions to choose from and there are no strong prior reasons for choosing any one of them. The simplest (and therefore probably the best) definition is called M_1. This consists of currency (notes and coins) plus current account deposits at banks. A wider definition of money is called M_3 which includes deposit accounts at banks as well as currency and current account deposits.

We could, of course, expand our definition to include, for example, deposits in building societies and in the National Savings Bank, accounts held in Britain in currencies other than sterling, and so on. Table 5.1 defines the various monetary aggregates which were officially in existence in 1985, together with an indication of their size. As can be seen, the dividing line between money and other assets which are not money is not at all clear-cut and the definition of the money supply owes more to convention than to any real difference between the various money-like substances.

We can, however, make a very clear distinction between the cash-base of the system, which is money issued by the central bank, and credit money, which is money created by the commercial banking system through the process of multiple credit creation, explained below.

Table 5.1

Name	Definition	Amount (mid 1985) £ bn.
Main measures		
M_0	Notes and coins in circulation with the public + banks' till money + banks' operational balances with the Bank of England	12.5
M_1	Notes and coins in circulation with the public + sterling sight bank deposits held by the UK private sector	56.5
$£M_3$	M_1 + sterling time bank deposits held by UK residents in the private sector	118.5
M_3	$£M_3$ + UK private sector deposits in other currencies	138.2
Other measures		
M_2	M_1 minus sterling interest-bearing wholesale sight deposits with banks + sterling retail deposits held by the UK private sector with Building Societies and in the National Savings Bank Ordinary Account	139.7
PSLI	$£M_3$ minus deposits of over two years original maturity + private sector holdings of money-markets instruments and certificates of tax deposit.	121.7
PSL2	PSLI + the more liquid Building Society shares and deposits and similar forms of National Savings instruments minus Building Society holdings of money-market instruments and bank desposits etc	204.7

Source: *Bank of England Quarterly Bulletin*, September 1985, Tables 11.1 and 11.2. (for notes and definitions see the March Bulletin)

5.3 The process of multiple credit creation

Currency is the so-called cash base of the system. It is money created by the central bank, in our case the Bank of England, and the amount in existence can therefore be controlled by them. Credit money, on the other hand, is money created by the

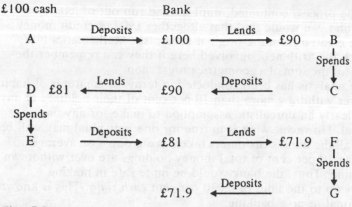

Fig. 5.1

commercial banking system through the process of credit creation. If a bank grants one of its customers an overdraft it has thereby increased the stock of credit money. The stock of credit money is not directly controlled by the Bank of England, and this may have important implications for the ability of the central bank to control the overall money stock, as we shall see later.

We can illustrate the principle whereby the banks create credit money with the following example. The practice is somewhat different, depending as it does on the particular institutional arrangements.

Suppose that individual A deposits £100 cash with his bank, and that the bank knows that A, who is a creature of habit, never withdraws more than 10 per cent of his total deposit at any time. The bank can therefore safely lend out the other 90 per cent (or £90 in this example), which it will do quite willingly since it is a profit-seeking institution whose main source of revenue is the interest charged to borrowers. Thus, it will want to lend out as much as possible, subject to the requirement that it must retain enough cash to satisfy any withdrawal that A is likely to make. The bank therefore lends £90 to B, who uses the money to buy goods valued at £90 from C, who promptly banks the receipts. Provided C, like A, is not expected to withdraw more than 10 per cent of his holdings at any one time, the bank will then re-lend the other 90 per cent (90 per cent of £90 = £81) to another customer, D, who uses it to buy goods from E who banks the receipts, and so on.

By the time this process gets to the letter G in Fig. 5.1 the total amount of money in existence is £100 + £90 + £81 + £71.9 = £342.9, of which £100 was the cash originally in existence, and the other £242.9 is credit money created by the banking system.

If the process continued, until we had run out of letters and way beyond, we would find that altogether £900 of credit money could be created from the original £100 cash. Mathematics buffs can check the arithmetic involved here if they can remember the formula for the sum of a geometric progression.

Our analysis has been conducted in terms of creatures of habit who never withdraw more than 10 per cent of their holdings at any time – clearly an unrealistic assumption to make for any one individual. However, what is untrue for one individual may well be true for all the bank's customers taken as a group – on average no more than 10 per cent of total money holdings are ever withdrawn at one time. Thus, the bank would be quite safe in making advances up to the limit of its 10 per cent *cash ratio*. This is known as fractional reserve banking.

5.4 The control of the money supply via control of the cash base

In the past, commercial banks have been obliged by the Bank of England to adhere to a cash ratio of the sort described above. However, as we have seen, since banks get their income from lending money at interest, they will attempt to lend as much as possible, so as to make their profits as large as possible. That is, they will seek ways to circumvent the reserve ratio imposed upon them by the central bank and therefore, on a cash base of a given size, they will try to create as much credit money as possible.

Because cash ratios proved an ineffective method of controlling banks' multiple credit-creating activities, the reserve requirements introduced in 1971, known as the 'Competition and Credit Control System' (CCC), were defined not on the ratio of cash to total liabilities, but on the ratio of a narrowly-defined range of liquid assets to total liabilities.

If the CCC reserve requirements had effectively limited the amount of credit money that could be created on a given cash base, then we can see how the Bank of England could have controlled the total money supply via its control over the cash base. A given reduction in the cash base would have been followed by a (much larger) reduction in the amount of credit money created by the banks. In practice, what happens is that the banks reduce the amount of credit money created by reducing their lending to customers.

However, there is disagreement amongst specialists in this field as to whether the CCC reserve requirements did effectively limit the ability of financial institutions to create credit money, or whether they could be circumvented, as the cash ratio was.

In any case, by 1980 recognition of the shortcomings of the

CCC system lead the Bank of England to propose its abolition, to be replaced by some form of 'monetary base control'. Under this system, the Bank of England would control the monetary base – that is, principally cash (notes and coins) plus some balances which the commercial banks were obliged to hold at the Bank of England. This control of base money would directly affect each bank's liquidity position, that is, the extent to which it was able to fulfil its immediate obligations to creditors. Normal banking prudence would then ensure, in theory, that the banks did not overstretch themselves by lending too much, but the liquidity position of each bank would be monitored by the Bank of England. Thus the system of monetary base control which evolved after 1980 was akin to a cash ratio system except that there was no externally imposed cash ratio to which the banks had to adhere. Rather there was a self-imposed prudential ratio set by each individual bank which would reflect that bank's overall liquidity position both immediately and in the near future. The Bank of England monitors this overall liquidity status rather than concentrating on any particular cash or liquid asset ratio.

An alternative method of attempting to control monetary growth is to operate not on the supply of money but on the demand for it. By increasing the rate of interest at which it is willing to lend (known as the Minimum Lending Rate (MLR) under the CCC system), the Bank of England can engineer an increase in the overall level of interest rates, which will, they hope, reduce people's willingness to borrow money. That is, the increase in interest rates reduces the demand for money. If this happens, then banks will not be able to create as much credit money as they would like, simply because people are not prepared to borrow at the high interest rates.

There is a two-fold difficulty with such a policy. First, the higher the rate of interest, the greater the incentive for banks to lend money since the greater the profits they can thereby earn; and second, the high interest rates may have a damaging effect on the economy, as we shall see in the next section.

5.5 The connection between government spending and the money supply

We saw in section 5.1 that government spending can be financed either by:
(a) taxation,
(b) borrowing from the public, or
(c) a process which involves monetary expansion – 'printing money'.
Consider the impact on the money supply of an extra £10 m.

of public spending which is financed by taxation. The government expenditure adds £10 m. to the supply of money but this is exactly cancelled out by a £10 m. decrease in the supply of money brought about as a result of the increased taxes that people have to pay to government. Thus, we say that the monetary effect is neutral.

Similarly, if the government finances spending by borrowing, the increase in the money supply brought about by the extra spending is offset by an equivalent decrease in the money supply which results when the public lend the government money by purchasing National Savings Certificates, Treasury Bills and so on. The monetary effect is again neutral.

Even though these methods of financing do not result directly in any increase in the money supply, they may have certain undesirable effects. Raising taxes in order to pay for increased public expenditure is understandably unpopular since, other things being equal, it reduces people's real disposable income. If income tax is increased then take-home pay falls, and if VAT is increased the increase in the price level which this brings about reduces the real value of a given money income. Thus, in both cases, people's ability to purchase goods and services with their income is reduced, and consumption in real terms will fall. This, by definition, will lead to a fall in society's welfare, which may or may not be offset by the increase in social welfare brought about by the increased public spending. The reduced consumer spending may also have deleterious long-term effects on investment in those consumer goods industries which are most affected by the fall in demand.

Lastly, it has been claimed that direct taxes have a disincentive effect on work effort. It should be noted that there are no prior reasons for supposing that this will necessarily be the case. If the individual's objective is to obtain a certain amount of post-tax income, then an increase in income tax will mean that he has to work harder to meet his objective. What is more likely, however, is that the individual will seek ways of avoiding the payment of income tax, either by tax-avoidance (which is legal) or tax-evasion (which is illegal). He may, for example, prefer to take part of his income in the form of benefits-in-kind, or 'perks', which are either not taxed as highly as money income or not taxed at all. Company cars and expense account lunches are examples of tax avoidance. Alternatively, slightly lower down the social scale, the individual may resort to 'moonlighting' or taking on jobs for which he is paid in cash and which he does not declare for tax purposes. It has been claimed that this has become increasingly prevalent in recent years, and the existence of a sizeable 'cash economy' or 'black economy' therefore leads to a substantial underestimate of national income, since many transactions take place which are not officially recorded.

Financing government spending by borrowing from the public can also have undesirable side effects. The money which the government borrows may be funds which would otherwise have been spent on consumption; or they may be funds which would otherwise have been lent to some other sector, such as private industry. If this is the case, the government spending is said to have displaced or 'crowded out' the investment in private industry which would ·therwise have taken place. The assumption implicit here is that there is a fixed amount of investable funds and, if the government pre-empts a large part of those funds, there will be less left for other sectors. We consider this crowding out hypothesis in more detail in section 10.6.

The way in which the government attracts investment funds is to offer interest rates which are higher than those the investor can get elsewhere. This, of course, leads to an increase in the overall level of interest rates, which is undesirable for a number of reasons. First, as we have already noted, it may lead to a fall in the investment undertaken by private sector firms, and this, in the long run, may have adverse effects on productivity growth and on the growth of output. Second, the increased interest rates lead to an increase in the price index (and may thus contribute to inflation), since they increase the cost of borrowing generally and, in particular, they increase the cost of borrowing for house purchase, which is the largest single item in many people's expenditure. The high interest rates will also increase industry's costs and these increased costs may be passed on in the form of increased prices, thus exacerbating the inflationary effects. Lastly, high interest rates increase the burden of debt of the government, which means that the government will have to raise more money just to pay the increased interest charges.

To summarize, we can say that financing government spending through taxation or by borrowing from the public, although it does not increase the money supply, may have undesirable side effects.

Because of the damaging effect of high interest rates, the government may resort to raising funds in a way which results in monetary expansion (that is, by 'printing money'). If the government cannot persuade the public to buy Treasury Bills at the going rate, it can sell them to the banking sector. The banks can treat these Bills as a 'reserve asset' or 'liquid asset' so that they do not have to reduce their lending to customers. They have merely replaced one type of liquid asset (cash) with another (Treasury Bills) so their liquidity position remains unchanged.

Now, if the government uses the money it has raised by this means to finance spending, there will be a net increase in the money stock, since the increase in government spending is not this time offset by a corresponding decrease in people's bank balances as a result of increased tax payments or increased lending to the government. This increase in the money supply may, according to the monetarists, lead to a fall in the value of money – that is, inflation.

5.6 The money supply as a determinant of aggregate demand

The monetarist school, which has been growing in influence in recent years, would claim that, as a matter of empirical fact, variations in the level of aggregate demand can be explained better by variations in the money supply, rather than by the Keynesian explanation which emphasizes injections and withdrawals. Inflation, monetarists would argue, is the inevitable result of a situation in which the money supply is expanded too fast, allowing aggregate demand to exceed the capacity of the economy to produce goods. They point out that every single inflation in history has been associated with an expansion of the money supply. Since an over expansion of the money supply is the one factor which is common to *all* inflationary situations, then the cause of inflation must be attributed to excessive monetary growth.

The monetarists thus elevate the money supply to a position of prime importance in macroeconomics, a position which it formerly occupied before the Keynesians relegated it to a more inferior one.

5.7 The quantity theory of money

The pre-Keynesian (or 'classical') thinking about the role which money plays in determining economic activity is often illustrated by reference to the so-called Quantity Theory of Money. The famous 'Equation of Exchange'

$$MV = PT \tag{5.1}$$

states that the money supply (M) multiplied by its velocity of circulation (V) must always be equal to the number of transactions (T) multiplied by the average price of each transaction (P). Since one pound note creates one pound's worth of spending every time it changes hands, MV must therefore represent total spending in the economy, or aggregate demand. What this equation is therefore saying is that the total amount of money spent on buying goods and services in the economy in the year must be equal to the total value of all the goods and services sold in the economy in the year. As such it is a tautology. It is similar, though not the same, as the statement we make in microeconomics that when trade takes place in the market for a particular good, the amount demanded (and the amount bought) must equal the amount supplied (or the amount sold).

The quantity theory of money, in its crudest form, used the equation of exchange to show that if V (the velocity of circulation), and T (the physical volume of goods produced) were fixed, then there would be a directly proportional relationship between variations in the money supply and variations in the price level. A 10 per cent increase in the money supply would result in a 10 per cent rise in the price level.

Clearly, once one has accepted the crucial assumption that the velocity of circulation is fixed, then aggregate demand is determined solely by the money supply. The way in which the classical economists justified this assumption of a fixed velocity was to argue that, since it depended upon institutional factors which would change only slowly over time, then in the short run the velocity could be treated as fixed. These institutional factors – the length of payment periods (that is, whether people are paid daily, weekly or monthly), the nature of the banking system (for example, the speed at which cheques can be cleared through the banking system, bank opening hours, the extent to which credit cards are accepted as a means of payment) – will certainly remain relatively fixed in the short run, but Keynes argued that the velocity did not depend solely on these institutional factors. He went further in fact, to argue that the velocity of circulation was a quite unstable magnitude, so that a given money stock could finance widely differing levels of aggregate demand, depending on the velocity of circulation.

5.8 Keynesian and monetarist views of the role of the money supply

We saw above how the monetarist school claimed that, throughout history, inflation is always associated with an increase in the supply of money. It may seem paradoxical that Keynesians would not dispute this as a statement of fact. What they would dispute is the fact that, simply because there is an *association* between increases in the money stock and inflation, that increases in the money stock are necessarily the *cause* of inflation.

Both schools would agree that there is a correlation between increases in the money stock and increases in aggregate demand, and that in a situation in which the economy is utilizing all the available resources of manpower and capital, then real output cannot increase, and an increase in aggregate demand will result in inflation or a rise in spending on imported goods, or both. The fact that a correlation exists between changes in the money stock and changes in aggregate demand is not all that surprising. It is difficult to see how spending can increase unless there is an expansion of the money supply, but correlation is not proof of causality. The causality could run from the rise in the money stock to the rise in aggregate demand or, equally logically, it could run the other way round, from the rise in aggregate demand to the rise in the money stock. The monetarists, while accepting this point, argue that if it can be shown that increases in the money supply *precede* increases in aggregate demand, then this, on the face of it, is evidence that the causality runs from the money supply to aggregate demand, and not the other way round. A number of prominent monetarists have attempted to show, in the contexts of the American and British economies, that changes in the money supply do in fact precede changes in aggregate demand. The Keynesian riposte has been first of all to dispute the validity of the statistical evidence, and secondly to point out that precedence in time is not proof of causality. To illustrate this, one could point to the increase in the money supply which occurs in November and December each year, which is followed by a sharp rise in consumer spending. The cause of the spending spree is the general bonhomie engendered by the Christmas season (reinforced if not invented by the advertising industry), rather than the increase in the money supply *per se*. This is a clear example of the monetary authorities anticipating an increase in spending and therefore expanding the money supply so that consumers and traders will not run short of cash.

The general Keynesian view, therefore, is that the money supply is a passive variable. It responds to increases in aggregate demand (and may even anticipate them) but it does not play an active role in determining economic activity.

5.8.1 The transmission mechanism

The dispute between the Keynesians and the monetarists about the role played by the money stock in determining the level of economic activity has taken various forms. First, as we have seen, the statistical evidence has been disputed. Second, the mechanism whereby changes in the money supply induce changes in aggregate demand – the so-called transmission mechanism – has been argued about at length.

5.8.2 The Keynesian view of the transmission mechanism (first version)

The account that one is normally given of the Keynesian transmission mechanism is as follows. The interest rate is the price of borrowing money. This price is therefore determined by the demand and supply of money, as in Fig. 5.2.

The demand for money is shown to be inversely related to interest rates. This is because holding money involves an *opportunity cost*, which is the interest one could have earned by

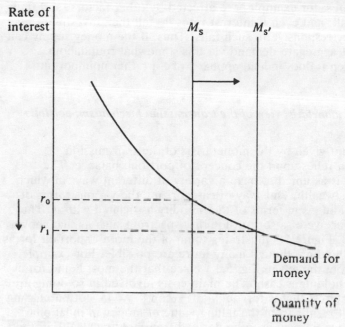

Fig. 5.2

lending one's money to a bank or building society or some other institution. As interest rates rise, so the cost of holding money rises and people will wish to hold less – that is, the demand for money will be less. The supply of money is represented as being fixed by the monetary authorities at some particular level, and is thus not dependent on interest rates.

An increase in the supply of money, shown by a rightward shift of the money supply curve, will lead to a drop in equilibrium interest rates and the fall in interest rates will encourage investment spending, which is itself a component of aggregate demand. Thus, the money supply affects aggregate demand through the interest rate effect on investment.

Increase in money supply
    leads to
fall in interest rates
    leads to
rise in investment and thus a rise in aggregate demand.
Thus, in this view, the link between the money supply and aggregate demand is somewhat tenuous. Hence the view that money is not very important in determining aggregate demand. If the transmission mechanism is of this form, then it is likely to involve considerable time lags and a large amount of uncertainty.

Interest rates, for example, are affected by other factors, and they may not fall; and even if interest rates do fall then investment may not be very responsive to such falls. Thus, if the money supply can only affect aggregate demand via this somewhat roundabout process then it does indeed appear to be a rather unimportant variable.

5.8.3 The monetarist view of the transmission mechanism: portfolio balance

The account given by the monetarists of the transmission mechanism relies upon the concept of portfolio balance. The individual is assumed to have a variety of different ways in which to hold his wealth. One way of categorizing the various forms of wealth holding is in terms of the liquidity associated with it. Thus, we can conceive of a sort of liquidity spectrum such as that shown in Fig. 5.3. Figure 5.3 illustrates some of the more important forms of wealth holding, though many more are possible. For example, reading from the left in Fig. 5.3 we see that the most liquid form of wealth holding is cash. The main costs involved in so doing are first the interest that is forgone and, second, the loss of purchasing power that results from the falling value of money in inflationary times. The main benefit to be derived from holding wealth in the form of cash is convenience – one does not have to bother to go to the bank if one wishes to make a purchase, since cash is universally accepted as a means of payment. Holding cash may, however, involve some risk of theft. Putting one's money in a bank account reduces the risk of theft, but may also involve some loss of convenience.

The important point, however, is that the costs and benefits associated with each of the various forms of wealth holding will differ from one individual to another – or, at least, their assessment of the costs and benefits will differ. Thus, an individual will weigh up the costs and benefits of each form of wealth-holding and will then proceed to arrange his wealth portfolio in a way that yields him maximum utility (that is, yields him maximum personal satisfaction). This condition will be satisfied when it is impossible to increase his utility by rearranging his portfolio; for example, by holding more bonds and fewer shares. His portfolio will then be in a state of equilibrium or balance.

Now consider the effect of an increase in the money supply. Some individuals will now find themselves holding more cash than previously, and this will disturb the equilibrium of their portfolios, which are now too liquid. In an attempt to re-establish equilibrium in their portfolios these individuals will therefore use part of their money to buy assets – and this spending spills over not just on to

Liquid ◄——————————————————————————————► Illiquid

Form of wealth holding	Cash	Current bank account	Deposit account or building society a/c	Bonds, e.g. local authority bonds	Shares	Physical assets, e.g. cars, TVs, boats	'Real property', houses
Costs	Interest forgone – Value eroded by inflation – Risk of theft	Interest forgone – Value eroded by inflation – May not be accepted as means of payment	Loss of liquidity – cannot withdraw money immediately	Less liquid than bank – money tied up	Risky – could go down in value – may be difficult to sell without incurring capital loss	Very illiquid	Very illiquid
Benefits	Convenience	Less risk of theft than cash	Rate of interest	Usually higher rates of interest than bank	May go up in value	Yields stream of services – Value not eroded by inflation	Yields stream of services – May appreciate in value

◄—— Money ——► ◄—— Financial assets ——► ◄—— Physical assets ——►

Fig. 5.3

financial assets but also into the realm of physical assets and even on to goods and services which are not normally considered as assets at all. As this spending takes place, so it may change the costs and benefits (either real or perceived) of the various forms of wealth holding, causing further adjustments to be made to get back to a state of portfolio balance.

The basic idea, then, is that an increase in the supply of money causes an increase in spending, as individuals attempt to re-establish equilibrium in their wealth portfolio. The resultant increased spending on any particular asset or class of assets cannot be predicted with accuracy, since the process of portfolio adjustment involves individuals' subjective assessments of the costs or benefits associated with very many different types of wealth holding. However, in the aggregate, the monetarists would argue, the increased spending resulting from monetary expansion is clearly discernable in empirical studies.

5.8.4 Portfolio balance: the Keynesian view

In explaining the transmission mechanism, most contemporary Keynesians would probably accept the portfolio balance view – with one important difference. For the Keynesians, the increase in the money supply directly affects other financial assets – but the effect does not spread directly to the realm of physical assets, as the monetarists would claim it does. Rather, any impact which monetary expansion or contraction ultimately has on demand in other sectors of the economy occurs as a result of the changes brought about in the market for financial assets. For example, an increase in the supply of money will result in some portfolios becoming excessively liquid and, in an attempt to correct this imbalance, part of the cash will be used to purchase financial assets. The increased demand for financial assets will cause their price to rise and this, in turn, will cause their yield to drop (for reasons explained below). Thus, interest rates generally will fall and, in response to this, both consumption and investment spending will increase. Thus, even though the contemporary Keynesians acknowledge the validity of the portfolio balance approach, they still maintain that the effect that monetary factors have on spending is indirect, operating via interest rate changes in financial markets.

Before concluding this section we should explain how these interest rate changes are brought about. Consider a bond (that is, a fixed interest security) whose nominal value is £100. Suppose it pays interest of £10 per year, thus giving it a nominal rate of interest of 10 per cent. If the actual market value, as opposed to nominal value, of the bond is £100 then it will yield an actual return of 10 per cent. But suppose now that its market value increases to £200 because of a strong demand for such securities. Since it gives a return of only £10 per year, its actual yield will now fall to 5 per cent per year (that is, $\frac{10}{200} \times \frac{100}{1}$). This demonstrates that the market price of fixed interest securities is inversely related to their yield.

5.9 Monetarists and Keynesians; waxing and waning

In the battle that raged between the Keynesians and the monetarists during the 1970s and early 1980s the Keynesians may have won the intellectual skirmishes but the monetarists won control of the political high ground. In the immediate post war period Keynesianism was the conventional wisdom of academics and governments alike. Spawned in the depression years of the 1920s and 1930s, the message of Keynesianism was one of hope; governments could spend their way out of a recession and thereby eliminate the scourge of unemployment. There is absolutely no doubt that the Keynesian medicine worked. And it was easy for Keynesianism to win the hearts and minds of the people, for the medicine was pleasant to take. Just inject more spending into the economy and prosperity will follow with no nasty side effects – or so it seemed at the time.

But, in the late 1960s and 1970s, the disease which seemed to be attacking the economies of the Western world was of a different kind. Inflation was becoming the major concern. The Keynesian prescription for this was a much more bitter pill to swallow. Deflation, with its attendant slow down in the growth of prosperity and consequent rise in unemployment, meant that, to get well again, the patient had to undergo a rather painful treatment. And, moreover, the treatment seemed to be becoming increasingly ineffective. It was almost as if the patient had developed a sort of immunity to the drugs that the Keynesian doctors prescribed, so that larger and larger doses of deflation and reflation were required to bring about the desired effect. Could a new treatment be found? It was in these circumstances that the monetarists started to gain intellectual and ideological support. True, the medicine that they prescribed would be no more pleasant to endure but it might, some thought, be more effective. The monetarist diagnosis of the problem attributed the cause of the disease, in part at least, to the medicine that had been prescribed in the past. The behaviour of governments in increasing public spending had, they claimed, had a four-fold impact. First, in as much as it had been financed by borrowing, it had made it increasingly costly and difficult for governments to service the ever growing burden of the National

Debt. Second, increasing public borrowing had tended to pre-empt the lion's share of the available loanable funds, crowding out private sector investment and thus hindering the growth of the private sector. Third, in as much as increasing public spending had necessitated monetary expansion, which had resulted directly in inflation, it had engendered inflationary expectations amongst employers and employees alike, which had made the eventual curtailment of monetary expansion more difficult to achieve. And, fourth, the increasingly active role of the State in providing supportive services for individuals and for firms had led to a decline in the traditional values of self-reliance and self-advancement by one's own efforts. This moral degeneration had manifested itself at the personal level in a belief that the individual had the right to be maintained by the State, and at the company level by the belief that the State should cushion the firm from the unpleasant effects of market forces. The belief that the Lord will provide had been replaced by the belief that the State will provide.

It is immediately obvious from the above that, in addition to being an economic doctrine, monetarism is also a political ideology. This, of course, is equally true of Keynesianism. Neither is value free, since it is impossible to have a value-free social science. Monetarism, then, is normally identified with the right of the political spectrum; it deprecates the growing influence of the State on people's lives and advocates a greater reliance on market forces. Keynesianism, normally identified with the left of the political spectrum, advocates increasing State intervention to regulate the vagaries of the market mechanism.

The extent to which one accepts either monetarist or Keynesian ideas therefore depends to some extent on one's political beliefs. These beliefs are themselves a product of the social and political environment. It is important to understand the changing nature of this environment for this is the context within which disillusionment with Keynesianism set in and governments espoused what appeared to be a new doctrine. In Britain in particular the Conservative Government of the early 1980s was wedded to the idea that the level of demand in the economy was determined by the money supply.

The greatest irony is perhaps that in the analysis of inflation traditional monetarists have much in common with traditional Keynesians. Both regard inflation as resulting from excess demand. It follows from this that the appropriate counter-inflation policy is to reduce demand – that is to deflate the economy. Recently, however, many Keynesian economists, though not denying that inflation can be the result of excess demand, have argued that the principal cause of inflation in the late 1970s and early 1980s is cost-push factors and it is to this view which we now turn.

Questions

1. What do you understand by the term 'a budget deficit'? What impact does it have on aggregate demand?

2. 'An increase in teachers' salaries will mean that the government has to increase taxes to pay for them.' Discuss.

3. What are the three functions of money?

4. Explain under what circumstances the following were (or could have been) used as money, and consider the drawbacks of so doing:

   (a) cigarettes;
   (b) salt;
   (c) cowrie shells;
   (d) cows;
   (e) coffee;
   (f) gold coins.

5. Give four definitions of the money supply.

6. Explain what the following terms mean:

   (a) PSBR;
   (b) The National Debt.

7. Which of the following are ways of financing a budget deficit?

   (a) Selling Treasury Bills.
   (b) Persuading the public to buy more National Savings Certificates.
   (c) Printing more £5 notes.
   (d) Selling off assets.
   (e) Selling local authority bonds.
   (f) IMF loan.
   (g) Increasing the 'divi' paid by the Co-op.
   (h) Persuading the public to buy more 'Ernie' Bonds.

8. In the Quantity Theory of Money

$$MV = PT$$

What do the four symbols, M, V, P and T stand for?
What factors might determine the magnitude of V and why therefore might V change (according to Keynes)?
What is likely to happen to V in a hyperinflation?

9. The following causal chain represents the interest rate effect on investment of an expansion in the money supply:

$$\text{increase in money supply}$$
$$\downarrow$$
$$\text{effect on interest rates}$$
$$\downarrow$$
$$\text{effect on investment}$$
$$\downarrow$$
$$\text{effect on Aggregate Demand}$$

Indicate in each case the direction of the supposed effect and what other factors may be present to reduce (or eliminate) the expansionary effect of an increase in the money supply.

10. Which of the following statements most nearly describes the view of the transmission mechanism between money and spending held by (a) a contemporary monetarist and (b) a contemporary Keynesian:

(a) An increase in the money supply will cause a reduction in interest rates and this in turn will stimulate investment.

(b) An increase in the money supply means people have more income and they base their consumption spending on their income.

(c) An increase in the money supply will result in some people's wealth portfolios becoming too liquid. Hence they swap money for goods in an attempt to re-establish equilibrium in their portfolios.

(d) An increase in the money supply will result in some people's wealth portfolios becoming too liquid. Hence they buy less liquid financial assets, e.g. bonds. This causes an increase in the price of bonds and hence a fall in interest rates.

11. Consider an individual whose portfolio of assets is currently 'in balance'. What does it mean to say that the portfolio is 'in balance'? What effect on his holdings of various types of asset will result from the following:

(a) an increase in the market price of bonds;
(b) an increase in the rate of inflation;
(c) increasing optimism on the stock market;
(d) an increase in bank charges for overdrawn balances;
(e) an increase in share prices.

12. What will happen to the market price of a bond whose nominal value is £100, which pays 10 per cent of its nominal value annually, if market interest rates rise to 15 per cent?

13. Explain the distinction between Bonds and Bills, e.g. Treasury Bonds and Treasury Bills.

14. The extreme Keynesian view is that the money supply is unmeasurable, uncontrollable and irrelevant. Explain why they take this view.

Chapter 6
Cost inflation

6.1 Wage inflation

In Chapter 3 we saw how the causes of inflation could be explained in terms of demand pressures or in terms of autonomous increases in costs. We argued that autonomous increases in costs would result in a sustained increase in prices only if the level of demand was allowed to expand to enable the same volume of goods to be bought at the higher prices. If aggregate demand was fixed, increases in wages would lead to falling output and employment. In practice, however, we recognized that there was considerable political pressure on governments to allow the level of demand to expand, and thus prevent the unemployment that would otherwise occur.

Since the Keynesian revolution some forty years ago it has been widely acknowledged that governments have the responsibility for maintaining a level of effective demand which is sufficient to ensure the full or reasonably full employment of resources, particularly labour. Thus, for the first half of the post-war period, at least, the maintenance of 'full employment' was arguably the government's top priority. Since high levels of unemployment are embarrassing for governments, there is an expectation amongst the electorate that the government will take steps to alleviate the problem. This means that there is an expectation that the government *will* allow the level of demand to rise to prevent unemployment.

In such a situation autonomous increases in costs, particularly wage costs, may be an important determinant of the rate of inflation. Thus the use of the term 'wage inflation' implies that the cause of the increases in the price level can be traced to increases in wage costs. This explanation of the causes of inflation, however, implicitly assumes that the government will act in an accommodating fashion, allowing demand to expand, and that there is a widespread expectation that the government will, in fact, behave in this way. Thus the union *expects* that an increase in wage rates will not lead to a fall in the demand for its labour because the increased wage costs will be passed on in the form of higher prices. The employer *expects* that, as a result of the increased costs which he has passed on to his customers in the form of higher prices, the demand for his product will not fall because there will be an increase in purchasing power and because his competitors are announcing similar price increases. Thus, everyone expects inflation to continue, and wage increases are therefore negotiated which ensure that inflation does indeed continue. Deflationary demand management policies could in theory prevent inflation from proceeding and thus change people's expectations. But this process of changing people's expectations by holding down the level of aggregate demand would involve a painful period of adjustment, with high unemployment and falling living standards for a time at least. Hence, for most governments whose time horizon is necessarily short, the price (in terms of political popularity) of getting inflation down is too high, and they cannot afford to pay it.

6.2 Incomes policies

Hence governments resort to other means, such as incomes policies, which appear to offer a way out of the dilemma. If wage costs can be held down in the short run, it is argued that this will bring down the rate of price inflation. This will, in turn, reduce the expected rate of inflation, and hence the wage increases that are negotiated in the following time period will be more modest. Thus, a progressive reduction in the rate of inflation is achieved.

There are, however, certain difficulties inherent in the operation of incomes policies. Nevertheless, in recent times governments in Britain have come to place increasing reliance on incomes policies as a policy weapon. In the remainder of this section we discuss the difficulties involved in using incomes policy as an instrument of macroeconomic management and we look at the possible effects of the use of such policies.

6.2.1 Statutory or 'voluntary'

In what is still fundamentally a free enterprise economy it is not really feasible to enforce laws governing the price to be paid for a particular good or service unless the overwhelming majority of the populace believe those laws to be just, and thus voluntarily comply with them. The difficulty is not in putting the laws on the statute book – any government with a parliamentary majority can do that. The difficulty is in enforcing the laws. By analogy, it is easy to pass a law making the use of seat belts in cars compulsory, but extremely difficult to enforce it. It would require an enormous amount of resources (a policeman on every street corner) to ensure that no one broke the law. In such a case people either act within the law voluntarily or they break the law with impunity apart from the tiny majority who are unlucky enough to get caught. Moreover, if people believe in the wisdom of wearing seat belts they will do so whether or not the law tells them to, and in this case the law is superfluous.

At this point, however, the analogy between the wearing of seat belts and the actions of employees in seeking to increase their income breaks down. In the seat-belt case you are asking people to behave in a way which is, in fact, in their own interest. The major beneficiary is the individual himself, though society as a whole may experience some benefit in terms of a smaller burden on the National Health Service. In the latter case, however, by asking the individual to refrain from seeking wage increases, you are asking him to behave in a way which runs counter to his own best interests, though society as a whole may benefit from it. If it were universally agreed that this act of self-sacrifice would, in fact, benefit society, it might be possible for sufficient moral suasion to be exercised to persuade the individual to act against his own interests, but since there is no such universal agreement that wage restraint will bring down the rate of inflation and preserve real living standards, such moral suasion is weak and ineffective.

Because of the inherent difficulties with statutory incomes policies, governments have often opted for what have been euphemistically called 'voluntary' incomes policies. They are 'voluntary' in the sense that no legislation has been placed on the statute book, though governments have attempted to ensure compliance with their directives by a variety of means, the legality of which is sometimes open to question. Most frequently this has taken the form of 'agreements' reached between the employees' organization, the Trades Union Congress (TUC), the employers' organization, the Confederation of British Industry (CBI), and the government. Since neither the TUC nor the CBI has any power to compel its members to abide by these agreements, however, the effectiveness of such agreements depends to a large extent on the degree to which a consensus exists on the desirability of price or wage restraint. Whether or not such a consensus is feasible is discussed in section 6.2.4 below.

6.2.2 Sanctions

Whether the incomes policy is statutory or voluntary, it will be difficult to enforce. First, as we have already noted, the administrative cost of monitoring the millions of pricing decisions that are made in the economy every year is very high. Second is the problem of what sanctions can be applied to those who do not abide by the government's directives.

In the past, society has punished those who transgress the law in a variety of ways – fines, imprisonment, deportation, hanging and so on – and the motive for so doing has been threefold. First, to set an example so that others will be more easily persuaded not to break the law (*pour encourager les autres*), second, to ensure that some restitution takes place, and third, so that society can extort retribution from the lawbreaker. Although the retributive motive figures prominently in some people's attitudes towards trade union legislation, it is the other two motives which concern us here. Clearly, whatever sanctions are taken, to be effective they should encourage others not to break the law in the same way and they should take from the lawbreakers the fruits of their illegal act.

In the context of a wage settlement in excess of the government's directive, one can attempt to impose a fine, the magnitude of which is related to the degree to which the wage settlement was deemed to be excessive. A very real problem arises, however, as to who should pay the fine – the employee or the employer – since both were party to the illegal act. A second and more serious problem arises if one or both parties refuse to pay the fine. The only sanction that then remains is imprisonment and, although the imprisonment of trade union officials is not an uncommon occurrence in some countries, we do not need to elaborate on the undesirability and impracticality of such a solution.

An alternative solution, and one which some writers regard as a practical possibility, is to use the income tax system to tax away wage increases in excess of the governement's directive. Such a tax-based incomes policy would, of course, require a substantial increase in the resources of the Inland Revenue, and the feasibility of such a scheme is open to question. At this moment in time it is difficult to see how such a scheme could be applied fairly and efficiently.

6.2.3 Formulating the policy

The limit on wage increases can either be in the form of a lump sum or a fixed percentage increase (or some combination of the two). There could possibly be some relaxation of the controls for the low paid.

Wage increases which could be wholly financed through increased productivity could be encouraged. If these were genuine productivity increases then *wage costs* per unit of output would not rise – and this is presumably the objective of the incomes policy, rather than keeping down wages as such. The danger of relaxing controls in this way, however, is that in many occupations, labour productivity – defined as the value of output per unit of labour input – is difficult to measure, or difficult to improve, or both. In teaching, for example, the value of output cannot be measured. It would be possible for teachers to teach bigger classes but this does not necessarily increase the teacher's productivity, since the quality of the education that they give to each child might deteriorate. An incomes policy which encourages 'productivity deals' would discriminate against groups such as the teachers. If, however, the salaries of groups such as the teachers were allowed to increase under some sort of 'comparability principle' then there would be a tendency for the general level of wage increases to be lifted to the level of those industries where productivity increases are easiest to secure. In other occupations where, as we have seen, it may be difficult to measure productivity, the possibility of measuring it in some spurious fashion is opened up, and this provides employers and employees with the opportunity of circumventing the controls by negotiating spurious productivity deals.

For these reasons a wage *freeze* may be a simpler and more effective policy. Whatever form of incomes policy is imposed, however, the distribution of earnings between different occupations will be affected, or one could say *distorted*, by the policy. In the absence of any sort of government policy on incomes, occupational differentials will ultimately be determined by market forces. The forces of demand and supply, or relative *scarcity*, must in the long run determine the wage that any particular type of labour can command. Over time, relative scarcities will change and thus occupational differentials will change also. For example, fifty years ago the average wage of blue-collar workers was less than that of the lowest grade of white-collar worker. Nowadays, the situation is reversed. This change has not been brought about by the increased recognition of the nobility of manual labour; it merely reflects changes in the relative scarcities of the two types of labour.

In essence, it is impossible for any form of incomes policy to be sufficiently flexible to allow the pattern of differentials to change in response to changing relative scarcities. Thus, we can argue that the 'successful' application of an incomes policy leads to a pattern of differentials which is different from that which would be produced in the absence of any policy.

It is interesting to note that there are two possible interpretations of the word 'successful' in this context.

The primary objective of an incomes policy is normally regarded as being the control of the rate of inflation. Thus, 'successful' can be interpreted as meaning that the incomes policy leads to a lower rate of inflation than would otherwise have occurred. Therefore, the degree of 'success' of various incomes policies is an empirical question which we will consider later in section 6.3.

Second, we could argue that in addition to controlling inflation, incomes policy has another objective, namely, to produce a different set of differentials to that which would be produced by the market mechanism (or, if preferred, by 'free collective bargaining'). For example, it could be argued that the differentials between highly paid workers and low paid workers are too great and should be narrowed by allowing larger increases for low paid workers. Implicit in this view is the belief that the set of differentials produced by the market mechanism is undesirable, and that it is the explicit objective of incomes policy to amend it. The success of an incomes policy can thus be judged by the extent to which it modifies the set of differentials that would have existed in the absence of the policy.

6.2.4 *Is a consensus possible?*

Wage control is frequently associated with industrial unrest, which often has far-reaching consequences. The 'May events' in France in 1968 and the fall of the Conservative Government in Britain in 1974 and the Labour Government in 1979 were all caused, in part at least, by industrial troubles brought about by incomes policies. As a result, many people have asked whether there might not be a less painful way of settling differentials. Is it not possible, they ask, for a society to arrive at a consensus view on the pattern of differentials. In essence they are asking the question whether, given the size of the national cake, it is possible for everyone to agree how that cake should be divided up. Is there any criterion which would be universally accepted, by which an impartial arbiter could work out how much a nurse should earn relative to a doctor, a dustman and a carworker?

The answer to this question is yes, but it will prove to be a disappointing answer, as we shall presently show. In order to fully appreciate the answer, however, we need to consider the question of how wage differentials are in fact determined in our society, and whether or not there is an economically founded pattern of wage differentials.

Before tackling this question the reader may like to study Fig. 6.1 and Table 6.1 which illustrate the earnings differentials in the United Kingdom in 1985. Figure 6.1 shows the average earnings of various occupational groups. It also shows the 80 percentile range. For example, 80 per cent of accountants earned between £140 and £382 per week (in April 1985) and average earnings for accountants were £252 per week. As can be seen from Fig. 6.1, doctors head the list of income earners. The most highly paid

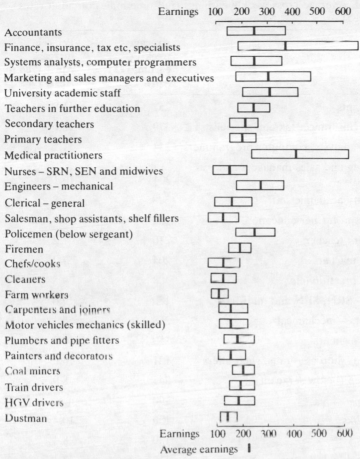

Fig. 6.1 Weekly gross earnings (£) (excluding top 10% and bottom 10%) Adult males
Source: *New Earnings Survey 1985* Part A, Table 8.

nurses earn less than the most lowly paid doctors (excluding the top and bottom 10 per cent).

6.2.5 *Is there an economically founded pattern of wage differentials?*

The price that any particular factor of production can command must ultimately depend on its scarcity. In other words, the laws of demand and supply are inexorable. Like the law of gravity, which states that there will be a mutual attraction between two bodies proportional to their masses, the laws of supply and demand (which were discovered rather than invented by economists) state that, when goods or services are traded on markets, there exists an

Table 6.1 Average gross weekly earnings (full-time males on adult rates – April 1985)

	Average weekly earnings (£) April 1985	Per cent increase April 1984 to April 1985
Accountants	252	11.9
Finance, insurance, tax etc. specialists	379	12.6
Systems analysts, computer programmers	254	11.1
Marketing and sales managers and executives	304	10.1
University academic staff	308	5.8
Teachers in further education	252	6.9
Secondary teachers	210	7.2
Primary teachers	204	7.2
Medical practitioners	408	9.8
Nurses – SRN, SEN and midwives	150	9.6
Engineers – mechanical	268	6.3
Clerical – general	159	10.2
Salesmen, shop assistants, shelf-fillers	121	10.0
Policemen (below sergeant)	245	8.9
Firemen	190	n.a.
Chef/cooks	130	10.4
Cleaners	130	8.0
Farm workers	116	7.1
Carpenters and joiners	153	6.6
Motor vehicles mechanics (skilled)	153	7.6
Plumbers, pipe fitters	173	7.3
Painters and decorators	144	5.6
Coal miners	200	n.a.
Train drivers	192	9.4
HGV drivers	177	8.0
Dustmen	139	5.1

Source: *New Earnings Survey 1985*, Part A, Table 8.

equilibrium price which is determined by the forces of demand
and supply. Transactions can take place at prices which differ from
the equilibrium price, but there will normally be a tendency for
prices to move towards the equilibrium. Thus, in the labour
market, though short-term aberrations are possible, in the long-run
the reward that any particular type of labour receives will depend
upon the forces of demand and supply. Thus, there exists an
economically founded pattern of wage differentials.

This much would be agreed by most economists, though not
all. It represents the view of the mainstream of economic theory
(what is normally called neo-classical economics) to which most
practitioners of the art and teachers of the discipline subscribe.
There are, of course, alternative views – such as the Marxist
interpretation – but it is not the intention to discuss them here. We
shall content ourselves with a more detailed examination of the
neo-classical analysis of wage differentials.

Consider three groups of workers – airline pilots, doctors and
nurses. We shall attempt to explain the differences in the earnings
of these groups in terms of neo-classical price theory.

Consider the labour market for airline pilots.

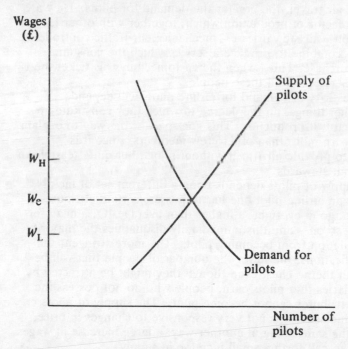

Fig. 6.2

We can argue that there will be an equilibrium wage, W_e, for pilots' services, and that the actual wage will tend towards this equilibrium level. Thus, if the actual wage is less than W_e, say at W_L, there will be an excess demand for pilots. Airlines will find they cannot service all their schedules with their existing staff and they will try to hire more staff by offering higher wages. Thus, the actual wage tends towards the equilibrium wage. Similarly, if the actual wage is above the equilibrium level, say at W_H, there will be an excess supply of pilots. In their wage negotiations pilots will now be in a weak bargaining position, since there are now more people seeking jobs as pilots than there are jobs available. Thus, pilots' wages will tend to decline, perhaps not in absolute terms (though this is possible if their wages do not keep pace with inflation), but more likely in *relative* terms, that is, relative to other groups of workers.

However, if the equilibrium wage is in fact determined by demand and supply, we then have to ask what determines the demand for and supply of pilots.

Clearly the demand for pilots is derived from the demand for air travel. If no one wished to travel by air, there would be no demand for commercial airline pilots. Similarly, the greater the demand for air travel, the greater the demand for pilots. They are an essential factor of production which, together with other factors of production – air stewardesses, mechanics, air-traffic controllers and so on – combine to produce a service which the consumer is willing to purchase. Thus, when the customer buys his ticket, he is buying the services of all these people.

The elasticity of demand for airline pilots will depend, amongst other things, on the degree to which they constitute an essential factor of production. This goes part of the way to explain why pilots earn more than other crew members, since it is impossible to provide air travel without pilots, but quite feasible to do so without stewards.

The supply of pilots depends upon a different set of factors. To become an airline pilot one has to possess certain attributes – good health, good eyesight, a higher than average IQ, a head for heights and so on – and this immediately disqualifies the majority of the population from becoming pilots. The more stringent the entry qualifications, the fewer the number of people that will be able to meet them. Thus, even though they might be attracted by the high salaries that pilots earn, people who do not possess the necessary attributes cannot become pilots. The supply of pilots is thus fairly inelastic; it is not very responsive to changes in price, or, to put the same thing in another way, a large increase in wages is required to call forth a small increase in supply.

The supply of pilots is further restricted by the establishment of a professional organization, or pilots' trade union, which can limit entry into the profession, or establish operating standards which are more stringent than is strictly necessary. If the union is well organized and successful, the effect of this will be, in terms of our analysis, to push the supply curve to the left, thus raising the equilibrium wage for pilots.

Taking all these factors together, we could argue that, because there is a high demand for pilots, because the demand is inelastic and because the supply of pilots is inelastic, this will tend to keep the equilibrium wage high and rising.

Doctors are another group who earn high wages. Unlike airline pilots, however, the service that they help to produce is not sold to consumers, since in Britain under the National Health Service medical care is provided free, or almost free, to consumers and financed out of general taxation. Thus, the demand for doctors does not depend upon market forces; rather it is the result of a complex set of decisions taken by hospital administrators, civil servants, government ministers and so on. Nevertheless, we can still describe the demand for doctors as a derived demand since they are, in effect, a factor of production which combines with other factors to produce health care, a service for which consumers would be willing to pay. Indeed, the very existence of private medicine in Britain illustrates that consumers are willing to pay for health care. However, because in the NHS health care is provided publicly, the government in effect decides when it allocates spending how much health care will be produced and consumed. In so doing, the government also determines the demand for doctors, though if the services of the doctors became very expensive we might expect hospital administrators to substitute other factors of production   technicians, nurses, clerical staff and so on – in order to minimize the cost of producing a given amount of health care. The degree to which doctors can be substituted by other factors of production will determine the elasticity of demand for doctors. As with airline pilots, where we argued that because of the essential role they played the elasticity of demand for their labour would be low, so with doctors we could argue that the demand for their services will be inelastic because of the essential role they play in providing health care.

On the supply side, we can argue that the supply of doctors will be highly inelastic for the same reasons as the supply of pilots is inelastic, namely that to become a doctor requires high academic qualifications, a lengthy training period and so on, and that this disqualifies most of the population from taking up jobs as doctors, however much they might be attracted by the high salaries. As with pilots, the establishment of a professional organization, or doctors' trade union, can restrict the supply of doctors still further – imposing minimum entry requirements into the profession over and above what would be required to safeguard the interests of the patient.

Thus, an analysis of the labour market for doctors would look similar to that for pilots in Fig. 6.2, the combination of an inelastic demand and supply ensuring a high equilibrium wage.

The wages that nurses earn in the NHS on the other hand are notoriously low. If the wage that they earn is, in fact, the equilibrium wage (and we discuss this below) then the fact that the equilibrium wage is low must be because the demand for nurses is low in relation to the supply of nurses.

As with doctors, the demand for nurses within the NHS is determined not by market forces but by a set of administrative decisions. The demand for nurses is still a derived demand, since they too combine with other factors (including doctors) to produce health care. The elasticity of demand for nurses will depend upon how easily the services of a trained nurse can be substituted by other factors of production – ancillary staff, ward orderlies and so on – and on *a priori* grounds we could argue that they will be less essential and hence face a more elastic demand for their services than doctors or airline pilots.

A more marked difference is apparent on the supply side of the market, however. The entry requirements into the training schools are much lower than for doctors or pilots, there is a highly elastic supply of foreign-trained nurses and, with no effective trade union organization to restrict the supply of nurses by imposing strict entry requirements or restrictive codes of conduct, the supply of nurses in Britain is highly elastic. Hence a small increase in wages calls forth a greatly increased supply, thus ensuring that the equilibrium wage remains low.

By this stage some readers will have been moved to indignation. Surely nurses should be paid more than they get at present? How can one seek to justify the low pay of nurses in terms of the workings of the so-called laws of demand and supply?

In response to this understandable indignation, the neo-classical economist would reply that what the above analysis has attempted to do is explain *why* some occupations earn more than others. The analysis does not attempt to say what differentials *ought* to exist, nor does it say that the existing differentials are 'just' or 'fair'. This is the way the market mechanism works. To say that the laws of demand and supply are 'unfair' is rather like saying that the law of gravity is unfair because bodies with a larger mass exert a larger gravitational pull.

If nurses formed a strong trade union and succeeded in restricting the supply of nurses, this would, *ceteris paribus*, raise the equilibrium wage and the actual wage would in the long run rise towards the equilibrium level. The particular economic analysis we have been using does not suggest that the higher wage is more justifiable or less justifiable than the lower one. It merely explains how in the long run relative scarcity, or the laws of demand and supply, determine the wage that a particular occupational group can command.

6.2.6 A consensus solution

In section 6.2.4 we asked whether it was possible for a consensus to emerge as to how the national cake should be divided up between the various occupational groups. Was it possible, we wondered, for an impartial arbiter to establish a set of criteria that could be used to work out how much each group of workers ought to earn relative to other groups?

Suppose that our impartial arbiter does establish some formula which everyone is persuaded to accept through some process of mass hypnosis. The formula could take into account variables such as the number of years' education or formal training required to do the job, the degree of physical or mental skill or physical strength required, the degree of unpleasantness associated with the job, the health risks involved and so on. Each of these variables could have a weighting associated with it, so that for each occupation the formula could be used to arrive at a single number which would thus represent the consensus view as to what this particular occupational group ought to be paid.

Suppose that the wage differentials established by the formula are accepted by all but there arises a shortage of, say, bus drivers. What is to be done? It appears that greater financial incentives have to be paid to persuade people to become bus drivers. But how can this be done? Can the formula be changed in some way so that bus-driving scores a higher number? Clearly either the weightings in the formula have to be changed or else additional variables have to be included in the formula, together with their associated weightings. Over time the formula could be adjusted and, given enough time, a formula could be arrived at which ensured that in each occupation there was neither an excess demand nor an excess supply of labour. Certainly this formula would be very complicated, containing many hundreds of different variables, including things such as the degree of skill involved in any particular job, society's evaluation of the worth of the good or service that this labour helped to create and how important a contribution any particular type of labour made in producing that good or service. Ironically, the set of wage differentials that would be produced by the super-formula would be identical to the set of differentials produced by the market mechanism. This is not surprising, since the many hundreds of variables which our formula would take into account would be precisely those variables which determine the supply of and demand for any particular type of labour. We would have established a surrogate price system.

6.2.7 Can an incomes policy permanently modify differentials?

The foregoing analysis should not be interpreted as suggesting that the set of differentials produced by the market mechanism is the only possible set. Government intervention, through an incomes policy or minimum wage legislation, can affect differentials but there will be a tendency for equilibrium differentials to be restored when the policy is relaxed. Under certain circumstances, however, it is possible to argue that government policy could permanently affect wage differentials. Consider the labour market for school teachers. The demand for school teachers will be inelastic, being the result of government policy, but since local authorities have some leeway as to what pupil–teacher ratio to apply, whether to provide nursery schools and so on, the demand for teachers will be affected by their salary levels. These salary levels will be determined more or less exogenously by a process of wage bargaining. What would be the effects on the labour market for teachers of a campaign which succeeded in securing a wage as high as W_H in Fig. 6.3? This is a disequilibrium situation and in the foregoing analysis we have argued that in the long run *price* will adjust to bring the market back into equilibrium.

It is possible, however, that the variable which adjusts to bring the market back into equilibrium is *quantity* not price. At a wage of W_H only q_1 teachers will be employed. This means that, if the market was formerly in equilibrium (when q_0 would have been employed), there will be a reduction in the numbers of teachers employed of $(q_0 - q_1)$. This reduction may be brought about by early retirement, or by natural wastage, or some redundancies may be involved. At the same time, the increase in wages will produce a movement along the supply curve so that the number of people wishing to be employed as teachers increases to q_2. There is thus substantial unemployment of $(q_2 - q_1)$.

The effect of this will be twofold. First, the government may instruct the colleges to reduce their output of newly trained teachers since there is little point in training new teachers when there is already a 'teacher surplus'. The colleges may reduce their intakes by making the examinations more difficult to pass, or the government may simply close down some colleges.

Second, teaching will become less attractive as a career since teachers will no longer enjoy the security of employment which

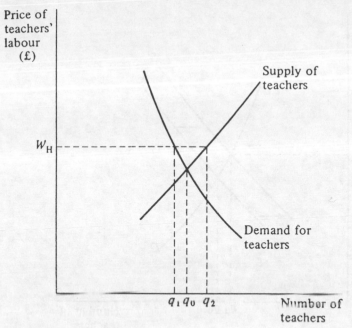

Price of
teachers'
labour
(£)

Supply of
teachers

W_H

Demand for
teachers

$q_1 q_0 q_2$ Number of
teachers

Fig. 6.3

they formerly had. Thus the number of people wishing to be
trained as teachers may fall.

In the long run both of these effects will tend to reduce the
supply of teachers, that is, to push the supply curve of teachers to
the left as in Fig. 6.4 so that the teacher surplus is eliminated and
the market is brought back to equilibrium at the new higher
equilibrium wage for teachers. Thus government policy has
succeeded in effecting a permanent increase in the salaries that
teachers receive, relative to other groups.

Whether the labour market for teachers is brought back to
equilibrium by price adjustments or by quantity adjustments is
impossible to tell a priori, depending as it does on the
circumstances of the particular case. The purpose of this analysis
has been to show that incomes policy can permanently affect
differentials for some groups since, although the forces of demand
and supply are very strong, they can be channelled in one direction
or another by conscious government policy.

6.3 The macroeconomic effects of incomes policies

We have spent some time discussing what we could call the

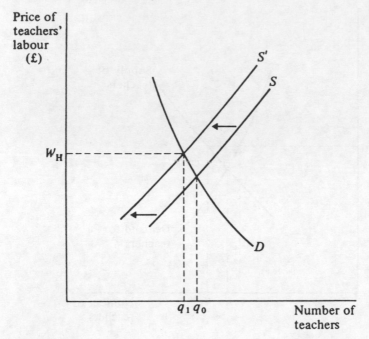

Fig. 6.4

microeconomic effects of incomes policy. That is, whether or not in the long run they can lead to a set of differentials different from that which would have occurred in the absence of policy, or whether they are policies which can only be applied for a limited period after which they are relaxed and the differentials produced by the market mechanism reassert themselves. These are important questions to which the economist can give no definite answer.

In the purely macroeconomic context, however, the effect of incomes policy is judged solely in terms of whether or not it reduces the rate of price inflation, and questions of distributive justice or allocative efficiency are not relevant. How can we judge the effect of incomes policy on moderating the rate of inflation? It is not sufficient merely to compare the rate of inflation in those years when incomes policy was in operation with those years when it was not, since incomes policy has only been introduced when the rate of inflation has been high. Clearly, what one needs to do is to try to estimate what the rate of inflation would have been in the absence of an incomes policy, and compare this with the rate of inflation that actually occurred with the policy. The difference between the two could thus be ascribed to the effects of incomes policy. What is needed therefore is a model that can be used to predict the rate of inflation from the values of certain other variables in the economy. As an illustration of the technique that could be used it will be helpful at this point to introduce the Phillips curve.

6.4 The Phillips curve

First of all it will be convenient to introduce a bowdlerized version of the Phillips curve to illustrate the main features before we look at some of the more esoteric issues connected with it.

The article by Professor Phillips[1] published in 1958 which was to provoke an enormous amount of subsequent research and criticism, was the result of an empirical investigation of the relationship between the rate of change of money wages and the level of unemployment. Phillips collected statistics for the British economy for the period 1861–1957 on these two variables, and plotted them on a graph such as that shown in Fig. 6.5. Using regression analysis, he fitted to this set of points the curve which now bears his name. Most of the observations appeared to lie quite close to the fitted line, apart from exceptional periods – such as periods of rapidly rising import prices. There appeared therefore to

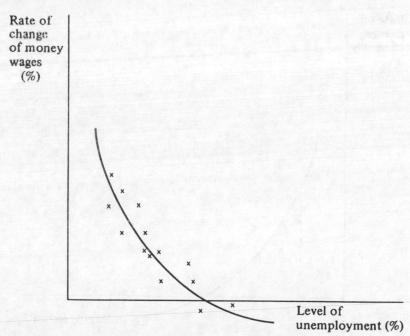

Fig. 6.5

be a fairly stable relationship between the level of unemployment and the rate of wage inflation in Britain. Similar experiments were conducted for other countries, which revealed similar Phillips – type relationships remaining stable over long time periods.

If the Phillips curve had been as simple and as unambiguously correct as was at first supposed, it would have been an enormously important discovery. Both the physical and the social sciences seek to establish stable functional relationships between variables. In physics, for example, Boyle's law tells us that there is a stable relationship between the volume, the temperature and the pressure of a gas. We can then use our knowledge of this stable relationship to 'explain' real world phenomena – such as the fact that gases become cold when they are allowed to expand – though it is a rather restricted type of 'explanation' since it relies on the acceptance of the general law to explain the particular event. So, in economics, if it were possible to demonstrate the existence of a stable relationship between one measurable variable and another, one could 'explain' changes in one variable in terms of changes in the other.

We could also use this relationship to predict, say, the rate of wage inflation that corresponds to any particular level of unemployment. For example, in Fig. 6.6 if the level of

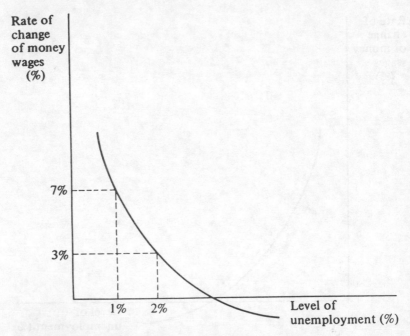

Fig. 6.6

unemployment is, say, 1 per cent, our Phillips curve model predicts that the rate of wage inflation will be 7 per cent.

We can use this as a way of measuring the effectiveness of incomes policies in moderating the rate of inflation. If, for example, in a particular year in which an incomes policy was in operation, the average level of unemployment was 2 per cent, we could predict from our Phillips curve that the rate of wage inflation would be 3 per cent. If the actual rate of wage inflation was, say, only 2½ per cent, then the difference between the two could be ascribed to the moderating influences of incomes policy. In other words, the incomes policy would have succeeded in reducing the rate of wage inflation by ½ per cent.

6.5 The effects of incomes policies

Tests such as these have in fact been used to try to assess the impact of incomes policies on reducing inflation. In practice, the models used have been more complicated than simple Phillips curve relationships; that is, they have used additional variables, not just unemployment levels, to predict the rate of inflation. In essence, the technique remains the same, however. First, construct a model which will predict the rate of wage inflation, given the values of certain other variables. Second, in those years when incomes policy is in operation, compare the 'predicted' rate of inflation with the actual rate of inflation. The difference between the two can then be ascribed to the effects of incomes policy.

Obviously, there are difficulties which the researcher encounters when he tries to apply this method, not the least of which is how to decide whether incomes policy is 'on' or 'off' (For example, do 'calls for restraint' constitute policy 'on', or is incomes policy only 'on' when it has the backing of the law?) The results of published research tend to suggest some modest success for incomes policies, as Table 6.2 shows. The effects are rather erratic however since, if the results are to be believed, in some periods incomes policy actually leads to a higher rate of inflation than would otherwise have occurred.

Overall in most periods the rate of inflation is not significantly lower than it would have been in the absence of incomes policies.

6.6 Criticisms of the Phillips curve

We introduced the Phillips curve as a way of illustrating the sort of model that could be used to estimate the effects of incomes policies. Its place in economics is much more important than this however, and the debate as to whether or not a stable relationship exists

Table 6.2 Estimated effects of incomes policy on the rate of wage inflation – results of two studies conducted by Lipsey–Parkin and Hines

+ =	number of quarters in which inflation was higher than predicted
− =	number of quarters in which inflation was lower than predicted
$\hat{\epsilon}$ =	estimated effect of incomes policy (% p.a.) mean
$\sigma_{\hat{\epsilon}}$ =	a measure of the degree of variability of the rate of inflation around its mean value. To be reasonably confident that incomes policy produces a significant reduction in inflation, the measured reduction should be at least twice as big as $\sigma_{\hat{\epsilon}}$ Lipsey-Parkin reductions in the rate of inflation of less than 2×1.038 could be the result of chance factors rather than the result of the incomes policy. Thus only in the early years 1948 (3rd quarter) to 1950 (3rd quarter) was there a significant reduction in inflation.

	Lipsey–Parkin			Hines		
Incomes Policy Years	+	−	$\hat{\epsilon}$	+	−	$\hat{\epsilon}$
1. 1948(3)–1950(3) 1949(1)H	0	9	−2.369	0	7	−1.440
2 1956(1)–1956(4)	2	2	−1.050	2	2	−0.073
3. 1961(3)–1967(2) 1968(2)H	11	13	−0.127	14	14	−0.050
4. 1968(3)–1969(4) Hines only	—	—	—	2	4	−0.056
All periods	13	24	−0.772	18	27	−0.267
		$\sigma_{\hat{\epsilon}} = 1.058$			$\sigma_{\hat{\epsilon}} = 0.851$	

Source: R. G. Lipsey and M. Parkin 'Incomes policy: a re-appraisal' in M. Parkin and M. T. Sumner (eds) *Incomes Policy and Inflation* (1972) p. 101, Manchester University Press.

between unemployment and wage inflation has received considerable attention in recent years. The reason for this is twofold.

First, in recent years, combinations of high unemployment and high inflation have been observed which do not lie on the Phillips curve, but lie somewhere to the right of it. Thus, it was said, the Phillips relationship has 'broken down' in recent years.

This view, however, is the result of an incorrect reading of Phillips' original work. We explained above that Phillips anticipated that the relationship between unemployment and changes in money wages would not hold good during periods when import prices were rising very rapidly. Since the late 1960s and 1970s have been a period of rapidly rising import prices, it is not surprising that the model breaks down for those years.

6.7 The vertical Phillips curve

The major criticism of Phillips' work has, however, come from those writers such as Phelps[2] and Friedman[3] who have argued that Phillips was fundamentally incorrect in trying to discover a relationship between unemployment and the rate of change of money wages. The variable which is determined by the level of unemployment, they argued, is not the rate of change of money wages, but the rate of change of *real* wages, that is, money wages deflated by the change in the price index. Phillips' original hypothesis had been that, for any commodity or service, when the demand is high relative to the supply of it, we expect the price to rise, the rate of rise being greater the greater the excess demand. In the labour market, he argued, excess demand can be measured by the level of registered unemployment (the two will be negatively correlated) and this will therefore determine the rate of change of the price of labour, which he took to be money wages. Friedman, however, argues that the price of labour is, in fact, real wages – that is, money wages relative to what those wages can purchase.

If this is the case, it is argued, there will be not one Phillips curve but a whole family of such curves, each corresponding to a particular rate of price inflation as in Fig. 6.7. Consider what would happen if the economy were initially operating at a level of unemployment of U_N with no price inflation and the government, in an attempt to reduce unemployment, expands demand. The effect will be felt initially in the goods market but will be rapidly transmitted to the labour market where the expansion of demand for labour reduces unemployment to U_0 but also pushes up wages by, say, 2 per cent. That is, we move north-west along the zero price inflation Phillips curve. However, because of excess demand in the goods market, prices begin to rise by, say, 2 per cent, and the economy therefore shifts to the 2 per cent price inflation curve.

We can see from Fig. 6.7 that, with 2 per cent price inflation, a money wage increase of only 2 per cent will cause the level of unemployment to rise again towards U_N. The reason for this is that to preserve a level of unemployment of U_0, increases in *real wages* of 2 per cent would be necessary, but since prices are now rising by 2 per cent, the *money wage* increase of 2 per cent is equivalent to a zero per cent increase in real wages – the real wage increase compatible with a level of unemployment of U_N.

If the government expands demand again, attempting to reduce

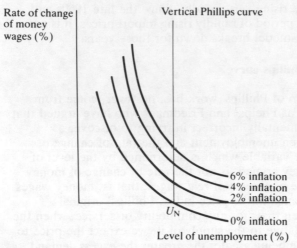

Fig. 6.7

unemployment to U_0, the economy will now move along the 2 per cent price inflation curve. Money wages increase by 4 per cent, as do prices, and the level of unemployment drifts back towards U_N as we shift to the 4 per cent price inflation curve, and so the process continues.

This analysis suggests, then, that trying to keep the level of unemployment down to U_o results in a continually increasing rate of inflation. Only by allowing the level of unemployment to rise to U_N (where the zero price inflation Phillips curve cuts the axis) can the rise in the rate of inflation be halted. Friedman calls this the 'natural level' of unemployment. It is that level of unemployment which is consistent with a steady – that is, non-increasing – rate of inflation. The rate of inflation could be zero per cent, or 4 or 10 per cent, but the crucial point is that labour market conditions are such that there is no tendency for the rate of inflation to increase. To achieve a reduction in the rate of inflation from an initially higher level, requires that the level of unemployment be held above U_N so that the level of demand in the labour market is damped to a sufficient extent to bring about a fall in real wages.

There are two further implications which follow from this analysis. First, the 'trade-off' between inflation and unemployment, which the Phillips curve appeared to illustrate, now disappears. There is no longer a downward sloping relationship between inflation and unemployment. Since the level of unemployment continually drifts back towards the natural level, the Phillips curve, if it exists at all, should be thought of as a vertical line at U_N, as in Fig. 6.8 illustrating that in the long run society can choose either a

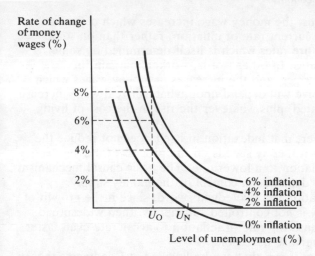

Rate of change of money wages (%)

8%

6%

4%

2%

6% inflation
4% inflation
2% inflation

U_O U_N

0% inflation

Level of unemployment (%)

Fig. 6.8

high rate of inflation coupled with the natural rate of unemployment or a low rate of inflation coupled with the natural rate of unemployment. In other words, as far as the level of unemployment goes, there is no choice at all in the long run.

Second, and more important, this analysis highlights the importance of expectations in the inflationary process. If people expect a certain rate of price inflation, they incorporate this into their money wage claims. The higher the expected rate of inflation, the higher the increase in money wages which they will seek. Thus, expectations play a reinforcing role in sustaining the inflationary process once it has got under way.

The role of expectations is something which is stressed by Friedman and other monetarists. They point out that once the government has allowed an inflationary situation to develop, it will be extremely difficult to reduce the rate of inflation because people acquire expectations of inflation which lead them to behave in such a way that inflation does, in fact, result. The rate of inflation can only be reduced if expectations are changed and this can only be brought about, Friedman argues, by reducing the level of demand so that unemployment rises above the natural level.

Bringing down the rate of inflation by keeping the level of unemployment somewhere above its natural level may be a protracted process, since expectations change only slowly in response to events. However, the process by which expectations are adjusted can be speeded up by the widespread use of *indexation* of wage settlements. Indexation means that current money wage increases will be tied to the current increase in the cost of living. Thus, the money wage increases which occur will depend upon the current rate of inflation, rather than on some expectation of future rates which is itself determined by some average of past rates. In other words, workers bargain for increases in real wages, and the increases in money wages which they actually receive will depend upon whatever real wage increase they have negotiated, plus whatever the rise in the cost of living turns out to be.

Note, however, that indexation in itself does not reduce the rate of inflation – it merely speeds up the process of moving from a higher rate of inflation to a lower one. The basic causal mechanism is the restraint of demand via control of the money supply. Therefore, indexation is a two-edged sword, since if the growth of the money supply is not controlled sufficiently, then widespread indexation will cause the rate of inflation to accelerate even faster than it would otherwise have done.

One serious criticism that can be levelled at Friedman's theory of the 'vertical Phillips curve' is that the analysis does not tell us how high a level of unemployment is required to prevent accelerating inflation – that is, it does not tell us what level of unemployment corresponds to the 'natural level'. We can define the natural level of unemployment as that level which is compatible with non-accelerating inflation, but in recent years it would appear that the natural level of unemployment has itself been rising.

Notes

1. **Phillips A. W.** (1958) 'The relation between unemployment and the rate of change of wage rates in the United Kingdom 1862–1957', *Economica*, Vol. 25 (Nov.), pp. 283–99 (reprinted in *Inflation*, **Ball R. J. and Doyle P.** (eds) Harmondsworth, Penguin)
2. **Phelps E. S.** (1970) *Microeconomic Foundations of Employment and Inflation Theory* (Norton)
3. **Friedman M.** (1968) 'The role of monetary policy', *American Economic Review*, Vol. 58 (March), pp. 1–17

Questions

1. Some economists argue that inflation can be caused by autonomous increases in wage costs. Explain what is meant by the term autonomous in this context.

2. The following are all types of wage/price restraint policies which have been attempted in Britain. What are the drawbacks (and the advantages) of each particular form?

    (a) wage freeze;
    (b) freeze on earnings and prices;
    (c) lump sum increase in wages;
    (d) fixed percentage increases;
    (e) wage restraint with special allowances for low paid and/or for special duties, e.g. unsocial hours;
    (f) policies which allow wage increases which can be covered by productivity increases.

3. In what ways can firms circumvent controls on

    (a) wages;
    (b) prices?

4. In Britain the SDP supports incomes policy, the Tory Government is fundamentally opposed to a formal policy and the Labour Party is opposed to a formal policy but for different reasons. Explain and evaluate the position of each party.

5. How can a government make an incomes policy 'stock'?

6. The following factors may affect (to a greater or lesser extent) wages for different occupational groups.

    (a) Market forces, i.e. relative scarcity.
    (b) Notions of social status
    (c) Notions of comparability.
    (d) Power to determine your own wages.
    (e) Equity.
    (f) Trade union bargaining power.

Consider which of these factors are important in determining wages for the following occupational groups:

    (i) computer programmers;
    (ii) printing workers;
   (iii) teachers;
   (iv) footballers in Division 3;
    (v) cabinet ministers;
   (vi) ministers in the Shadow Cabinet;
   (vii) accountants;
  (viii) water workers;
   (ix) judges.

If relative scarcity is thought important assess the elasticity of demand for the labour in question and the elasticity of supply.

7. Is the Phillips curve compatible with a demand-pull or cost-push interpretation of inflation?

8. Suggest reasons why the Phillips curve may have 'broken down' in the 1970s.

9. If inflation were always fully anticipated would we need to bother about inflation?

10. What do you understand by indexation? Give examples of this and explain what role this would play in a counter inflation policy.

11. Why don't they have inflation in Russia?

Chapter 7
International aspects of inflation

7.1 The inflation of the 1970s: demand pull or cost-push?

In Chapter 3 we began our investigation of the inflationary process
by looking at some statistics on the rate of inflation in some
OECD countries in the 1970s. Any satisfactory explanation of the
causes of inflation, we argued, should be able to offer a convincing
interpretation of these facts. In Chapters 4 and 5 we looked at the
Keynesian and monetarist versions of demand-induced inflation
and, in Chapter 6, we looked at a third explanation, which many
contemporary Keynesians support, that of cost-push inflation. We
shall now consider the extent to which any of these provide a
convincing explanation of the inflation of the 1970s, as evidenced
by the statistics in section 3.1.

7.2 Cost-push inflation

Consider first the cost-push interpretation. The root cause of
inflation, according to this view, was autonomous increases in
costs, and these cost increases fell into two main types:
(a) increases in wage costs;
(b) increases in the cost of imports.
    The very rapid increase in inflation rates experienced by all
countries in 1973 cannot, without stretching credulity too far, be
totally explained by autonomous increases in wage costs. It would
be too much of a coincidence to suppose that suddenly and
simultaneously workers throughout the Western world became
more forceful in their wage demands, or employers became more
submissive in acceding to those demands. Clearly, on its own, this
cannot be an adequate explanation of the causes of inflation.
    The increase in the cost of imported raw materials seems a
more plausible explanation. Oil prices increased very rapidly in the
wake of the Yom Kippur war in late 1973, and other commodity
prices had been increasing steadily since the beginning of 1972.
    Table 7.1 gives some information on this. It is worth noting
from the table that the increase in world commodity prices

Table 7.1 World commodity prices and oil prices, 1970–76

	All commodities index 1970 = 100	Petroleum: dollars per barrel
1970	100.0	1.30
1971	94.1	1.65
1972	107.2	1.90
1973	166.0	2.70
1974	212.3	9.76
1975	174.3	10.72
1976	195.7	11.51

Source: *International Financial Statistics*, Oct. 1977, Vol. XXX, no. 10

preceded the oil price increase, though in percentage terms the oil price increase was more dramatic, being of the order of 260 per cent in 1974. It seems reasonable to ascribe much of the acceleration in the rate of inflation that occurred in 1973–74 to this increase in the price of oil and other commodities. There remains, however, an important unanswered question, namely –

Why was the acceleration in the rate of inflation so rapid in some countries and so modest in others? Could it be that some countries are more dependant upon imports – and in particular raw material imports – than others?

Table 7.2 gives some indication of the relative importance of imports in GDP for a number of countries and there is no obvious correlation between dependence on imports and inflation rates. However, the composition of the basket of goods and services imported differs from country to country and therefore the impact of rising world prices would also differ from country to country.

Table 7.2 Imports as a percentage of GDP

	UK	France	West Germany	Italy	USA	Japan
Average, 1951–55	25	14	15	13	4	11
Average, 1971–75	27	19	21	24	7	11

Source: OECD National Accounts, quoted in *Economic Progress Report*, July 1978

For example, those countries having a high oil content in their basket would be affected more severely than those with a low oil content by the rapid increase in oil prices in 1974.

Table 7.3(a) gives some information on movements in import prices. The difference between the countries in this table are due to differences in the composition of the import baskets, countries like Japan, for example, experiencing a larger increase in prices because her basket contained relatively more of those commodities which were increasing in price the fastest. Note, however, that Table 7.3(a) is based on import prices expressed in US dollars. The impact which rising import prices have on the domestic rate of inflation in any particular country will, of course, depend on these movements in the dollar price of imports plus the effect of movements in the exchange rate, by which these dollar prices are converted to sterling, francs, yen and so on. For example, an

Table 7.3(a) Movements in import prices: index of prices expressed in US dollars, 1970 = 100

	1972	1973	1974	1975	1976
UK	113.5	141.0	204.8	217.4	216.1
France	115.0	139.8	190.1	209.5	207.7
West Germany	110.0	140.6	181.7	191.3	193.5
Italy	116.3	149.1	231.8	245.2	240.6
USA	113.0	133.0	200.1	216.1	222.9
Japan	110.1	140.1	232.5	249.0	251.5

Table 7.3(b) Movements in import prices: index of prices expressed in national currencies, 1970 = 100

	1971	1972	1973	1974	1975	1976
UK	104.9	109.1	138.1	210.3	235.9	288.6
France	103.5	104.4	112.1	164.6	161.7	178.7
West Germany	99.0	96.5	102.7	128.7	128.6	133.1
Italy	105.5	108.5	139.1	241.2	256.1	320.4
USA	105.2	113.0	133.0	200.1	216.1	222.9
Japan	101.8	94.2	105.9	188.3	205.3	207.2

Source: *International Financial Statistics*, Jan. 1977, Vol. XXX, no. 1 and Oct. 1977, Vol. XXX, no. 10

appreciation of the Deutschmark *vis-á-vis* the dollar would partly offset the increase in the dollar price of German imports so that the effect on the domestic rate of inflation in Germany would be less than it would otherwise have been. Table 7.3(b) shows the net effect of movements in dollar prices of imports plus movements in exchange rates, since it is based on movements in import prices expressed in national currencies.

Table 7.3(b) shows that there were considerable differences in the extent to which different countries were affected by rising import prices. Taken together with our measure of the degree of dependence on imports (spending on imports as a percentage of total expenditure), this should give us a rough indication of the contribution which imported inflation made to the overall increase in consumer prices. The results of such an exercise for the period 1973–74 are shown in Table 7.4. Column 1 shows the percentage increase in import prices measured in dollars. Movements in the exchange rate shown in col. 2 will either exacerbate or mitigate this, depending upon whether the exchange rate depreciates or appreciates. Thus col. 3, which shows the percentage increase in import prices measured in national currencies, is approximately equal to the net effect of cols 1 and 2. Column 4 shows imports as a percentage of GNP in 1974. The product of cols 3 and 4 (shown in col. 5) therefore gives us our measure of imported inflation in 1974 in these countries. By comparing this with col. 6, which shows the total rise in consumer prices, we can see what proportion of the total rise in consumer prices is attributable to imported inflation and what proportion therefore is attributable to domestic factors (col. 7).

The method employed here is fairly rough and ready. One of its principal drawbacks may be that it is unduly sensitive to the exact time periods chosen and, had we chosen a different period to study, the results might have been quite different. It does provide us with a valuable indication however of the extent to which imported inflation could *potentially* have contributed to the overall increase in consumer prices in 1974. Note that, in this exercise, we cannot evaluate the extent to which imported inflation actually *did* contribute to the overall rise in consumer prices, merely the extent to which it could *potentially*, have done so. It is, of course, quite possible that all or part of the increase in import prices was absorbed by manufacturers and retailers and not passed on in the form of higher prices. It is also possible that firms do not base their prices on costs at all – rather they look at the demand conditions for their product and they charge what the market will bear. We showed in Chapter 2 (in the discussion of car prices in various countries) that there was considerable evidence to suggest that this interpretation of firms' pricing behaviour was substantially

Table 7.4 The contribution of imported inflation to the rise in consumer prices, 1973–74

	Col. 1 dollar import prices % increase	Col. 2 % change in exchange rate	Col. 3 import prices measured in national currency, % increase	Col. 4 imports as % of GNP (1974)	Col. 5 Col 3 × Col 4 'imported inflation' (%)	Col. 6 total increase in consumer prices (%)	Col. 7 Col. 6 minus Col. 5 inflation caused by domestic factors (%)
UK	45.2	down 4.6	52.3	32.1	16.7	23.8	7.1
France	36.0	down 7.7	46.8	24.0	11.2	15.0	3.8
West Germany	29.2	up 2.4	25.3	25.0	6.6	6.4	-0.2
Italy	55.5	down 11.9	73.4	29.9	21.9	24.7	2.8
USA	50.3	—	50.3	8.9	4.5	12.1	7.6
Japan	65.9	down 6.9	77.8	15.6	12.1	23.8	11.7

Notes

(i) Cols 1, 2 and 3 measure the percentage change between the average 1973 figure and the average 1974 figure. Col 6 is the percentage increase in consumer prices between the fourth quarter of 1973 and the fourth quarter of 1974. Thus we are allowing for a slight time lag for the increase in import prices to feed through into consumer prices.

(ii) Col 2 is the percentage change in the exchange rate index *vis-à-vis* the US dollar.

Source: *International Financial Statistics*, Oct. 1977, Vol. XXX, no. 10.

correct. If it is correct then, in a situation where costs are rising, firms would not automatically respond by increasing prices, and the exercise of decomposing the total rise in consumer prices into the 'imported' element and the 'domestic' element is invalid. We shall pick up this point again in section 7.6, when we discuss alternative views on the nature of the mechanism by which inflation is transmitted from one country to another.

Leaving aside this objection for the moment, however, there remains to be explained the residual shown in col. 7 of Table 7.4 – which we have described as purely domestic inflation. What determines the strength of these domestic inflationary forces? One possible explanation is that, in the high inflation countries, increases in the cost of living, caused by increases in import prices, provoked high wage demands which led to increases in unit labour costs and hence to wage-push inflation. These countries therefore experienced high rates of price inflation which can be traced directly to wage push forces and ultimately to import price push forces. In such a situation, economists would call the wage increases the *proximate* cause of inflation, that is, the nearest identifiable cause, even though they recognize it may not be the ultimate cause.

It is unfortunately difficult to test empirically the validity of this seemingly plausible interpretation. The first problem is that it is difficult to determine what constitutes a 'high' wage demand (for the reasons set out in Chapter 6). Second, the wage settlements that are actually made will depend to some extent on the willingness of employers, in both the public and private sector, to grant wage increases. This in turn will depend upon the rate at which demand is expanding (for employers in the private sector) and the rate of increase in public spending and hence of monetary growth (for employers in the public sector). Thus demand pressures cannot be ignored and any 'explanation' of the causes of inflation which confines itself to cost factors must be at best a partial explanation.

7.3 Demand pull inflation

Could we, however, argue that the inflation of the mid-1970s was the result of excess demand pressures? Whether we regard aggregate demand as being determined by injections and withdrawals or by the money supply, it seems unlikely that an increase in aggregate demand sufficient to trigger off such an acceleration in the rate of inflation could have occurred simultaneously in all those countries in the early 1970s. Unless there is some way in which the economies of the world are linked, so that excess demand in one country spills over to other countries, we must regard the level of demand in any particular economy as being determined by the government and the monetary authorities within that country. As such, it is implausible that governments and monetary authorities throughout the Western world should have all decided to create excess aggregate demand at approximately the same point in time. According to this line of reasoning, then (which we shall subsequently qualify in section 7.5), the inflation of the 1970s cannot have been initiated by excess demand.

However, even though an expansion of demand may not have initiated the inflation, it may have been responsible for allowing it to proceed. We have seen how some countries managed to keep inflation rates lower than others when faced with comparable amounts of imported inflation (cols. 5 and 6 in Table 7.4). We could argue that those countries who were successful in keeping inflation to relatively modest levels may have been those who kept demand in check. Those countries who were not so successful may have been those who allowed demand to increase, thus allowing inflation to proceed and gather momentum.

7.4 A methodological note

It seems quite plausible to argue on *a priori* grounds that the pressure of demand had a significant influence on inflation, though this explanation is quite different from our previous plausible explanation. One of the problems faced in applied economics, and in the social sciences generally, is that one can frequently offer a variety of seemingly plausible interpretations of observed phenomena and it is extremely difficult to decide empirically which is correct. It is not simply a question of having recourse to the empirical evidence, for the empirical evidence itself is often subject to differing interpretations. In other words, there are no 'hard facts'.

However, if we did set out to try to decide empirically which of our explanations remained most plausible when confronted with the evidence, what sort of questions should we ask and what sort of evidence should we look for? The following would appear to be a preliminary list. If we compare a high inflation country such as the UK with a low inflation country such as Germany then we should ask:
1. How severe were the external inflationary pressures facing each economy? To what extent was this the effect of exchange rate changes, which were themselves partly dependent on the level of demand in the economy?

2. Did either country show evidence of excess aggregate demand? How could we measure this? Did unemployment rise faster in one country than in the other, and is this symptomatic of insufficient demand, or are other factors more important in determining unemployment rates?
3. What was happening to public spending, and to what extent was public spending financed through taxation or through borrowing? What therefore was happening to the growth of the money supply?
4. Was the level of wage settlements higher in one country than in the other? Taking account of differential changes in productivity growth, did this represent differential changes in unit labour costs?

We would have to collect data on these things not just for one year but over a number of years, and as such this represents quite a large informational requirement. Even if we had all this information, however, it would not be possible to devise tests which would show conclusively which of our interpretations was correct. Moreover, some epistemologists would argue that it does not necessarily follow that the more information we collect the more certain we can become that one interpretation is correct and the other incorrect.

The essential shortcoming of the empiricist method is illustrated by the story of the empiricist chicken. Every morning the empiricist chicken was fed grain by the farmer. The chicken, being an empiricist, thought 'I do not know for certain whether the farmer is going to kill me or whether he is my friend and is going to keep me as a pet and feed me every morning. But every morning I get more evidence that the second interpretation is correct. Every time that he feeds me increases the probability that the second interpretation is correct and reduces the probability that the first is correct.'

After almost a year the empiricist chicken felt that there was an overwhelming weight of evidence in favour of the second interpretation, that the farmer was going to keep him as a pet. The next day the farmer killed him and had a plump chicken for his dinner.

This cautionary tale is not meant to imply that we should not seek to verify or falsify our theories by an appeal to the evidence. It merely illustrates the difficulty, some might say the impossibility, of so doing. The fact that there is disagreement amongst economists about the correct interpretation of real world events is in itself evidence of how difficult it is to refute a false hypothesis. Economics, however, would be a very boring subject if everything were known for certain.

7.5 International monetary forces

In section 7.3 we argued that the level of demand within a particular economy is determined by the government and the monetary authorities within that country, and therefore, since it is implausible that all countries should have decided to expand demand simultaneously, that the cause of the simultaneous increase in inflation rates cannot be attributed to demand pull forces. However, there is a school of thought which argues that, because of the nature of the international monetary system, the economies of the world are linked more or less closely together so that an expansion of demand in one country causes demand to be expanded in other countries and that this is how inflation is initiated and transmitted from one country to another.

In theory, excessive monetary expansion in one country can only produce inflation in another country if both countries are linked by a fixed exchange rate. If the exchange rate is immutably fixed then, in effect, the two countries share the same currency, since a given amount of one currency can always be exchanged for a fixed amount of the other. Floating exchange rates on the other hand act as a sort of 'flexible joint' between the two economies.

International monetarists would argue that the expansion in the world's money supply in the early 1970s was caused by an over expansion of the major currency, the dollar. The United States, they would argue, was paying for the Vietnam war with excessive domestic monetary expansion which caused both domestic inflation and balance of payments deficits. Thus the world was flooded with dollars. On international money markets there would thus be an excess supply of dollars and an excess demand for, say, Deutschmarks. In order to prevent the price of Deutschmarks appreciating against the dollar, the German central bank would have to step in and buy up the excess dollars, paying for them in marks. These marks might be bought by American firms importing German products who would use them to pay German exporters, who would in turn use them to pay their workforce and so on. Thus, there would be a tendency for the domestic money supply in Germany to expand, as a direct result of the expansion of the American money supply. As long as the two economies were linked by a fixed exchange rate then the larger the American balance of payment deficit with Germany, the greater the tendency for the German money supply to expand. Thus there is a tendency for inflation in one country caused by excessive monetary expansion to generate a sympathetic monetary expansion – and hence inflation – in those countries with which it is linked in a fixed exchange rate system. This tendency will be stronger the more immutably fixed is the (nominally) fixed exchange rate.

This is not the end of the story, however. The simultaneous increase in inflation rates in the 1970s could have been caused, we argued, by increases in the cost of imported raw materials experienced by all importing countries. These increases in raw material prices could have been caused by the action of individual producer cartels (such as OPEC), but since most if not all raw material prices were rising simultaneously and the rise in commodity prices preceded the oil price rise (see Table 7.1), it seems more plausible that these price increases were caused by demand pressures. International monetarists would argue that these demand pressures were generated by an over-expansion of the world money supply through a process such as that described in the previous paragraph.

7.6 The transmission of inflation across national frontiers

The international nature of the inflationary process has been noted and two interpretations of the way in which it passes from one country to another have been described, namely:
1. Directly, as a result of rising import prices via a simple cost-push mechanism. Implicit in this explanation is the view that firms base their prices principally on costs. The rising import prices themselves could have been caused either by the actions of producer cartels (such as OPEC) or as the result of worldwide demand pressure resulting from a too-rapid expansion of the world money supply.
2. As a result of the simultaneous over-expansion of the money supplies of various countries, which caused excess demand inflation in these countries. The reason why all these monetary expansions occurred at the same time was because the over-expansion of the American money supply led to expansion of the domestic money supplies of those countries linked with her in a fixed or fairly fixed exchange rate system.

A third interpretation of the way in which inflation crosses national boundaries was provided in section 2.4. This interpretation, generally known as international price arbitrage, will be restated briefly here.

Assume two countries operate a fixed exchange rate and there are absolutely no restrictions on trade between the two countries, and that they both have the same rate of sales tax. In such a situation, if there are appreciable differences between the price of goods in one country and the price of the same goods in the other country, then it will be profitable to buy up goods in the cheap country and re-sell in the expensive one. To the extent that this process takes place the effect will be to lower prices in the expensive country and raise prices in the cheap one. In theory, the process would continue until prices of goods in the two countries were equalized, making due allowance for transport costs.

This process of course occurs initially in the tradables sector – those commodities which are or could be traded internationally – but it spreads to the non-tradables sector as a result of pressures in the labour market as workers in the non-tradables sector seek comparable pay increases with those in the tradables sector.

The explanations of the way in which inflation spreads from one country to another are, of course, not mutually exclusive. From the standpoint of the policy maker, however, it is vital to know which explanation is closest to reality at any particular point in time, since only then can effective policies be formulated. The fundamental point of disagreement from which these divergent views stem relates to the way in which prices are set. Are prices basically demand determined or are they cost determined? This was the question with which we began our discussion of inflation back in Chapter 3.

The answer to this question, of which the reader must by now be aware, is that both interpretations are correct a priori. *A posteriori* – that is, when we look at the evidence – there are some situations in which demand seems to be the principal factor in determining prices, and other situations in which costs seem to play the dominant role. As with all important questions, there are no easy answers.

Questions

1. Table 7.5 provides data on world exports and the price of commodities. Both are in the form of an index number with 1980 = 100. Graph the two series (on the same graph) and comment on the relationship between them. What in particular does this susggest about the way in which commodity prices are determined? What was happening to the world economy after 1980?

Table 7.5 World exports and commodity prices (index 1980 = 100)

	World exports	Commodity prices
1973	28	57
1974	42	74
1975	43	59
1976	49	68
1977	56	83
1978	64	79
1979	82	92
1980	100	100
1981	98	85
1982	91	74
1983	89	80
1984	94	82

World exports = world exports in billions of US dollars expressed as an index.

Commodity prices = weighted average of the prices of all commodities expressed as an index.

Source: *International Financial Statistics Yearbook 1985*.

2. Table 7.6 contains enough information to enable you to repeat the exercise described in section 8.2 for the period 1979–84. That is, by filling in the blanks in the table marked with an arrow you can calculate:

    (a) an index of import prices in sterling (line 3) and therefore,
    (b) the percentage increase in this index (line 4).
        This will enable you to work out the amount of
    (c) 'imported' inflation (line 6)
        By subtracting this from
    (d) the overall rate of inflation (line 8)
        you can work out the residual, which is
    (e) inflation due to domestic factors (line 9)

As was stated earlier, the procedure is very approximate but it yields some interesting results. You will of course need a calculator.

Table 7.6

	1978	1979	1980	1981	1982	1983	1984
1. Index of import prices expressed in US dollars (1980 = 100)	85	91	100	108	117	128	139
2. Exchange rate ($ per £) period average	1.92	2.12	2.33	2.03	1.75	1.52	1.34
Import prices in sterling							
3. index →	..	..	..	..	..	..	..
4. percentage increase →	..	..	..	..	..	..	..
5 Imports as a percentage of GNP	27	28	25	24	24	25	28
6. 'Imported' inflation (i.e. line 4 × line 5) →		..	..	..	..	..	..
7. Consumer price index	74.7	84.8	100	111.9	121.5	127.1	133.4
8. Rate of inflation →		..	..	..	..	..	..
9. 'domestic inflation' (i.e. line 8 − line 6)		..	..	..	..	..	..

Source: *International Financial Statistics Yearbook 1985.*

3. Classify the following goods and services into tradables, non-tradables: houses, haircuts, hamburgers, postal charges, holidays, clothes. Why will inflation in the tradables sector tend to spread to the non-tradables sector?

Chapter 8
Exchange rates, competitiveness and trade flows

8.1 The effective exchange rate

The value of sterling – that is, the exchange rate between sterling and other currencies – is of great importance because of its influence on import and export prices and import and export flows. These in turn affect domestic prices, domestic output and hence employment and unemployment. In Chapter 2 we discussed how the exchange rate was determined in foreign exchange markets by the interaction of the demand for pounds and the supply of pounds. The exchange rate we discussed then was a *bilateral rate* – the sterling/deutschemark rate, the sterling/dollar rate, the dollar/deutschemark rate, the dollar/yen rate and so on. Bilateral exchange rates have the great merit of being easy to understand. The disadvantage of comparing sterling's value with only one other currency, however, is that movements in the bilateral rate tell us as much about what is happening to the other currency as what is happening to sterling. For example, a depreciation in the sterling/dollar rate (say from £1 = \$1.3 to £1 = \$1.2) represents a 'fall in the value of the pound', but only against the dollar. Measured against other currencies the pound may be rising.

Figure 8.1 illustrates the movements in the value of sterling since 1975. The value of each currency is expressed as an index number which stood at 100 in 1975. A fall in the index represents a depreciation in the value of the pound. As can be seen, since 1980 sterling has fallen *vis-à-vis* the deutschemark, the dollar and the yen, but has risen against the French franc and the Italian lira. These movements of course tell us as much about what has been happening to the German, American, Japanese, French and Italian currencies (in that order) as they tell us about what has been happening to sterling.

Rather than comparing the value of sterling against any one specific foreign currency it would be convenient to compare the value of sterling against a weighted average of foreign currencies. Clearly the weights used should reflect the importance of the currency in question – the US dollar should have a larger weight than the Spanish peseta and the Austrian schilling. An obvious set

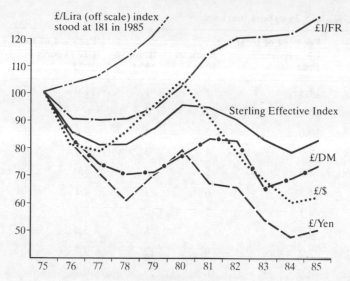

Fig. 8.1 Exchange rate indices

of weights to use is trade shares. That is, the weight attached to a
particular currency should reflect the proportion of UK exports
which go to the country in question. For example, as Table 8.1
shows, the United States took 14.5 per cent of Britain's exports in
1984. Thus the weight attached to the US dollar should be 0.145,
the weight attached to the German mark should be 0.106 and so
on. Of course the trade shares – and hence the weights – are
different on the import side from the export side as a comparison
of Tables 8.1 and 8.2 shows. Some sort of averaging process would
therefore have to be used in calculating a 'trade weighted index' of
the value of sterling.

A more commonly used index is the *Sterling Index*, which is
shown in Fig. 8.1. This index is known by a variety of different
names. Officially now referred to as the Sterling Exchange Rate
Index, it was formerly known as the Effective Exchange Rate for
Sterling – a rather misleading title which, unfortunately, is still in
common usage and is likely to persist. We shall refer to it as the
Sterling Effective Index, thus retaining the adjective 'effective'
which is understood by economists and misunderstood by everyone
else. The Sterling Effective Index is a weighted average of the
sterling exchange rate against seventeen other currencies ranging
from the dollar to the Finnish mark. The weights used are akin to
trade weights, though they are in fact calculated from a rather
complicated multi-lateral exchange rate model (MERM) at the IMF.

Table 8.1 UK's top 25 export markets

	Per cent of total UK exports 1984	Rank in 1984	Rank in 1974	Per cent of total UK exports 1974
USA	14.5	1	1	11.0
West Germany	10.6	2	2	6.3
France	10.0	3	4	5.6
Netherlands	8.7	4	3	6.1
Irish Republic	4.8	5	5	5.0
Benelux	4.3	6	7	4.1
Italy	4.1	7	10	3.1
Sweden	4.1	8	6	4.4
Switzerland	2.2	9	12	2.7
Saudi Arabia	2.0	10	29	0.7
Spain	1.9	11	16	1.8
South Africa	1.7	12	9	3.2
Denmark	1.7	13	13	2.6
Australia	1.7	14	8	3.7
Canada	1.7	15	11	3.0
Norway	1.4	16	14	2.1
Japan	1.3	17	15	2.0
Hong Kong	1.3	18	23	1.0
India	1.1	19	28	0.8
Nigeria	1.1	20	20	1.4
Soviet Union	1.0	21	31	0.7
Iran	1.0	22	17	1.7
Finland	1.0	23	19	1.4
Singapore	0.8	24	24	0.9
Egypt	0.6	25	47	0.3

Source: *Monthly Review of External Trade Statistics*, Annual Supplement 1985, Table F7.

Table 8.2 UK's top 25 import sources

	Per cent of total UK imports 1984	Rank in 1984	Rank in 1974	Per cent of total UK imports 1974
West Germany	14.1	1	2	8.2
USA	12.1	2	1	9.9
Netherlands	7.8	3	3	7.1
France	7.5	4	4	5.8
Norway	4.9	5	18	1.8
Italy	4.8	6	10	3.1
Japan	4.8	7	13	2.5
Benelux	4.7	8	9	3.2
Irish Republic	3.3	9	8	3.5
Switzerland	3.2	10	11	3.0
Sweden	3.1	11	7	4.0
Spain	2.1	12	22	1.3
Denmark	2.1	13	12	2.5
Canada	2.1	14	6	4.3
Hong Kong	1.6	15	23	1.3
Finland	1.6	16	17	2.1
Soviet Union	1.1	17	26	1.0
South Africa	0.9	18	15	2.4
Portugal	0.8	19	25	1.0
Brazil	0.8	20	29	0.8
Australia	0.8	21	21	1.4
Taiwan	0.7	22	42	0.3
India	0.7	23	28	0.9
Saudi Arabia	0.7	24	5	5.1
Austria	0.7	25	27	0.9

Source: *Monthly Review of External Trade Statistics*, Annual Supplement 1985, Table F7.

8.2 Real rates

In section 8.1 we drew the distinction between a bi-lateral exchange rate and a multi-lateral exchange rate – that is, a weighted average exchange rate such as the Sterling Effective Index. We now have to make a further distinction – that between *nominal* exchange rates and *real* exchange rates. The concept of a real exchange rate (or inflation-adjusted exchange rate) is based on the recognition that relative rates of domestic inflation must in the long run be reflected in changes in nominal exchange rates if these nominal exchange rates are themselves to reflect domestic purchasing power parities. (Refer to section 2.4 to revise purchasing power parities.)

To illustrate this point suppose two countries, Britain and France, have different rates of domestic inflation – say the annual rate of inflation in France is 10 per cent and that in Britain is zero. Suppose now that over a twelve-month period the nominal exchange rate between sterling and the franc – that is, the rate actually paid by dealers in foreign exchange markets – rises from 10 francs = £1 to 11 francs = £1. This, of course, represents a fall in the value of the franc of approximately 10 per cent against sterling in nominal terms. Clearly, however, the movement in nominal rates offsets exactly movements in domestic price (or cost) levels between the two countries. A bottle of Château Neuf du Pape (a French good) which last year cost 100 francs to produce and sold at £10 in Britain would this year cost 10 per cent more to produce, that is 110 francs, but would still sell at £10 in Britain. Thus the real rate of exchange between the pound and the franc is unchanged.

In summary, and to reinforce what has just been said, it may be helpful to refer to Table 8.3 where the distinction is drawn firstly between a bilateral and a multilateral rate and secondly between a nominal and a real rate. As can be seen, this gives us four different types of exchange rate. The first of these – the nominal bilateral rate – is easy to understand but may not be adequate for our purposes. The last of these – the real effective rate – may overcome our objections to the use of other measures, but is rather difficult to understand (and, of course, to measure). Moreover, and this creates further difficulties of interpretation, we cannot at any particular point in time measure the *level* of the effective exchange rate. All we can measure is the *movements* in the effective exchange rate since some arbitrarily chosen point in the past. Thus effective exchange rates (both nominal and real) are always measured as an index number. The Sterling Effective Rate is shown in this way in Fig. 8.1. To summarize: if the Sterling Effective Index falls this means that sterling is falling in value

Table 8.3

Bi-lateral	Multi-lateral
Nominal Easily understood, e.g. sterling/dollar rate	Known as 'effective' exchange rate. A weighted average of exchange rates, e.g. the Sterling Effective Index
Real i.e. nominal exchange rate adjusted for differences in domestic rates of inflation in the countries concerned.	Known as 'real effective rate', i.e. weighted average exchange rate adjusted for the difference in domestic inflation rates between Britain and the rest of the world.

against a weighted average of other currencies. That is, more foreign currency is required to buy one pound than was required previously.

8.3 Interpreting movements in the exchange rate

Movements in some macroeconomic variables have an unambiguous interpretation. For example, an increase in GNP, *ceteris paribus*, is 'a good thing'. An increase in unemployment, or in prices is, *ceteris paribus*, 'a bad thing'. How, therefore, are we to interpret a fall in the exchange rate?

In George Orwell's *Animal Farm* the pigs, when they took control of the farm, wrote a slogan on the barn door:

Four legs good. Two legs bad.

In other words animals who walked on two legs (humans) were bad, others were good. A slogan you see was necessary for the other animals who were none-too-bright and could not think things out for themselves. Later on, of course, the pigs began to emulate the behaviour of their former human captors and walked upright on two legs. Then the slogan painted on the barn door was changed:

Two legs good. Four legs bad.

Few of the animals noticed.

Thus it is with movements in exchange rates. One can point to certain periods in the past (for example, the late 1960s) when a fall in the value of sterling was regarded, if not with horror, then certainly as something to be avoided if at all possible. At other times, for example in the early 1980s, a fall in the value of sterling

139

was something to be encouraged, at least according to the received wisdom as written on the equivalent of the barn door. If, dear reader, we are not to accept uncritically what the pigs tell us then we have to think things out for ourselves.

8.3.1 Competitiveness

Movements in the exchange rate will clearly have an effect both on trade prices and on trade volumes. Consider first the effect on the price of UK exports. Assume that exporters set their foreign currency prices by converting sterling prices into a foreign currency price using the exchange rate (this was the behaviour described in Model One in section 2.5). A depreciation in the value of the pound will therefore lead to a fall in the foreign currency price of UK exports – in other words, UK exports become more competitive; that is they become cheaper relative to the exports of other countries.

An index which measures competitiveness in this way is shown in Fig. 8.2. It is labelled 'relative export prices' and it is defined as the price of UK exports divided by the price of competitors' exports, both measured in a common currency. A fall in the index thus represents an improvement in competitiveness. Note that movements in the index measure *changes* in competitiveness. Competitiveness in an absolute sense at any particular point in time cannot be measured by this index.

In section 2.5 we also described a behaviour pattern (labelled as Model Two) in which exporters set their foreign currency prices at a level similar to that of their competitors. According to this model of behaviour, even if UK exporters' foreign currency prices remain unchanged, their export revenues measured in sterling will rise following a depreciation of the pound. Hence export sales become more profitable relative to home sales. Thus the *relative profitability of exports* – or rather, movements in this variable – could be used as an indicator of changes in competitiveness. This variable is defined as an index of export prices (of UK goods) divided by an index of prices on the home market (both being measured in a common currency). It is one of the standard indices of competitiveness and it is shown in Fig. 8.2.

There are, of course, other ways of measuring competitiveness. One of these is *relative unit labour costs*, defined as an index of unit labour costs in the United Kingdom divided by an index of unit labour costs abroad (both in a common currency). Suppose, for simplicity, that unit labour costs measured in local currency are constant in both Britain and America. A fall in the value of the pound relative to the dollar will therefore mean that relative unit labour costs measured in a common currency will fall.

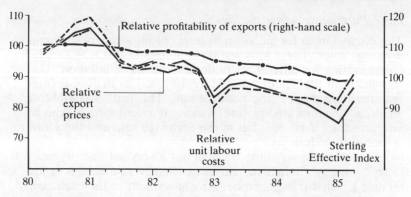

Fig. 8.2 Measures of competitiveness; a fall indicates an improvement in competitiveness

Source: *Monthly Review of External Trade Statistics and Economic Trends*

Thus, in Fig. 8.2, a fall in relative unit labour costs indicates an improvement in competitiveness.

In summary, no matter how we choose to measure it, competitiveness will be increased if the pound falls in value. Increased competitiveness on the face of it seems to be 'a good thing' but note in Fig. 8.2 the strong correlation between our various measures of competitiveness and the exchange rate. Clearly the indices which are conventionally used to measure what we call competitiveness are highly influenced by changes in the nominal exchange rate. Indeed, on the basis of Fig. 8.2 one could go as far as to say that movements in the exchange rate lead to equivalent movements in measured competitiveness. In periods when there have been rapid movements in the exchange rate (such as the 1980s) changes in the exchange rate and changes in competitiveness are more or less the same thing.

The extent to which export volumes rise as a result of an improvement in competitiveness will of course depend upon the relative-price elasticity of demand for UK exports and on the extent to which producers respond to the relative profitability of exports (that is, the profitability of exports relative to home sales). However, as we mentioned when discussing the *J* curve in section 2.5, the improvement in competitiveness brought about by a depreciation of the exchange rate will be partially offset by the resulting rise in import prices. This rise in import prices will tend to raise domestic costs and prices. If this induced rise is significant it will significantly reduce the competitive advantage gained by the initiating fall in the exchange rate.

8.3.2 *Purchasing power parities*

The discussion so far has been in terms of movements in nominal exchange rates. These movements in nominal rates may simply be compensating for differences in domestic rates of inflation. The movement in the *real* exchange rate may be less than or greater than the movement in the nominal rate. This further complicates an already complicated picture, making it even more difficult to interpret the effects of a fall in the exchange rate and therefore to appraise its desirability.

One possible way out – though not a very satisfactory one – is to try to assess whether the current exchange rate is high or low relative to what it ought to be. Any movement in the exchange rate which moves it towards where it ought to be is therefore a 'good thing'. Our assessment of what the exchange rate ought to be must be based on some notion of an equilibrium rate. One could argue, of course, that the current market rate is the equilibrium rate. In a sense this is true but the logical conclusion to be drawn from this is that the current rate is the correct rate, by definition. Movements up or down have certain effects, but they are neither beneficial nor detrimental, merely neutral. This is a defensible view to hold.

However, we could argue that there is a notion of a 'correct' exchange rate which does make some sense. This is based on the idea of purchasing power parities introduced in section 2.4. The purchasing power parity of a currency is the ratio of the price of a representative basket of goods in country A relative to the price of the same basket of goods in country B. The currency is in 'equilibrium' when the purchasing power parity is equal to the exchange rate parity. This solution to an intractable problem does have an intuitive appeal. In practice, however, estimates of purchasing power parities are calculated only on an infrequent basis, though, of course, lack of data should not deter us if we feel this procedure is fundamentally correct. Comparisons of purchasing power parities and exchange rate parities can sometimes be very revealing. Figure 8.3 shows the relationship between the exchange rate parity and the purchasing power parity of sterling in comparison to the German mark. Between 1976 and 1979 both exchange rate parity and purchasing power parity decline, the e.r.p. declining more sharply than the p.p.p. After 1979, however, the e.r.p. rises while the p.p.p. continues to fall. The curves cross in 1980. At that particular point in time the exchange rate parity is equal to the purchasing power parity. What this means is that if one were to take £1 and convert it into marks, the amount of goods one could buy in the shops in Germany is exactly the same as if one had spent the original £1 in the shops in England. Note,

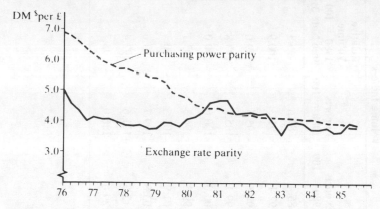

Fig. 8.3 £ versus DM: Exchange rate parity and purchasing power parity

however, that after 1980 the exchange rate 'overshoots'. The external purchasing power of the currency (the exchange rate) becomes 'too high' relative to its internal purchasing power and remains so until mid-1982 after which it overshoots again and becomes 'too low'. This overshooting behaviour is a common feature of exchange rates and was observed again in the dollar–sterling rate in the 1980s.

8.4 Trade volume, value and unit value indices

The purpose of this section is to introduce the reader to some terminology which he or she will probably encounter in newspapers, textbooks or statistical sources at some time in the future – and would almost certainly have misinterpreted had they not been forewarned. Most of the confusion surrounds the use of the terms 'import volume' and 'export volume'. In the minds of the uninitiated this conjures up a picture of physical quantities of goods – aggregated in some way – so many tonnes of coal plus so many sacks of rice plus so many cars and so on. It is nothing of the sort of course because the heterogeneous nature of imports makes aggregation in anything other than money terms impossible. Thus imports (and exports) are measured initially in *value* terms – so many million pounds worth of coal plus so many million pounds worth of rice plus so many million pounds worth of cars. This gives us a figure for the value of imports in £ million.

Now over time the price of these imports (measured in sterling) will change. For example, a fall in the pound and an

Table 8.4 Visible trade

	Exports (£ m.)	Imports (£ m.)	Visible Balance (£ m.)	Relative Value (see Note 1)	Unit Value Indices			Volume Indices		
					Exports 1980 = 100	Imports 1980 = 100	Terms of Trade (see Note 2)	Exports 1980 = 100	Imports 1980 = 100	Relative Volume 1980 = 100 (see Note 3)
1976	25191	29121	−3930	87	60.8	70.9	85.7	85.4	89.6	95.3
1977	31728	34012	−2284	93	72.0	82.1	87.7	92.1	91.3	100.9
1978	35063	36605	−1542	96	79.1	85.2	92.7	94.5	95.5	99.0
1979	40686	44135	−3449	92	87.6	90.9	96.4	99.1	105.7	93.8
1980	47422	46061	+1361	103	100.0	100.0	100.0	100.0	100.0	100.0
1981	50977	47617	+3360	107	108.8	108.2	100.5	99.3	96.3	103.1
1982	55565	53234	+2332	104	116.2	116.7	99.6	101.9	101.5	100.4
1983	60776	61611	− 836	99	125.7	127.5	98.6	103.8	109.7	94.6
1984	70409	74510	−4101	94	136.0	139.5	97.5	112.3	121.6	92.4
1985	81092	84102	−3010	96	146.0	148.0	98.6	120.6	126.0	95.7

Note 1 Export Value as a percentage of Import Value.
Note 2 Export Unit Value Index as a percentage of the Import Unit Value Index.
Note 3 Export Volume Index as a percentage of the Import Volume Index.

Source: *Monthly Review of External Trade Statistics*, September 1985, Table A2.

increase in world prices will both tend to increase the price of imports. We can compute an index of import prices in a similar way to the way in which we compute an index for domestic prices (the RPI). The price index for imports is known, somewhat misleadingly, as **unit value index** (UVI). Using such an index of unit values we can adjust the data on the value of imports to take account of changes in the price of imports. The statistical series so derived – which is normally turned into an index number – is known as a *volume index*. The procedure, therefore, is similar to that performed in the National Accounts and explained in section 4.10.2 when we deflate current price estimates using a price deflator to produce constant price estimates. That is, volume indices for imports and exports are akin to constant price estimates of imports and exports.

Table 8.4 shows some recent data for the United Kingdom on trade values, unit value indices and volume indices. The table will repay some detailed study. Note particularly the way in which the columns headed Relative Value and Relative Volume are made up and the way in which the Terms of Trade are calculated.

8.5 Does devaluation work?

Earlier, in Chapter 2, we distinguished between the terms *depreciation* and *devaluation*. Depreciation, we said, referred to a decrease in a floating exchange rate whereas devaluation referred to a fall in a (nominally fixed) parity. Even though we recognize that since 1972 there has been no official parity, we shall in this section refer to a fall in the exchange rate as a 'devaluation'. We do so in order to emphasize that a lowering of the exchange rate can be a conscious act of policy designed to bring about certain consequences. That is, a lowering of the exchange rate ('devaluation'), whether a step decrease or a more gradual decline, can be a purposeful act rather than something which just happens as a result of market forces. The purpose of a devaluation is of course to improve competitiveness, thus increasing exports (both in value and volume terms) and reducing imports. In fact a reduction in imports is not necessary for the devaluation to be considered successful. What is required is that the rise in exports in value terms in the long run outweighs any induced rise in imports in value terms. In short, a devaluation is successful if it improves the balance of trade.

Whether or not a devaluation does in fact improve the trade balance – or could in principle be capable of doing so – is one of the most important policy questions facing the UK economy. As we have indicated in this chapter, the question is complex. It is

difficult to estimate empirically how trade flows have responded to
movements in the exchange rate in the past – hence it is difficult to
forecast the likely future response of trade flows to a devaluation.

The crucial issue is whether or not in the long run devaluation
produces a sustained improvement in competitiveness. We know
(from Fig. 8.2 for instance) that the immediate impact of a
devaluation is to increase measured competitiveness. We also
know, however (from our discussion in Chapter 7), that increased
import prices feed through into an increase in the retail price
index. This rise in domestic prices will reduce the improvement in
competitiveness brought about initially by the fall in the nominal
exchange rate. In the long run the induced rise in domestic prices
and costs may completely eliminate the improvement in
competitiveness gained by devaluation. If there is no long-term
improvement in competitiveness then devaluation cannot improve
the balance of trade. If we accept this view, as some economists
do, then we must look elsewhere for ways of improving
competitiveness. The labour market seems a natural place to turn
to. In Chapter 6 we looked at the possibility of reducing wage
inflation and thus, *ceteris paribus*, improving competitiveness. In
the next chapter we again focus our attention on the labour
market.

Questions

1. The price elasticity of demand for UK exports is defined as:

$$E_D = \frac{\text{per centage change in quantity of exports}}{\text{per centage change in the price (in foreign currency) of UK exports}}$$

If this elasticity were equal to one, which of the following will necessarily
result from a 10 per cent fall in the exchange value of the £, assuming
exporters change their foreign currency prices by the full extent of the
devaluation:

  (a) The amount of foreign currency we earn from exporting will rise.
  (b) We will have to sell a larger volume of exports to maintain our
      pre-existing level of export earnings.
  (c) Our exports become more competitive so export volume and
      value will increase.
  (d) Export volume will increase but the value of our exports will
      remain unchanged.

2. Suppose a UK exporter sells abroad on markets where the prices he
charges are determined by local market conditions. Suppose the £ were
devalued by 10 per cent. Which of the following statements are true?

   (a) The exporter would receive more foreign currency for each item
       sold.
   (b) The exporter would increase his sales volume.
   (c) Exporting would become more profitable in comparison to selling
       on the home market.

3. Assume that the Government's revenue from North Sea oil is based on
the sterling value of the oil exploited. Will an appreciation in the value of
the £ reduce/increase/leave unchanged the tax revenue from Petroleum
Revenue Tax?

Hint: The oil at the well-head is measured in barrels and its value is
denominated in dollars, which then have to be converted to sterling for
the purposes of calculating liability for PRT.

4. Assume initially that £1 exchanges for $2 or DM 4. If the value of the
DM in terms of dollars rises by 25 per cent (to DM 3 = $2) but the
sterling–dollar relationship remains unchanged, what do you expect would
happen to the sterling–DM rate? If the sterling–DM rate remained
unchanged what would be the best way for a German resident to acquire
pounds for spending during his British holiday?
What ensures that the currency relationships are consistent:

   (a) arbitrage;
   (b) the EEC;

5. Referring to Fig. 8.1, which of the following statements are true. Since
1980:

   (a) The fall in the Sterling Index shows that the pound has fallen
       against all the major currencies.
   (b) The French franc and the Italian lira have fallen against the
       pound.
   (c) The pound has fallen against the French franc and Italian lira.
   (d) Britain has become more competitive *vis-à-vis* West Germany and
       Japan.
   (e) Japanese exports have become less competitive
   (f) Italy has gained competitiveness *vis-à-vis* Britain.

You may of course wish to qualify your answers or amend the statements
above.

6. In section 8.2 the distinction was drawn between nominal and real
exchange rates. A similar distinction exists, of course, between nominal
and real interest rates (i.e. inflation adjusted interest rates.) State which of
the following are correct.
The willingness of non-residents to buy UK government securities (in
preference to German or American securities) will depend on:

   (a) the nominal interest rate offered (in London relative to those
       overseas);
   (b) the real interest rate offered;
   (c) the nominal interest rate offered, but investors will also take

account of the likely future movement in the nominal exchange
rate;

(d) the nominal interest rate offered, but investors will also
take account of the likely future movements in the real exchange rate;

(e) some other combination not elsewhere specified.

7. Suppose a UK resident travels to Germany in 1981, exchanging his
pounds for marks at the official exchange rate. He then goes shopping in
Germany. Is he likely to find that, on average:

(a) goods seem expensive in Germany;

(b) goods seem cheap in Germany;

(c) goods seem about the same price in Germany as in the UK.
(You may need to consult Fig. 8.3).

8. Which of the following will result from a rise in the value of the
pound?

(a) the import UV1 (import prices measured in sterling) will increase.

(b) The import UV1 will decrease.

(c) The terms of trade will improve.

(d) The terms of trade will deteriorate.

(e) The volume of imports will increase.

(f) The volume of imports will fall.

(g) The value of imports will rise.

(h) The value of imports will fall.

(i) The value of imports may rise or they may fall.

Chapter 9
The labour market: unemployment

9.1 The meaning of unemployment

This chapter will be primarily concerned with an analysis of
unemployment. The question we shall be trying to answer is:
'What determines the level of unemployment in the economy?'
This is an area in which the gulf between textbook theory and
applied economics is very wide, and the analysis which follows will
attempt to provide a bridge between the two.

A major difficulty which we face initially is to define what we
mean by the term 'unemployment'. The published unemployment
statistics record all those people who register themselves as
unemployed by 'signing-on' each week at their local employment
office. In the United Kingdom by the end of 1985 this figure
seemed to have stabilized at about 3.3 m., having risen
dramatically from 1980 to 1983. The total population of the United
Kingdom in 1985 was about 56.5 m. and the working population
slightly less than half that – about 27 m. Registered unemployment
thus constituted about 12 per cent of the working population.

However, as the figures above show, more than half the
population of Britain is not working, or more exactly is not in the
employed labour force. Such people are said to be *economically
inactive* – that is, they do not form part of the working population.

What then determines the size of the working population?
This is not equal to that proportion of the total population who are
aged 18–65 (or in the case of women 18–60). One has to add to
this figure those people who go on working past the normal
retiring age – some MPs, judges, university professors and self-
employed people – and one has to subtract those in full-time
further education, in prison, those who, because of some physical
or mental disability are unable to work, and those who choose not
to work. This last group will include all those married women who
do not go out to work but prefer to stay at home to look after the
home and family. It will also include some men and women who
prefer not to work because their income from social security
benefits is almost as great, or in some cases greater than, the
income that they could earn from full-time employment. In these

circumstances, the unemployment which these last two groups are experiencing would correctly be defined as *voluntary unemployment* – they would prefer not to work given the circumstances in which they find themselves. These last two groups will be treated very differently in the official statistics, however. The full-time housewives will not be regarded as part of the working population even though the task of child-rearing may be particularly onerous, and they will not be counted in the unemployment statistics, since they do not register themselves as unemployed. They do not form part of the 'economically active population'. Those people in the second group, however, would normally register themselves as unemployed in order to qualify for social security benefits. Thus, even though they choose to be unemployed in the same way that the housewives do, they will be counted as part of the 'economically active population' and they *will* be counted in the unemployment statistics as involuntary unemployed.

The term 'voluntary unemployment', however, should not be taken to imply that those so classified are necessarily satisfied with the circumstances in which they find themselves. The housewife, for example, may be anxious to go out to work but unable to do so because of the inadequate nursery school provision in her area. Similarly, the father of a large family who finds that he can earn more by living on social security than he can in full-time employment may regret that his employment earnings potential is so low and resent the lack of status that society affords him as an unemployed person.

The fact that we have suggested that some people who could work prefer not to do so implies no moral condemnation of them, whether they be fathers of large families, childless housewives, single-parent families, people who stay home to look after aged relatives, or people with substantial inherited wealth. The choice of whether or not to engage in paid employment is a decision which each individual makes, having regard to his own circumstances. He or she will take into account not only the potential income to be earned but also the degree of job satisfaction likely to be experienced. The individual will also take account of the *opportunity cost* of working – what he or she has to give up in order to earn income from employment. In some cases, this opportunity cost may be so high in comparison to potential net earnings from employment that the rational individual chooses not to enter the labour market.

Figure 9.1 is an attempt to show how the total population of Great Britain is broken down into the various categories. An alternative presentation is given in Table 9.1 which also shows the distribution between males and females. This table, including the

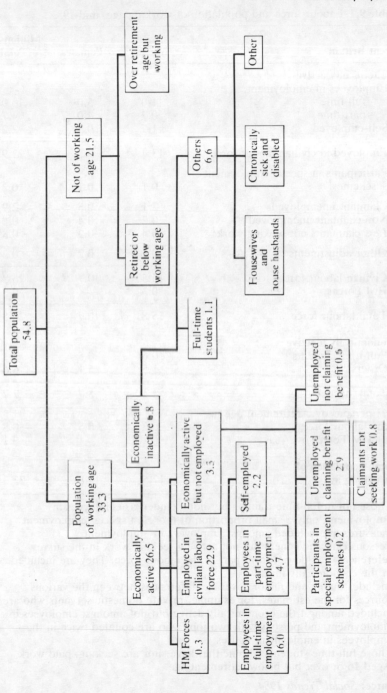

Fig. 9.1 Population Great Britain 1983 (millions) Source: *Social Trends 1984*

Table 9.1 Labour force and population of working age, mid-1983

Great Britain	Males	Females	Millions Total
Economically active			
Employees in employment			
– full-time	11.0	5.0	16.0
– part-time	0.7	4.0	4.7
Self-employed	1.7	0.5	2.2
Employed in civilian labour force	13.4	9.5	22.9
Participants in special employment schemes[1]	0.1	0.1	0.2
Claimant unemployed	2.1	0.8	2.9
Non-claimant unemployed	0.2	0.4	0.6
Less claimants not seeking work[2]	−0.4	−0.3	−0.8
Other adjustments[3]	0.1	0.2	0.3
Civilian labour force	15.5	10.7	26.2
HM Forces	0.3	—	0.3
Total labour force	15.8	10.7	26.5
Economically inactive			
Full-time students[4,5]	0.6	0.5	1.1
Others[5]	1.5	5.1	6.6
Total inactive[2,5]	2.1	5.7	7.7
Less persons over retirement age in the labour force	−0.3	−0.5	−0.8
Less HM Forces overseas	−0.1	—	−0.1
Home population of working age	17.5	15.8	33.3

[1] Those not in full-time training but not included as employees in employment; only a small proportion of those on special employment measures are included amongst employees in employment.

[2] Persons claiming benefit but not actively seeking work in the survey reference week do not form part of the labour force. They are included in the economically inactive.

[3] Includes timing and minor coverage differences between the various sources for the estimates, for example, private domestic servants who are included amongst the economically active but not amongst employees in employment and persons with two jobs who are counted twice in the employees in employment figures.

[4] Those full-time students who neither have, nor are seeking, paid work.

[5] Aged 16 or over but below retirement age.

Source: *Social Trends 1984.*

Table 9.2 Different estimates of 'unemployment' (Great Britain 1983) (millions)

A. unemployed claiming benefit	2.9
plus	
unemployed not claiming benefit	0.6
plus	
participants in special employment schemes	0.2
	―――
	3.7
	―――
B. as in A above but excluding participants in special employment schemes (0.2 m.)	――― 3.5
	―――
C. as in B above but excluding unemployed not claiming benefit (0.6 m)	――― 2.9
	―――
D. as in C above but excluding claimants not seeking work (0.8 m.)	2.1

Source: derived from *Social Trends 1984*, Ch 4

footnotes, is reproduced verbatim from *Social Trends*, an annual publication of the CSO.

Careful study of Fig. 9.1 reveals that the level of unemployment can be calculated in several different ways, depending upon whether one wishes to arrive at a relatively high figure or a relatively low figure. Some of the possible ways of calculating the level of unemployment are summarized in Table 9.2 though this by no means exhausts all the possibilities. The essential point is that the concept of unemployment is not an unambiguous one. What the unemployment statistics record is simply the number of people who register themselves as unemployed – no more, no less. As we shall see, this does not necessarily correspond to the theoretical definition of unemployment which we explain in the next section.

9.2 The causes of unemployment

The analysis which follows will go part of the way towards answering the question – 'What determines the level of unemployment?' In looking at the workings of the labour market, the approach we shall adopt would be accepted by most Keynesian economists, but its origins are firmly rooted in the classical (or pre-Keynesian) tradition.

As we saw in Chapter 4, where we looked at the pre-

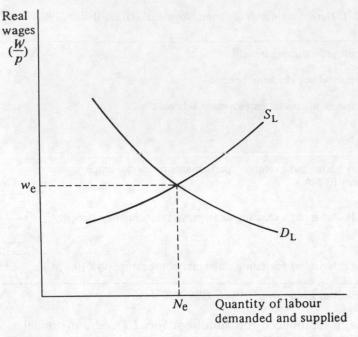

Fig. 9.2

Keynesian views on the determination of the level of savings and investment, the classical view of the workings of the macroeconomy relied heavily on the theory of value. It was natural for the classical economists to apply the same sort of reasoning to the study of the labour market, and this we do below.

In analysing the labour market we assume, for simplicity, that labour is a homogeneous commodity – an hour of one employee's time is equivalent to an hour of any other employee's time. This simplifying assumption will be relaxed later when we consider the problem of structural unemployment.

In Fig. 9.2 we measure, on the horizontal axis, the quantity of labour demanded and supplied and, on the vertical axis, the price of labour (the wage rate). It is very important to note that this is measured in real terms, that is, it is the money wage divided by the price index.

The number of people offering themselves for employment (the supply of labour) is assumed to be positively related to real wage rates. The higher the reward for work then, other things being equal, the greater the number of people who will want to work. This will not necessarily be so under all circumstances, but it is a convenient working hypothesis.

The demand for labour we assumed to be inversely related to the price of labour. implying that the demand for labour will fall as the price of labour increases.

The *equilibrium level* of employment, N_e, is thus determined by the intersection of the demand and supply curves, and this occurs at the equilibrium wage rate, W_e. At this wage rate, N_e people will offer themselves for employment, and this will be equal to the number of people that employers are willing to hire at that wage rate. Thus there is no unemployment, or rather there is no *involuntary* unemployment.

Now consider what would happen if the demand for labour shifted to the left, implying a fall in the demand for labour, as in Fig. 9.3. If real wages are flexible downwards, then a new equilibrium level of employment will be established at N_e' at a real wage of W_e'. Actual employment has, of course, fallen by ($N_e - N_e'$) but this movement along the supply curve represents a fall in the number of people *willing* to work, that is, a rise in voluntary unemployment, and these individuals, you will recall, like the housewives who stay at home to look after families, are not recorded in the official unemployment statistics.

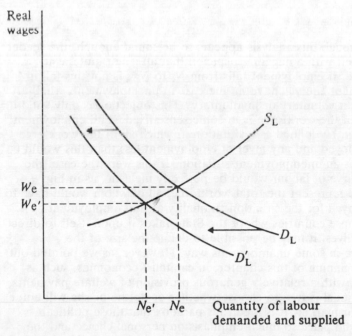

Fig. 9.3

155

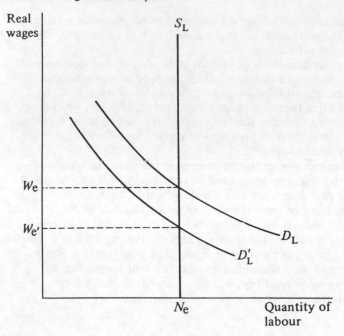

Fig. 9.4

Although this analysis appears to be sound enough, the reader may be left with a nagging suspicion that all is not quite as it should be. If employment falls from N_e to N_e', is not this fall in employment equivalent to an increase in unemployment, whether one calls it voluntary or involuntary? This objection is only valid if the size of the workforce is in some sense fixed. 'Full employment' could then be defined as a situation in which all of the workforce was employed and any level of employment less than this would be defined as an unemployment situation. If this were the case, the supply curve of labour would be perfectly inelastic, as in Fig. 9.4. N_e would represent the total workforce, all of whom would have to be employed for the situation to qualify as 'full employment'.

In those countries where the State takes it upon itself to direct people's lives, it may be possible to define the size of the workforce in some unambiguous way. However, as we pointed out at the beginning of this chapter, in capitalist economies, such as our own, with a relatively generous provision of welfare payments, the individual is free to choose whether or not he or she will enter the labour market. It is a curious paradox that those political parties who place so much emphasis on personal choice and the freedom of the individual should complain so loudly when certain members of our society should choose to exercise that choice and opt out of the labour market.

However, for those readers who find the concept of voluntary unemployment difficult to accept, a compromise can be reached. Henceforth, the supply curve for labour will be drawn as a relatively steep curve, indicating that the number of people offering themselves for employment is relatively insensitive to changes in wage rates. In terms of our model, the supply of labour can then be treated as something which is a relatively fixed magnitude.

To continue with our analysis, consider what would happen if wages did not fall, as a result of a shift in the demand for labour, but remained at W_e as in Fig. 9.5. Actual employment would then fall to N'' and unemployment equal to $(N_e - N'')$ would emerge. All of this unemployment could be regarded as involuntary since, at a wage of W_e when N_e people were offering themselves for employment, only N'' would actually be employed.

It is important to note that this is a disequilibrium situation.

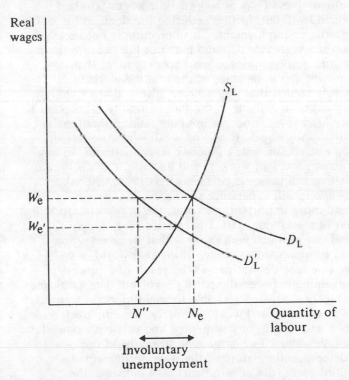

Fig. 9.5

The existence of involuntary unemployment occurs as a result of the downward inflexibility of wages, which prevents them falling to the equilibrium level $W_e{'}$.

This was the explanation that the pre-Keynesian economists gave for the existence of unemployment. It was a disequilibrium phenomenon caused by monopolistic elements in the labour market which prevented the real wage from falling as it ought to do. Eventually, however, the market would adjust to the new equilibrium position and unemployment would then be eliminated. Government intervention was unnecessary as, in the long run, the market would adjust of its own accord.

This argument, though seemingly logical, is now widely regarded as fallacious, for the following reasons.

First, the demand for labour is what is known as a *derived demand*. It is derived from the demand for the final product which the labour helps to create. The sum of the demands for all the goods and services in the economy – aggregate demand – thus determines the total demand for labour. By far the largest component of aggregate demand is the consumption spending of the workers themselves. Thus, it is argued, if wages fall then aggregate demand will fall, further reducing the demand for labour and creating more unemployment. This objection is not necessarily correct, however. Aggregate demand may not fall because the rise in incomes of the newly employed workers may more than compensate for the fall in incomes of the existing workers.

Second, it is argued that wages *never* fall, so that an analysis that says they ought to is flying in the face of reality. This point is easily answered, however, since we are here talking about *real* wages and not money wages. Real wages fall when the rate of price inflation exceeds the rate of money wage increases. In any given year, many groups of workers will be suffering falls in real income and there will be some years, such as 1974, when the majority of workers will experience such a decline.

Third, and more important, however, this way of interpreting the behaviour of the labour market is criticized for being unrealistic and out of touch with the way that wage rates are determined in contemporary society. In the real world, it is argued, wage rates are determined as the result of a process of collective bargaining between the parties involved. The employees' side may be highly organized and able to wield monopoly power, or it may be fragmented and weak. Similarly, the employers' side may be unified and strong, or fragmented and relatively powerless to resist union demands. The bargaining strengths of the two parties will determine the nature of the wage settlement. In addition, a third party (the government) may influence the outcome of the bargaining process.

This last point is very important. A sizeable fraction of the workforce in this country is employed in what could loosely be termed the 'public sector'. This fraction could be one third more or less, depending upon how one defines the term 'public sector'. Wage rates and employment levels in the public sector are determined not so much by market forces – the pressures of demand and supply – as by institutional factors. The number of people employed in any particular part of central or local government will depend upon a complex set of political decisions, made at various levels of the decision-making governmental hierarchy. Thus, the number of teachers that a local authority employs in its schools will depend on a directive from central government about required class sizes, and on how the local authority interprets that directive. Teachers' salaries will be agreed nationally by a process where arguments about relativities and differentials play a more important role than arguments about teacher shortages or oversupply.

9.3 Summary and preview

Before proceeding with our analysis it may be useful to summarize the argument so far. We set out to try to analyse the determinants of the level of unemployment. Unemployment, we discovered, could be either voluntary or involuntary. The official statistics record involuntary unemployment but may also erroneously include some voluntary unemployment. Furthermore, some people who are actively seeking work may not register themselves as unemployed. Thus, the unemployment statistics may over or under estimate the true level of involuntary unemployment.

A more fruitful line of enquiry may be to ask what determines the level of *employment*, and this, we saw, can be explained in terms of the demand and supply of labour. If, for the time being, we treat the supply of labour as fixed (invariant with respect to wage rates) then the level of unemployment will be determined as a residual – it will be the difference between the level of employment and the size of the workforce (or the supply of labour). After discussing in section 9.4 the determinants of the demand for labour, we shall therefore proceed in section 9.5 to discuss the determinants of the level of employment.

9.4 The determinants of the demand for labour

As we saw above, the demand for labour is determined by the level of aggregate demand (though this statement is really true only of the people employed in the private sector). In Chapters 4 and 5 we discussed at length the views of the two major conflicting schools of thought – Keynesian and monetarist – about the determinants of the level of aggregate demand. We said that the level of aggregate demand was crucial in determining the rate of inflation. We have now seen that the level of aggregate demand is equally crucial in determining the demand for labour in the private sector.

In the public sector, the demand for labour is determined by administrative decisions. In this context, the term 'public sector' refers to all the activities of central and local government, that is, spending on education, health, social services, roads, parks, defence of the realm and so on. In addition, the demand for labour in certain State-owned industries, such as British Rail, will be influenced by administrative decisions as well as market forces.

The demand for labour in the public sector, even though it is formally determined by administrative decisions, may also be influenced by the level of aggregate demand. In the health service, for example, the demand for labour will be determined by the amount of funds which the government allocates for health care. In a recession, when the level of aggregate demand is low, government tax revenues will be correspondingly low and, because funds are short, expenditure cuts can be expected in all government departments, including those concerned with health care. Thus, the state of demand in the economy indirectly affects the demand for labour in the public sector.

To sum up then, the primary determinant of the demand for labour is aggregate demand, with administrative decisions being important for those in the public sector.

9.5 The determinants of the level of employment

We argued above that, in an advanced capitalist society, the price of labour cannot be explained solely in terms of market forces. Wage rates, we argued, are the result of a complex bargaining process between parties with varying degrees of monopoly power where attitudes and expectations play an important part in shaping the final outcome. In such a situation we can treat wage rates as being exogenous, that is, determined outside our model. If wage rates are treated as a given datum in this way then the level of employment will be determined solely by the demand for labour, as in Fig. 9.6.

We argued above that aggregate demand would be the principal determinant of the demand for labour. Since the demand for labour determines employment levels, we conclude that the level of aggregate demand is the most important determinant of the level of employment.

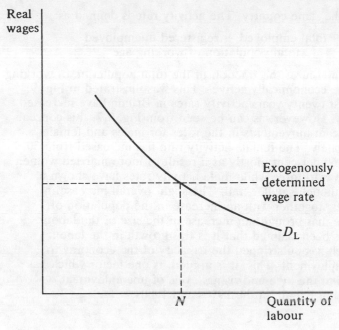

Fig. 9.6

9.6 The determinants of the level of unemployment

Up to this point we have been analysing the factors which determine the level of employment. The question with which we started this chapter was, however, 'What determines the level of unemployment?' Clearly, the level of unemployment must be determined as a residual. It is equal to the number of people who wish to work (at the going wage rates) minus the number of jobs which the economy sustains. The level of unemployment is thus affected by the level of demand in the economy. *Ceteris paribus*, the higher the level of aggregate demand, the higher will be the demand for labour and the higher the level of employment. The lower, therefore, will be the level of unemployment. It is a mistake, however, to regard the level of unemployment as being exclusively determined by aggregate demand since the supply of labour is equally important.

The supply of labour is itself determined by a complex set of socio-economic factors in addition to the obvious fact that the supply of labour will be affected by changes in the size of the population and its age-structure. These socio-economic factors are partly responsible for differences in *activity rates* between different

161

regions of the same country. The activity rate is defined as:

$$\frac{\text{total employed} + \text{registered unemployed}}{\text{total population of working age}}$$

and it thus measures the fraction of the total population of working age who are 'economically active'. This was illustrated in Fig. 9.1. Over the last twenty years activity rates in Britain have increased only slightly. However, as can be seen from Fig. 9.7, this conceals quite significant movements in the rates for males and females taken separately. The female activity rate has increased from 50 per cent to 60 per cent mostly as a result of more married women entering the workforce while male activity rates have shown a significant, though smaller, fall. The slight overall increase in activity rates, together with an increase in the population of working age, has brought an increase in the size of the labour force. It has been claimed that it is this growth in the labour supply which has outstripped the capacity of the economy to increase employment. This, it is argued, is one factor which has contributed to the high and rising levels of unemployment experienced in Britain in the 1970s and 1980s.

9.7 Monetarist and Keynesian views of the determinants of unemployment

Up to now, the analysis we have presented has been eclectic, owing no particular allegiance to either Keynesian or monetarist camps. We now want to highlight the crucial differences between these two schools in their analysis of the determinants of unemployment.

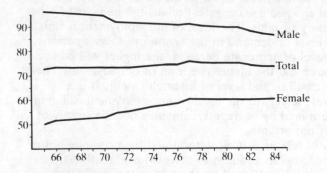

Fig. 9.7 UK Activity Rates 1965–85
Source: *OECD Labour Force Statistics* 1985

9.7.1 *Monetarist views*

Contemporary monetarist views on the determinants of
unemployment can best be understood in terms of the
'expectations augmented' Phillips curve analysis introduced in
section 6.7. Monetarists believe that the real wage and
employment levels are determined in the labour market and that
the market *clears*, that is, it is in equilibrium. They distinguish,
however, between short-run and long-run equilibrium. Short-run
equilibrium is a situation in which expectations are incorrect and
hence are unfulfilled, whereas in long-run equilibrium, the
expectations of all the parties involved are correct anticipations of
future events.

The suppliers of labour will be interested in the real wage.
Similarly, firms will hire labour only as long as the wage they have
to pay is less than the value of what that labour can produce. In
other words, they too will be interested in the real wage – the
money wage relative to the money value of the extra output that
the labour can produce. Monetarists believe that this real wage is
flexible in the long run (for example, if money wages fall less than
prices, the real wage will fall).This flexibility ensures that in the
long run a market-clearing real wage will rule in the labour
market, ensuring full employment or, more exactly, no involuntary
unemployment. Any registered unemployment that remains will be
'natural', since the economy will be at the 'natural level' of
unemployment.

Assume now, however, that the government undertakes
expansionary policies designed to reduce the level of
unemployment. The effect will be first of all to increase demand in
the market for goods and services, pushing up prices. The demand
for labour, therefore, increases because each employee becomes
more productive in the sense that the *value* of goods which he
produces per hour will rise. The disequilibrium situation in the
labour market caused by the increased demand for labour causes
money wages to rise and this results in an expansion of supply as
more individuals opt voluntarily for labour rather than leisure.
Thus, employment levels increase, along with money wages and
prices.

Note, however, that this short-run effect will only occur if
workers can be duped into supplying more labour by an increase in
the money wage, since real wages have not changed, prices and
wages having increased *pari passu*. Workers, in this case, are said
to suffer from 'money illusion'. In the longer run, however, the
scales fall from their eyes and they realize that increased prices
have completely offset the increase in their money wages.
Workers, therefore, revert to their former behaviour and those

who have newly entered employment drop out again, preferring leisure to labour at this real wage. This fall in the supply of labour results in labour shortages and consequently a further rise in money wages. This increase in money wages, however, which may also be a temporary increase in real wages, leads to a fall in the demand for labour, the net result being that the economy falls back to the natural level of unemployment.

The dynamics of the situation, that is, how the economy arrives at the long-run equilibrium position, may be involved and uncertain (they are considered in more detail in section 11.4). The essential point, however, is that deviations from the natural level of unemployment are purely temporary phenomena. In the long run, real wages determine both the amount of labour demanded and supplied and hence the 'natural rate of employment' as in Fig. 9.8.

In the long run, neither of the curves in Fig. 9.8 is altered by the sort of reflationary policies we have been considering, since each curve is based on the rational maximizing behaviour of individual firms and individual workers. This analysis, in fact, has been dubbed 'the New Microeconomic Approach' to the study of unemployment and inflation. The supply of labour is based on the

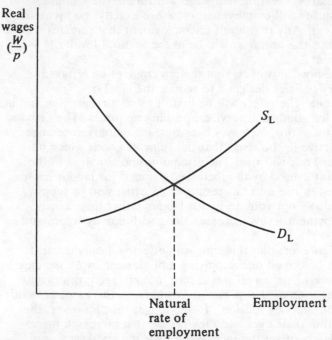

Fig. 9.8

labour-leisure choice facing each individual worker. This choice can be influenced by government policies, which make the reward for working higher relative to the reward for not working. A cut in income tax, for example, or a decrease in unemployment pay and social security benefit would have this effect. The demand for labour is based on the profit maximizing actions of firms in hiring labour up to the point where the cost of hiring additional labour exceeds the value of what that labour can produce. This analysis is known as Marginal Productivity Theory since the demand for labour depends upon the extra output – the marginal product – which each additional worker can produce. Marginal productivity theory lies at the heart of the neo-classical and monetarist analyses of the labour market and, as we shall see, it is the point at which critics have focused their attack. Note that, according to this analysis, the demand for labour depends upon the real wage and therefore it cannot be permanently raised by expansionary macroeconomic policies, since such policies result in wages rising in line with prices, leaving real wages unchanged. The demand for labour would increase permanently as a result of increased investment in new machinery, for example, which makes labour more productive, but the increased demand for labour brought about by reflationary policies will be purely temporary, and hence such policies cannot permanently reduce unemployment. Rather they result in accelerating inflation of both wages and prices.

9.7.2 The creed

So called 'Keynesian' views of the labour market cover a wide spectrum of opinion. The common feature which distinguishes their approach from that of the monetarists, however, centres around the use of the word 'market'. For monetarists, a market is a device for allocating resources which, in the absence of government regulation, functions smoothly and efficiently. It is a self-equilibrating mechanism, through which the transmission of appropriate signals to both buyers and sellers ensures that supply and demand are brought into equality by movements in prices. This concept of a market is an intellectual construction of sparkling clarity and elegant simplicity. But although it is an amazingly powerful analytical tool, it can also serve to block thought and hinder scientific progress because, for some people, it has transcended *theory* and become belief. Consider the following:

I believe that God created heaven and earth.
I believe in the market mechanism.

There is no difference in the meaning of the word 'believe' in each of these two sentences. In neither case does it mean 'I have a theory that...' Rather it means 'I support intellectually and emotionally, and accept the view that...' History is littered with examples where belief has stood in the way of understanding and scientific knowledge. In the seventeenth century, Gallileo was imprisoned for supporting the Copernican theory, that the planets revolved around the sun, because the theory was incompatible with the Church's belief that the earth was the centre of the universe. Gallileo knew that all the evidence was incompatible with the Church's belief but it is extremely difficult to argue with belief, whether it relates to the nature of the universe or the nature of the labour market.

9.7.3 Keynesian views

Thus, when we say that monetarists believe in the market mechanism, this statement has enormous philosophical and methodological implications. As regards the labour market, while Keynesians accept that *some* markets work in the way we have outlined, they maintain that the evidence is strongly at variance with the view that the labour market does. Although they concede that a market for labour exists, in the sense that there is a demand for labour and a supply, they point to the imperfections inherent in the market, which may prevent it clearing. On both the supply side and the demand side of the market, there are monopolistic elements which can influence wages and employment levels. Money wages are notoriously sticky in a downwards direction, and even real wages may exhibit such a tendency since institutional factors allow workers to resist cuts in their real wages.

More important, they argue that there is not one market for labour, but a number of distinct markets. Each market is separated from the rest by geographical, occupational and institutional factors. Thus, bus drivers in Birmingham and shop assistants in London constitute two non-competing groups.

Moreover, if we take any particular occupational group – say local authority manual workers – there may also be two distinct markets; an *internal* labour market comprising existing employees, and an *external* labour market comprising potential employees, all those who are actively or not-so-actively considering employment in this occupation. The internal market is governed by a different set of administrative procedures to that existing in the external market, and although the two markets are interconnected, the internal market is to a lesser or greater extent shielded from the competitive forces to which the external market is exposed.

In addition, some Keynesians would question the validity of Marginal Productivity Theory which underlies the analysis of the demand side of the labour market. The debate here is sufficiently important to warrant further investigation, which we do in the next section.

Table 9.3

Number of assistants	Net revenue from sales £ per week	Value of marginal product £ per week
1	100	100
2	180	80
3	245	65
4	300	55
5	320	20
6	320	0
7	310	−10

9.7.4 Marginal Productivity Theory

Consider the following example, where a shop manager whose objective is to maximize the profit he gets from his shop, can hire as many sales assistants as he wishes at the going rate. Generally speaking, the more staff he has, the greater will be his sales, but the more staff he hires, the smaller will be the extra contribution of each additional assistant. There will come a point when additional staff will actually reduce sales, not because the extra staff are less efficient or more surly, but simply because the size of the shop is fixed and the number of potential customers they could serve is limited. In other words, the staff get in each other's way and put off the customers by their excessive zeal. Clearly, there are too many staff in this situation, but what is the optimal number to hire?

Suppose that the shopkeeper knows the relationship between the number of staff and the net revenue from sales (that is, total sales revenue minus the bought-in prices of the goods he sells) as in Table 9.3 cols. 1 and 2. He can, therefore, calculate the extra net revenue attributable to each additional assistant. This is the value of the marginal product of each extra assistant (col. 3). The number of staff which the manager wishes to hire will depend upon the wage he has to pay. Suppose the going rate is £60 per week. The first assistant will be worth hiring because he adds £100 to net revenue but only £60 to costs, thus increasing profits by £40. Similarly, the second and third assistants add more to net revenue than they do to cost, so that they will be hired. But the fourth assistant adds only £55 to net revenue and a further £60 to costs, so that by employing him the manager will be reducing the shop's profits. Hence, he will not be employed. When the wage is £60, the manager will hire three assistants; that is, the demand for labour is three.

167

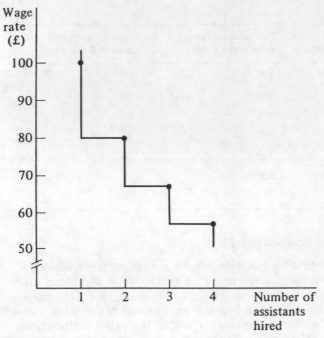

Fig. 9.9

If wages rise to say £70 per week but the productivity of the assistants remains unchanged then we can easily check that the third assistant will no longer be employed because the wage that he has to be paid exceeds the value of his marginal product. At the higher wage of £70, the demand for labour drops to two.

In fact, the value of marginal product curve is the manager's demand curve for labour, since it shows how many assistants will be hired at each wage level, as in Fig. 9.9. If the four points in Fig. 9.9 were joined up, they would constitute a demand curve for labour. In our particular example, this is a step function rather than a smooth curve, but one can readily appreciate that what Fig. 9.9 illustrates is an inverse relationship between the demand for labour and the wage rate.

This then is the microeconomic foundation of the neo-classical (or monetarist) analysis of the demand side of the labour market. Some Keynesians, while accepting that the analysis is logically consistent in the very restricted context of our example, deny that it can be validly applied in the real world, particularly in the macroeconomic context. There are a number of reasons for this.

First, it is argued that the assumption of profit maximization is unrealistic, particularly for labour employed in the public sector.

Second, even if one accepts that profit maximization is the goal that firms pursue, to do so successfully requires that they possess much more information about costs and revenues at the margin than they could ever hope to have in practice. In other words, it is impossible for firms to calculate the extra revenue attributable to the marginal employee. Third, the analysis presumes that all other factors of production are held constant; for example, the size of the shop cannot be increased, the number of checkouts is fixed and so on. In reality, a shop manager wishing to expand would be more likely to increase all his factors of production rather than holding all his factors fixed, save one. In the real world many technologies are characterized by fixed factor proportions and indivisibilities. For example, it takes one man to drive a bulldozer – three-quarters of a man is not enough and two men is too much. In short, critics of marginal productivity theory argue that, though the analysis may be internally consistent, it is a poor model of the determination of the demand for labour in contemporary societies, because it can only be applied to a very limited range of circumstances.

9.8 Structural unemployment

Our analysis so far has been somewhat theoretical. This is partly because we made the simplifying assumption that labour was a homogeneous commodity. This was necessary in order to be able to discuss the demand for labour and the supply of labour in aggregate terms, but, in reality of course, labour is not all of the same kind. Different people possess different skills and abilities which suit them for some forms of employment and not for others. This can give rise to a situation in which there is a mis-match between the demand for labour and the supply, not in terms of the numbers of people wanting work and the number of jobs offered, but in terms of the skills possessed by the people wanting jobs and the skills required by the employers. In one particular geographical area there could be, for example, a high and rising demand for bus drivers coexistent with severe unemployment amongst spot-welders. In such a situation, an overall expansion of demand in the economy will do little to alleviate the problem of unemployed spot-welders. The unemployment that exists in this case is due to structural factors rather than any overall deficiency in aggregate demand.

Structural unemployment, so called, arises either because there is a mis-match of skills available and skills required, or because there is a mis-match between the location where the jobs are available and where the unemployed labour is to be found.

This second type of structural unemployment could be described as regional unemployment, to emphasize the fact that unemployment, as it exists in the UK, is very much a regional phenomenon; Northern Ireland, the North of England and Scotland typically have unemployment rates higher than the rest of the UK and substantially higher than in the South East of England or East Anglia. Unemployment in these 'depressed' areas could be reduced by an overall expansion of demand – so, in this sense, it is still valid to think of it as being caused by a deficiency of aggregate demand; but, if such a policy were pursued, the result would be to cause the labour markets of the prosperous South East to become overheated, leading to wage-push inflation long before the unemployment in the depressed areas had been mopped up. Successive governments have, therefore, preferred to use policies which discriminate in favour of the less prosperous areas in order to try to reduce the disparities in unemployment rates between areas. Such regional policies have taken a variety of forms, but the most widely used have been policies designed to encourage the creation of new jobs in the depressed areas (or assisted areas, to use the official euphemism) through the provision of grants or other forms of financial incentives to employers.

Disparities in unemployment rates persist through all the stages of the 'business cycle', as Table 9.4 illustrates. Whether the overall level of unemployment is high or low, certain regions always have rates significantly above the national average, and the

Table 9.4 Percentage unemployment in selected regions 1978–85

	1978	1979	1980	1981	1982	1983	1984	1985
UK	5.7	5.3	6.8	10.4	12.1	12.9	13.1	13.5
South East	3.9	3.4	4.2	7.0	8.5	9.3	9.5	9.9
East Anglia	4.8	4.2	5.3	8.3	9.7	10.3	10.1	10.7
W. Midlands	5.3	5.2	7.3	12.5	14.7	15.7	15.3	15.3
North	8.6	8.3	10.4	14.7	16.6	17.9	18.3	18.7
Scotland	7.7	7.4	9.1	12.4	14.0	14.9	15.1	15.6
N. Ireland	11.0	10.8	13.0	16.8	18.7	20.2	20.9	20.7

Source: *Department of Employment Gazette.*

Note: Some reclassification took place during the 1980s. The effect of this was to reduce the pre-1980 estimates by about 1 per cent. That is, the revised figures shown here for the years prior to 1980 are about 1 per cent lower than those originally published.

unemployment that persists there when the rest of the economy is buoyant should therefore be ascribed to regional factors rather than to deficiencies of aggregate demand.

It should be noted that the two types of structural unemployment – the skills mis-match and the geographical mis-match – often occur together, the effect of one reinforcing the other. In many cases a whole area may be heavily dependent on one industry that is experiencing decline or rapid technological change which reduces the need for labour. This has occurred in Britain in the West Midlands, an area heavily dependent on the motor industry. As the motor industry has declined in importance as an employer of labour, so unemployment rates in the West Midlands have risen relative to other areas, as can be seen from Table 9.4. In 1978 the West Midlands had an unemployment rate which was lower than the national average. By 1980 it was above the national average, and it continues to be so.

Technological change, which reduces the demand for labour, produces what is sometimes referred to as 'technological unemployment'. This has become particularly associated of late with the so-called microelectronic revolution, though, in fact, its causes are much more widespread.

'Technological' unemployment has, in fact, been proceeding more or less rapidly since the dawn of time, though arguably – the process has now speeded up – it did, after all, take over one hundred years before the invention of the musket made the archer redundant. It is important to note, however, that in any dynamic economy – that is, one in which the pattern of consumer demand changes over time and in which technology also changes – a certain amount of temporary unemployment is, more or less, inevitable. Such 'frictional' unemployment, as it is known, arises because employees do not have perfect information about job vacancies and employers do not have perfect information about available unemployed labour. It therefore takes time to find a job and the unemployment statistics will always record some people who are in the process of changing jobs. Such frictional unemployment can be minimized by improving the flow of information; for example, by improving the services offered by labour exchanges and Job Centres, but can never be totally eliminated. Indeed, without a certain amount of frictional unemployment, changes in employment patterns would not occur.

9.9 Unemployment as an indicator of the level of economic activity

The level of unemployment is often taken as a crude indication of the state of aggregate demand in the economy. High levels of unemployment tend to be associated with situations in which the level of aggregate demand is relatively low and the economy is experiencing a recession; conversely, low levels of unemployment tend to be associated with a buoyant economy when the level of economic activity is high. Although this is a general tendency, it does not, however, follow as a matter of course. The level of economic activity determines, other things being equal, the demand for labour. This, together with the supply of labour, in turn determines the extent of unemployment.

The level of unemployment is more correctly thought of as the state of excess supply of labour and this may be more accurately measured by taking account of registered vacancies as well as registered unemployment. In Britain the Department of Employment publishes estimates of vacancies but it is acknowledged that the statistics may be inaccurate because of under-reporting. That is, firms may not notify the Job Centres when they have vacancies, preferring instead to recruit labour by other means. The extent of under-reporting may vary systematically with the unemployment rate.

It is accepted, however, that movements in unemployment rates do measure, albeit in a rather crude way, the state of demand in the economy. We should not be surprised to learn therefore that unemployment rates in different countries tend to move together, just as unemployment rates in different regions of the same country tend to move together. That is, in all of those countries linked by trade, unemployment rates tend to move in the same direction at the same time, as if moved by a common force. This force is, of course, the level of world economic activity. However,

Table 9.5 Unemployment rates in selected countries 1980–85

	1980	1981	1982	1983	1984	1985
Canada	7.5	7.5	10.9	11.8	11.2	10.1
United States	7.0	7.5	9.5	9.5	7.4	7.0
Japan	2.0	2.2	2.4	2.6	2.7	2.6
France	6.3	7.3	8.0	8.3	9.7	10.2
Germany	3.0	4.4	6.1	8.0	8.6	8.8
Italy	7.4	8.3	8.9	9.8	10.2	10.2
Netherlands	4.7	7.1	9.8	13.7	14.0	13.0
United Kingdom	7.1	11.0	12.8	12.7	13.0	13.2

Source: *OECD Main Economic Indicators.*

as we saw with the inflation statistics that we looked at in Chapter 3, some economies appear to be better able to hold unemployment in check than others. Table 9.5 illustrates this.

We have now identified three different types of unemployment – demand deficient, structural and frictional unemployment. It is, of course, not possible to say whether any one particular unemployed person is experiencing structural, frictional or demand deficient unemployment, since the categories are by no means mutually exclusive. Rather, the purpose of distinguishing the different types of unemployment is to identify their cause. This is the essential first step in devising appropriate policies to alleviate the problem.

Questions

1. 'An increase in employment levels of 1 m. implies an equal reduction in the numbers of the unemployed.' What is wrong with this statement?

2. How is it that a person can be 'economically active' yet be unemployed?

3. How do you measure the fraction of the total population of working age who are economically active? What do you think has happened to this statistic in recent years? Why?

4. Registered unemployment is supposed to measure the extent of 'involuntary unemployment' in the economy. State why it might either overestimate or underestimate the true extent of such 'involuntary unemployment'.

5. Given the official population census classifications, where would you place the following persons in terms of their employment status?

    (a) Persons detained in HM prisons.
    (b) Non-working housewives.
    (c) Full-time students.
    (d) Part-time students.
    (e) A 61-year-old man recently made redundant.
    (f) A 61-year-old woman recently made redundant.
    (g) A chronically sick person incapable of working.
    (h) A relative who stays at home to look after the above.

6. *Ceteris paribus*, what effect will each of the following have on the level of employment in the private sector (adopt a conventional Keynesian view of the determinants of employment).

    (a) a cut in income taxes;
    (b) an increased propensity to spend on imported goods;
    (c) an increase in the number of traffic wardens employed.

7. 'If people would agree to work for lower wages the unemployment problem would be solved.' Which of the following responses to this quote is most nearly correct?

(a) People never agree to work for lower wages because trade unions keep wages up.
(b) If people already in employment took a wage cut, their incomes would fall and hence spending would fall. This would further depress the demand for labour.
(c) The statement is correct because people have been pricing themselves out of jobs recently by asking for wage increases that exceed productivity increases.

8. Which of the following statements are correct:
(a) At the natural rate of unemployment there is no demand deficient unemployment.
(b) The natural rate of unemployment could be reduced if unemployment benefit and social security benefit were abolished.
(c) For the father of twelve dependent children the opportunity cost of working is very high.

9. What evidence suggests that the natural rate of unemployment has risen in recent years?

10. The difference between the number of people that want jobs at the prevailing wage rate and the number of jobs available is known as:

(a) The natural rate of unemployment.
(b) Voluntary unemployment.
(c) Involuntary unemployment.
(d) Registered unemployment.

11. A tomato farmer can hire tomato pickers at £20 per day and the relationship between pickers and yield is given below:

Number of pickers	Tomato output
1	60
2	110
3	135
4	154
5	164
6	169
7	170
8	170

If the farmer wants to maximize his profits he should hire only:

(a) one tomato picker because he picks most;
(b) three tomato pickers because the fourth costs more than he earns;
(c) Seven tomato pickers because that maximizes output.

The tomato pickers' union, in an attempt to make its members better off, manages to enforce a legal minimum wage of £26 per day. If our profit maximizing farmer complies, which of the following will be correct:

(a) Each of the tomato pickers our farmer had previously hired will become better off.
(b) The quantity of tomato output will fall.
(c) Unemployment amongst tomato pickers will increase.

If we had information on the number of pickers who would be hired at each wage rate we could trace out a schedule which would be the demand for tomato pickers' labour. This would depend on the value of their marginal product (VMP).

Say whether the following statements are true or false. If false correct them:

(a) The maximum wage that tomato pickers can earn is limited by the value of their marginal product.
(b) An increase in the market price of tomatoes will lead to a fall in the demand for tomato pickers' labour.
(c) If the supply of pickers is completely inelastic (i.e. fixed) the wage that they earn will not reflect their productivity.
(d) If employers were able to discriminate (i.e. pay each worker a different wage) the wages of each worker would be equal to the value of their marginal product.
(e) This analysis assumes that other factors of production are variable.
(f) In the long run pickers will be paid in accordance with what they produce.

12. Define and give examples of:

(a) regional unemployment;
(b) structural unemployment;
(c) demand deficient unemployment.

Are these categories mutually exclusive?
What types of unemployment do you think Britain is suffering from at the moment?

13. Given the statistics for percentage unemployment shown in Table 9.6.

Table 9.6

	1967	1970	1972	1974	1977	1984
South-East	1.6	1.6	2.1	1.6	4.5	9.6
North	3.9	4.7	6.3	4.7	8.4	18.1
Scotland	3.7	4.2	6.4	4.1	8.3	15.2
N. Ireland	7.5	6.8	8.0	5.8	11.1	21.0

Source: *Department of Employment Gazette.*

(a) Which area has the highest unemployment rate?
(b) Do you think the unemployment existing in this area in 1974 was due to cyclical factors (i.e. was it 'demand deficient' unemployment?). If not, what was it?

If income taxes were reduced, *ceteris paribus*, would this reduce the rate of unemployment in Scotland? If not what else can you suggest?

Chapter 10
Economic growth

10.1 A methodological note

Economic growth can be defined as an increase in real terms, in Gross National Product, or in GNP per capita. In other words, it is an increase in the volume of goods and services the economy produces in a given year. When allowance is made for any increase or decrease in population, the rate of economic growth therefore equates to the change in the average citizen's standard of living. It was not so very many years ago that economic growth was regarded as unequivocally a good thing – something to be pursued and maximized. These certainties have, however, given way in the minds of some people to a more sceptical attitude; indeed, some would now argue that continued economic growth is no longer either possible or desirable. We shall discuss these views in section 10.10 and 10.11, but first we shall consider the important question of why the performance of the British economy has been relatively poor in comparison to many of its competitors in the post-war period. We begin in sections 10.1 to 10.5 by considering the period up to the mid-1970s. Sections 10.6 to 10.9 then cover the period up to the mid-1980s, though it should be recognized that it is oversimplistic to compartmentalize the causes and effects of the continuing process of economic growth into discrete time periods.

Table 10.1 gives some comparative growth rates for a number of industrial countries. Clearly, in comparison with other countries, Britain has fared badly in the post-war period. One could offer literally dozens of explanations of this apparent failure – poor management expertise, restrictive practices on the part of trade unions, too much bureaucracy, a work-shy attitude and so on – but the problem with all these 'explanations' is that, although they may possibly contain an element of truth, they are insufficiently precise to merit the status of a scientific hypothesis. This is not to say that economists necessarily act in a more scientific way. In this particular area of enquiry, they seldom put forward testable hypotheses regarding the importance of any particular factor in promoting economic growth for the simple reason that it is almost impossible to formulate refutable hypotheses in this area.

Table 10.1 Real GDP Growth: 1951–76 (1970 prices)

	Percentages					
	UK	France	West Germany	Italy	USA	Japan*
Average growth rate, 1951–76	2.5	4.8	5.5	4.9	3.1	8.5
GDP in 1976 as a multiple of GDP in 1951	1.9	3.2	3.8	3.3	2.2	7.1

* Figures relate to 1952–76

Source: OECD National Accounts and CSO quoted in *Economic Progress Report*, July 1978

The major difficulty is that economic growth is the result of a very complex process, so that any explanation which attributes it to a single cause must necessarily be regarded with suspicion. This much is clear, but the difficulty comes in deciding whether any particular factor which has been identified is even a contributory cause, and if so, how important it is.

We shall not attempt to provide a solution to this methodological problem. One notable attempt to assess the quantitative significance of the various factors which could contribute towards economic growth – the work of Denison[1] – has been heavily criticized for its methodological arbitrariness. Indeed, we could argue that such an attempt is doomed to fail since it seeks to discover something which is, in essence, unknowable. The macroeconomy is a social organism whose properties cannot be discovered in the same way as the physicist or the biologist can discover, by experimentation, the properties of the physical world. The social world is different in two important and related respects. First, although experimentation is possible with the macroeconomy (though impractical), *controlled* experimentation is not possible. The essence of a controlled experiment is that all other factors, apart from the one whose influence the experimenter is trying to assess, should be held constant. This is possible under the laboratory conditions where the researcher in the physical sciences operates, but the researcher in the social sciences can never ensure that this condition is fulfilled; that is, the *ceteris paribus* assumption cannot be fulfilled in the real world.

Second, in the social sciences the process of experimentation may induce changes in the subject of the study. For example, if the Bank of England wishes to know what the effect will be on the demand for government securities of a 1 per cent rise in interest rates, it can raise interest rates and observe what happens. If it repeats the experiment, however, (that is, raising the interest rate a further 1 per cent), then the impact on sales of securities may not be the same as in the first experiment. This is because the responsiveness of demand for government securities to interest rate changes may have been changed by the Bank's previous action. Potential purchasers of securities now have a different set of experiences and expectations – they find themselves in a unique situation, just as the previous situation was unique, in the sense that an identical set of conditions had never prevailed before. Logically, because both situations are unique, one cannot infer anything about the properties of the second situation from experiments conducted in the first.

This is part of the general problem that, in the social sciences, the properties of the systems which the researcher is endeavouring to discover are constantly changing, whereas the laws of nature which the physical scientist investigates are essentially immutable. Thus, the 'law' of gravity is the same when Newton discovered it as it is now – gravitational attraction is 32 feet/second^2 – but social laws change over time; for example, the propensity to save out of aggregate income, the marginal propensity to save (MPS), will change as individuals slowly adjust their behaviour in response to a situation in which the value of savings is eroded by inflation.

In our analysis of the causes of the relatively slow rate of growth of the UK economy we shall not therefore attempt to attribute this slow growth to any single cause; nor shall we attempt to assess the quantitative significance of any single factor. Because of the sheer complexity of the growth process, economists have tended to concentrate on a few easily observable (and measurable) variables which common sense – sometimes an unreliable guide – tells one are important in promoting economic growth. We shall examine a few of these in the following sections.

10.2 The interaction of demand and supply

The cause of an increase in the output of goods and services of an economy could analytically be broken down into two parts, namely –
(a) A rise in output attributable to a rise in the inputs to the production process of the various factors of production, principally capital and labour.
(b) A rise in output resulting from the more efficient use of a fixed volume of factor inputs – that is, a rise in output per unit of input (or what is sometimes called productivity).

179

In practice, however, it may be difficult to distinguish between these two. Factor inputs, for example, are not directly observable. The input of the factor labour to the production process can be approximated by the number of people in employment multiplied by the number of hours worked. This, however, does not take account of differences in the amount of effort expended, or the skill with which this effort is applied. If one attempts to make allowance for the fact that highly paid skilled labour is more productive than low paid unskilled labour, by measuring labour input in value terms rather than in terms of the number of man-hours worked, then one runs up against the problem of whether wage relativities really do reflect differences in productivity levels, or whether the imperfections of the labour market have a more important determining role.

There are similar difficulties involved in measuring the input of capital into the production process. Because capital is a non-homogeneous commodity – that is, a mechanical earth mover is not the same as a capstan lathe – one has to measure capital input in terms of the *value* of capital employed. This raises a number of problems, not the least of which is that a new machine, which has the same value as an older machine which it is replacing, may be more technically efficient and thus able to produce more output per unit of labour and raw material input. Moreover, the value of an item of capital equipment purchased in the past may be difficult to determine objectively.

There is a further dimension to the problem. An increase in, say, the amount of labour employed in the production process is affected by both the supply of labour and the demand for it. The number of people in employment cannot increase unless there is an increase in the size of the workforce, but part of the increase in the workforce will remain unemployed unless there is also an increase in the demand for labour. Thus, both supply and demand factors affect labour input, and the same could be said of capital input.

In sections 10.3 to 10.5 below we shall examine the importance of capital input (that is, investment) and labour input, though in the light of what has been said above it should be appreciated that both demand and supply factors interact to produce a given amount of factor inputs.

10.3 Investment and economic growth

The idea that investment, by increasing the economy's stock of capital equipment, increases its productive potential and hence (potentially) the growth rate, seems self-evidently true. Thus, even though investment is not a sufficient condition for growth, and may not even be a necessary one, common sense tells us that it is very important. Other things being equal, we could argue that the greater the proportion of current output devoted to productive investment, the greater will be the resultant growth in output.

Table 10.2 Fixed investment as a percentage of GDP in major industrialized countries

	UK	France	West Germany	Italy	USA	Japan
Average, 1950–54	14	18	20	19	17½	21½*
Average, 1970–75	19	24	24	21	17½	33½
*Average, 1952–54						

Source: OECD National Accounts and CSO quoted in *Economic Progress Report*, July 1978

Empirically there is a high correlation between the proportion of current output devoted to investment and growth rates.

Table 10.2 gives some comparative figures for the post-war period, and it will be seen that there is a high correlation between the ranking of countries in Table 10.2 and that in Table 10.1; that is, countries who devote a high proportion of current output to investment tend to have high growth rates. Correlation, of course, is not evidence of causation and it is probable that a two-way causation is in operation here since, as we saw in Chapter 4, one of the determinants of the level of investment is itself the rate of growth of output. Therefore, the faster the rate of growth of output, the higher will be the level of induced investment and thus the growth process tends to be self-sustaining – high levels of investment lead to a growth in output which, in turn, induces higher levels of investment and so on.

10.4 The balance of payments constraint

However, we now have to ask why, if investment is so obviously conducive to economic growth, so little was undertaken in Britain. One widely held view is that, in post-war Britain, the balance of payments formed an effective constraint, preventing the expansion of aggregate demand and thereby the investment that would have followed it. According to this view, the effect of the weak balance of payments was to constrain the British economy to operate within a vicious circle characterized by 'stop-go' policies – periods of expansion followed rapidly by periods of deflation made necessary by a crisis in the balance of payments. A low level of investment in comparison with our competitors, and a fixed exchange rate, led to a situation where British exports became increasingly uncompetitive on foreign markets, whilst, on domestic markets, competition from foreign imports became increasingly severe. Thus, there was a continual tendency for the balance of payments to go into deficit, causing a continual run down of foreign exchange reserves to maintain the fixed parity of the pound. To remove the deficits, imports had to be reduced by deflationary fiscal and monetary measures. These measures – reducing aggregate demand by increasing taxes, cutting public spending and restricting monetary growth – also reduced domestic investment; directly, because investment depends upon the rate of growth of output, and indirectly, because a reduction in monetary growth usually goes hand in hand with high interest rates, and investment, as we saw in Chapter 4, is inversely related to interest rates. At times the authorities actively encouraged high interest rates as a means of attracting foreign capital and hence reducing the balance of payments deficit in the short term. Thus, short term measures which were necessary to control the balance of payments deficits had an adverse effect on domestic investment and hence, in the long term, on economic growth.

The circular nature of this process cannot be over-emphasized. It is, as we have said, a vicious circle from which it is proving extremely difficult to extricate the British economy. In direct contrast to this, countries such as Germany and Japan enjoyed a 'virtuous circle' of high growth rates and a persistent tendency for the balance of payments to go into surplus. Within these 'successful' economies a high rate of expansion of demand, much of which came from export demand, induced high levels of investment, which in turn produced rapid rises in output. Exports, which were initially encouraged by fiscal subsidies and the like, soon gathered their own momentum as the productivity gains derived from investment made exports more cost competitive on world markets. Thus, the expansion of demand could proceed unhindered by the constant need to check demand in order to check imports. The only constraint on the expansion of demand was a self-imposed one rather than one imposed externally, namely that the growth of demand should not overstretch the economy's capacity to increase output without creating inflationary pressures. The containment of inflation was, of course, made easier by the fact that, to the extent that the exchange rate appreciated – and balance of payments surpluses will always produce this tendency even though it may be checked under a fixed exchange rate regime – the price of imports fell, thus producing a fall in the overall price index.

Since the balance of payments seems to have been the crucial factor in restraining Britain's economic growth, we should perhaps ask why Britain's overseas trading position was so weak, and whether alternative policies might not have eased the constraint that it imposed. There were, of course, a number of relevant factors, but most writers seem agreed that the most important was the reserve currency role of sterling. The fact that the pound, alongside the dollar, was used as a reserve (or intervention) currency meant that foreign central banks would hold stocks of pounds and dollars to use in the event of their own currency being in excess supply on currency markets.

Of course, while these overseas sterling balances were being built up this was positively advantageous to Britain, since it allowed her to run balance of payments deficits, paying for them with money created by the Bank of England (often known as the right of seignorage). However, once these overseas sterling balances had accumulated, their existence posed a positive threat, since any apparent weakness in the pound would cause foreign holders of sterling to try to sell in order to avoid a capital loss in the event of sterling being devalued.

This selling pressure, of course, exacerbated the trading position of the pound, making a devaluation look still more likely, and thus further adding to the impetus to sell sterling.

Thus, repeatedly, there was pressure for a sterling devaluation, but precisely because of the reserve currency role of sterling, the monetary authorities in Britain felt that such a change in par values would be unwise. The par value system, which had worked so well in the post-war period, would, they felt, start to disintegrate if it were seen that one of the key currencies could no longer be relied upon for stability. Britain therefore resorted to alternative policies – domestic deflation to check imports and high interest rates as a means of attracting foreign capital, though this latter policy effectively increased the size of the overseas sterling balances, and hence stored up more trouble for the future. The fixed sterling parity was maintained until 1967, when the pressure for devaluation could no longer be resisted.

It is, of course, impossible to demonstrate conclusively that an alternative policy (such as devaluing earlier) would have been more successful in removing the balance of payments constraint and allowing growth to proceed at a faster rate, though with the benefit of hindsight the majority of writers would probably argue that the policy of protecting the external value of the pound, at the expense of other objectives, was unwise. However, as we saw in Chapter 3 and in Chapter 8, devaluation does not automatically bring the balance of payments into equilibrium; even if the elasticities of demand for imports and exports are favourable, there will be a considerable time lag before the benefits of devaluation become apparent. In the event, the devaluation of the pound in 1967 was to initiate a period of instability in the international monetary system, and five years later the British payments deficit was again so serious that the new parity was abandoned altogether and the pound allowed to float down rapidly.

10.5 Supply constraints: the role of labour supply

Up to this point the explanation for the low growth of the British economy that we have offered has concentrated on the role of *demand* in stimulating the investment needed for economic growth. According to this explanation, the reason for Britain's low growth can be traced to demand mismanagement, and the corollary is that if alternative policies had been pursued, which had made possible a steady and more rapid expansion of demand, then the level of investment, and therefore growth, would have been higher.

Some writers have tried to explain Britain's low growth in quite different terms, however. For these writers, it was the *supply* of factors – and particularly the supply of labour – which constrained the expansion of the post-war British economy. According to this line of argument, put forward by economists such as Kindleberger[2] and Kaldor[3], a necessary condition for economic growth is a relatively elastic supply of labour to the manufacturing sector. Countries which hitherto had large agricultural populations were able to satisfy this condition, as the movement of people off the land provided a potential source of recruitment for manufacturing employment. The size of the agricultural workforce in Britain, on the other hand, was already very small in 1945, so that no such source of labour was available. Consequently, so the argument runs, the expansion of the industrial sector was held back by a shortage of manpower.

The effect of this inelastic supply of labour would manifest itself as a tendency for labour markets to become 'tight' as an increasing demand for labour encountered a relatively fixed supply. This would tend to make wages rise, in excess of any rise brought about through changes in productivity, as employers bid against each other for this scarce resource. In this way, a process of wage-push inflation would be initiated. Increased costs would lead to increased prices which, under a fixed exchange rate, would lead to a deterioration in the overseas trading position. That is, exports would become uncompetitive and domestically produced goods would increasingly be unable to compete against imports on the home market, leading to a situation in which deflationary measures would have to be taken to preserve the sterling parity. Thus, the balance of payments again features as a restraining factor on growth, but this time the cause of the difficulties is the overvalued exchange rate which results from the process of wage inflation. The roots of the wage inflation, in turn, can be traced to the inelastic supply of labour to the manufacturing sector.

10.6 The importance of the manufacturing sector

Employment is conventionally classified into one of three sectors: primary (mostly agriculture but also including fishing and mining), secondary (manufacturing) and tertiary (all the service industries). Although this classification is rather crude, it is the one which underlies the foregoing analysis. In this view, the importance of the manufacturing sector in the growth process lies in the fact that it is in this area where most of the increases in productivity can be achieved. Technological advance, which allows a larger volume of output to be obtained from a given volume of inputs, although possible in the primary and tertiary sectors, is much more easily achieved in manufacturing production. Other things being equal, therefore, the larger the size of the secondary sector in relation to the primary and tertiary sector, the larger is the scope for productivity gains, and hence for growth.

Kaldor in 1968 argued that the cause of the slow rate of growth of the UK economy was that the manufacturing sector was too small and the service sector too large. There is a well-known tendency for employment in the tertiary sector to increase as a society evolves from a basically agrarian form to a developed industrial form, and the size of the service sector is an indication of the degree of maturity of the economy. In Kaldor's view, however, Britain was suffering from a 'premature maturity' – a large service sector swallowing up resources before a high level of output per head had been achieved. His policy prescription, implemented in the form of a Selective Employment Tax, was to encourage labour to move from the service sector to the manufacturing sector, where the potential productivity increases were greater.

10.7 The importance of marketed output

This theme – an overexpanded service sector depressing the overall growth rate of the economy – was taken up, though in a modified way, in 1975 by Bacon and Eltis[4]. Following Kaldor, they

185

recognized the importance of the manufacturing sector as a source of productivity growth, but they also stressed the fact that manufactures could be exported, whereas the output of the service industry, in general, could not be, so that if the service sector expanded at the expense of the manufacturing sector, this would necessarily have an adverse effect on the balance of payments.

They also recognized, however, that the classification of manufacturing sector output and service sector output was insufficiently precise, since some service sector output, such as the services of a UK pop group touring abroad, was sold directly on the market and made a contribution to the balance of payments, while some manufacturing sector output. such as Concorde, could not be sold at a profit and thus represented a drain on resources. They therefore proposed a revised classification – marketed and non-marketed output – a classification which corresponds approximately to what most people would understand by the distinction between the private sector and the public sector, though not exactly. British Airways, for instance, a public sector company, produces marketed output since it sells directly to consumers at home and abroad. Virtually all the activities of local government and most of those of central government would, however, be regarded as belonging to the non-market sector.

Bacon and Eltis's basic contention was that people employed in producing non-marketed output, although they themselves do not produce any 'wealth', nevertheless consume the 'wealth' being produced by the market sector. The larger the non-market sector, the larger will be the claims made by the drones on the workers within the hive. If the market sector is too small in relation to the claims being made upon it, then part of those claims will be satisfied from abroad – that is, there will be an increase in imports leading to a balance of payments deficit.

The basic analysis seems fairly sound, though many people would dispute the claim that only people working in the market sector produce wealth. However, whether the poor performance of the post-war British economy relative to our competitors can be ascribed to the excessive size of the non-market sector is basically an empirical question; is the non-market sector in Britain significantly larger than that in other countries at a similar stage of development? Bacon and Eltis presented evidence which purported to show that first, the non-market sector had expanded rapidly in recent years; and that second, it was now much bigger than in other countries. This evidence has been disputed, however, and a slightly different interpretation of the statistics produces the opposite result – that, although the post-war period has seen an expansion of the non-market sector, this sector is no larger in

Table 10.3 Taxation and government spending as a percentage of GDP –
some international comparisons

	1971		1978		1983	
	Tax revenue	Govern-ment spending	Tax revenue	Govern-ment spending	Tax revenue	Govern-ment spending
Sweden	43	41	51	51	51	52
Netherlands	—	—	45	48	47	52
Belgium	35	33	42	41	44	45
France	35	35	39	41	43	47
W. Germany	37	36	42	42	41	42
Italy	28	32	33	36	41	44
Austria	37	35	42	43	42	43
UK	34	32	33	35	38	39
USA	27	30	29	30	29	33

'Tax revenue' is revenue from direct taxes, indirect taxes and social
security contributions as a percentage of GDP.
'Government spending' is current expenditure on goods and services, gross
capital formation, current grants and subsidies as a percentage of GDP.

Source: derived from *OECD National Accounts*, detailed tables, Vol II
   1971–83 (1985 edn.).

Britain than in some comparable countries, and smaller than in
some others.

   Table 10.3 gives an indication that, according to
internationally accepted definitions, the size of the government
sector in Britain has grown more slowly than in most other
comparable countries and that Britain now has the smallest
proportion of output devoted to public spending of any Western
European country.

10.8 The deindustrialization of the British economy

It will be convenient at this point to introduce a topic which is
closely allied with the discussion of the previous two sections – the
so-called deindustrialization debate. The term 'deindustrialization'
is a somewhat emotive description of what is alleged to have
happened to the manufacturing sector in the UK in
recent years. Deindustrialization refers to a process whereby

employment in the manufacturing sector falls and there is a decline in the output of the manufacturing sector as a proportion of total output. This is associated with increased import penetration in manufactured goods.

There are a number of specific questions concerning the deindustrialization debate. Some of these are purely factual questions which can be answered by straightforward inspection of the data. Others are less straightforward. The more important questions are listed below:

1. Has the manufacturing sector declined in terms of employment in recent years?
2. Has the manufacturing sector declined in terms of its contribution to total output?
3. Is the decline in manufacturing peculiar to Britain? If not, is it more pronounced in Britain than elsewhere?
4. What trends have been observed in trade in manufactures between countries? Has import penetration increased?
5. If the process of deindustrialization in Britain is more marked than elsewhere then what is the explanation for this? Is it partly the result of government policies? Is deindustrialization an undesirable trend which appropriately designed policies could halt and possibly reverse? Alternatively is deindustrialization part of a widespread process of structural readjustment, common to all advanced industrial societies, which it would be unwise and damaging to attempt to reverse?

As regards employment, it is quite clear that the manufacturing sector has declined in importance. Since the mid 1960s in Britain employment in manufacturing has fallen by about one third, as the last line of Table 10.4 shows. Table 10.4 also gives an indication of those industries most affected.

The percentage of the workforce engaged in manufacturing has also declined as can be seen from Table 10.5 and Fig. 10.1, both of which also present data for other countries. In the UK in 1970 more than one in three people were engaged in manufacturing. By 1983 this had fallen to less than one in four. Careful inspection of Table 10.3 reveals that almost all the countries listed experienced a decline in manufacturing employment over the period 1960–83, the exceptions being Japan and, perhaps surprisingly, Italy.

If we compare the decline of manufacturing in the UK with that in other countries then it is apparent that the decline in the UK was somewhat more marked than elsewhere. However, this is mainly because in 1970 the proportion of the workforce engaged in manufacturing in Britain was comparatively large (exceeded only by West Germany). The rate of decline since then has been rapid

Table 10.4 Employment in manufacturing industry 1960–1981 (thousands)

Industry order	1960	1966	1970	1974	June 1981	% Decline from Peak Year to June 1981
Food, drink and tobacco	815.4	861.7	890.5	766	632	29.0 (since 1970)
Coal and petroleum products	—	—	63.3	40	37	19.0 (since 1961)
Chemical and allied industries	530.3	527.3	475.1	435	395	48.5 (since 1961)
Metal manufacture	617.1	623.0	591.7	507	326	48.5 (since 1961)
Mechanical engineering Instrument engineering Electrical engineering	2048.9	2576.9	2283.2	1980	1530	35.6 (since 1966)
Shipbuilding and marine engineering	278.8	213.6	199.0	185	144	54.0 (since 1956)
Vehicles	919.8	853.2	842.4	792	636	31.0 (since 1960)
Metal goods n.e.s.	546.0	599.0	639.9	582	428	33.1 (since 1970)
Textiles	901.8	810.8	716.0	585	364	67.0 (since 1951)
Leather, leather goods and fur	65.5	60.0	54.0	43	32	60.0 (since 1951)
Clothing and footwear	591.7	554.2	501.3	427	313	55.7 (since 1951)
Bricks, pottery, glass, cement	335.3	364.9	340.8	301	216	40.8 (since 1966)
Timber, furniture	292.9	319.0	299.8	283	227	30.4 (since 1968)
Paper, printing and publishing	603.0	650.9	654.9	589	493	24.7 (since 1970)
Other manufacturing industries	301.9	343.7	358.8	358	265	27.8 (since 1969)
Total manufacturing	8850.5	9153.1	8910.5	7871	6041	34.1 (since 1966)

Source: Thirwall A. P., 'De-industrialization in the United Kingdom', *Lloyds Bank Review*, April 1982.

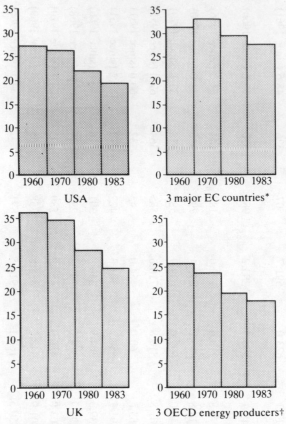

USA

3 major EC countries*

UK

3 OECD energy producers†

*France, West Germany, Italy – weighted average
†Canada, Netherlands, Norway – weighted average

Fig. 10.1 Employment in manufacturing – percentage of civilian employment

but by 1983 the proportion of the workforce engaged in manufacturing in Britain was still slightly above the OECD average.

These figures alone tell us little about the health of the manufacturing sector. Large numbers engaged in manufacturing could reflect low levels of labour productivity. Similarly a rapid decline in the manufacturing workforce could be evidence of rapidly increasing labour productivity so that the same – or more – output can now be produced by a much smaller workforce. Alternatively, a declining manufacturing workforce could be evidence of an ailing manufacturing sector with producers falling victim to foreign competition.

Table 10.5 Employment in manufacturing

| | Per cent of total civilian employment | | | | | | | | | | | | |
	1960	1970	1971	1972	1973	1974	1975	1976	1977	1978	1979	1980	1981	1982	1983
Canada	23.7	22.3	21.3	21.8	22.0	21.7	20.2	20.3	19.6	19.6	19.9	19.7	19.3	18.1	17.5
USA	27.1	26.4	24.7	24.3	24.8	24.2	22.7	22.8	22.7	22.7	22.7	22.1	21.7	20.4	19.8
Japan	21.5	27.0	27.0	27.0	27.4	27.2	25.8	25.5	25.1	24.5	24.3	24.7	24.8	24.5	24.5
France	27.5	27.8	28.0	28.1	28.3	28.4	27.9	27.4	27.1	26.6	26.1	25.8	25.1	24.7	24.3
W. Germany	37.0	39.4	37.4	36.8	36.7	36.4	35.6	35.1	35.1	34.8	34.5	24.3	33.6	33.1	32.5
Italy	23.0	27.8	27.8	27.8	28.0	28.3	28.2	28.0	27.5	27.1	26.7	26.7	26.1	25.7	24.7
Netherlands	30.6	26.4	26.1	25.6	25.4	25.6	25.0	23.8	23.2	23.0	22.3	21.5	20.9	20.5	20.3
Norway	25.3	26.7	25.3	23.8	23.5	23.6	24.1	23.2	22.4	21.3	20.5	20.3	20.2	19.7	18.2
UK	36.0	34.5	33.9	32.8	32.2	32.3	30.9	30.2	30.3	30.0	29.3	28.1	26.2	25.3	24.5

Source: *Economic Progress Report*, June–July 1985.

In addition to data on employment, therefore, we need to look at data which shows manufacturing output as a proportion of total output. This is shown in Table 10.6 and Fig. 10.2. As can be seen, the decline in manufacturing output (as a proportion of GDP) is perhaps even more dramatic than the decline in employment. In the United Kingdom in 1960 manufacturing accounted for almost one third of GDP. In 1983 this had shrunk to not much over one-fifth. However, as we noticed with the employment data, other countries have also experienced a decline. The decline in the UK may be said to be more marked because the UK manufacturing sector was large in comparison to other countries in 1960. Having said this, however, it is clear from careful inspection of Table 10.6 that certain other countries have experienced only a modest decline in manufacturing output – countries such as Japan, France, West Germany and Italy. These countries still retain a comparatively large manufacturing sector.

Before we go on to draw any conclusions from this it is important to point out that over time there will be a change in relative prices – that is, the price of manufacturing output relative to the output of the economy generally. The data in Table 10.6 are calculated from the following ratio

$$\frac{\text{value of manufacturing output}}{\text{value of total output}} \qquad [10.1]$$

Value is equal to price multiplied by quantity. Over time the price of manufacturing output will fall relative to the price of output generally because there is more scope for cost-saving technical change in the production of manufactures than there is in the production of services which are included in total output. For example, many electrical and electronic goods are cheaper now than they were ten years ago, not just relative to other goods and services, but also in absolute terms.

The implication of this is that the ratio shown in [10.1] above should be measured in current prices rather than in constant prices. (See section 4.10.2 for the distinction between current price and constant price data.) It follows that at least part of the decline in the share of manufacturing in GDP is the result of a fall in the price of manufacturing output relative to output generally. For example, suppose in volume terms manufacturing output and total output remained unchanged or – more likely – increased at the same rate. The ratio shown in [10.2] below would therefore remain unchanged:

$$\frac{\text{volume (i.e. quantity) of manufacturing output}}{\text{volume (i.e. quantity) of total output}} \qquad [10.2]$$

Table 10.6 Share of manufacturing in GDP*

(%)

	1960	1970	1971	1972	1973	1974	1975	1976	1977	1978	1979	1980	1981	1982	1983
Canada	23.3	20.4	19.9	20.2	20.2	20.2	19.2	18.6	18.0	18.4	19.1	18.8	18.3	15.6	15.9
USA	28.6	25.7	24.9	24.9	24.9	24.1	23.4	24.2	24.5	24.4	23.8	22.5	22.2	20.9	21.1
Japan	33.9	35.9	35.2	34.5	35.1	35.6	29.9	30.6	30.0	30.0	30.1	30.4	30.4	30.5	30.5
France	29.1	28.7	23.5	28.2	28.3	27.9	27.4	27.4	27.5	27.2	27.0	26.3	25.2	25.2	25.3
W. Germany	40.3	38.4	37.0	36.0	36.3	36.1	34.5	34.8	34.6	34.2	34.1	33.0	32.1	31.7	31.8
Italy	28.5	28.9	28.5	27.1	30.0	31.3	29.7	31.7	31.0	30.4	30.6	30.5	28.9	28.5	27.1
Netherlands	33.6	28.2	27.2	27.1	26.3	25.5	23.7	23.9	20.9	19.5	19.0	17.9	16.9	17.1	17.0
Norway	21.3	21.8	22.1	21.5	21.5	21.9	21.7	20.1	18.9	18.0	18.2	15.6	14.7	14.3	13.7
UK	32.1	28.1	27.4	28.3	28.5	27.2	26.3	25.4	26.6	26.6	24.9	23.1	21.4	21.3	21.0

*Value added in manufacturing as percentage of current price GDP.

Source: *Economic Progress Report*, June–July 1985.

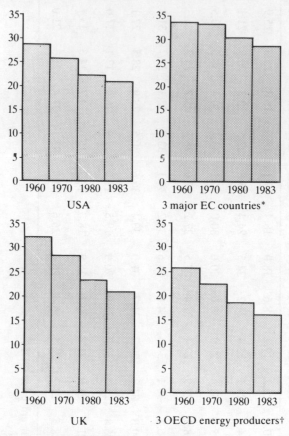

*France, West Germany, Italy – weighted average
†Canada, Netherlands, Norway – weighted average

Fig. 10.2 Share of manufacturing in GDP

Source: *Economic Progress Report*, June–July 1985

We cannot, however, measure quantities directly. All we can measure is value (i.e. quantity multiplied by price). If, as we have assumed, the price of manufactures falls relative to prices generally then in value terms manufacturing output will decline as a proportion of total output even though in volume terms there has been no decline.

This is a complicated index-number problem. It is, however, important to bear in mind when we look at the sort of data shown in Table 10.6. The decline in manufacturing output which it shows is at least partly the result of a fall in the price of manufactures relative to other goods and services.

We can now summarize our answers to the first three questions posed at the beginning of this section.

1. The manufacturing sector has declined in terms of employment in recent years.
2. The manufacturing sector has declined in terms of its contribution to total output (though the decline is magnified by the change in relative prices).
3. The decline in manufacturing is not peculiar to Britain. It does, however, appear to be more rapid than in some other countries with whom we might wish to compare ourselves.

Before we look at the impact this has had on our trade in manufactures with other countries it may be useful to consider a number of possible interpretations of why these changes have occurred.

One explanation which has been put forward to explain the decline of the manufacturing sector is that this simply reflects a change in the pattern of demand. As society becomes richer, it is said, it increases its demand for services at the expense of manufactured goods. However, it is known that the pattern of demand in all countries at a similar stage of development is approximately the same, so that such an explanation cannot be reconciled with the much smaller decline in the importance of the manufacturing sector experienced by some countries who are as rich or a good deal richer than us.

Moreover, the notion that as society becomes richer it increases its demands for services at the expense of manufactured goods is only partly correct, since the increased demand for a service often manifests itself as an increased demand for goods. For example, people no longer send their clothes to the laundry to be cleaned – they buy a washing machine and perform the service for themselves at home. When just a few people were rich and most people were poor, the rich could afford to employ servants to perform services. Now the relative cost of servants is too high, so that the rich (unless they are very rich) can no longer afford to employ them and hence their demand for services is satisfied by the purchase of various labour-saving devices which can be used for the 'home production' of services.

A different interpretation of the fall in manufacturing employment is that the manufacturing sector is experiencing an increase in labour productivity, so that the same (or increased) output can be produced with less labour. This is undoubtedly true, as the recent interest in microelectronics illustrates, but the increase in labour productivity is usually reckoned to be somewhat lower in Britain than in other countries. Such an interpretation, therefore, cannot readily be reconciled with the fact that countries with a more rapid growth of labour productivity – Japan, Germany – have not experienced a similar decline in manufacturing employment.

These interpretations, then, are clearly inadequate, and the only interpretation which seems plausible is that the demand for the output of the manufacturing sector in Britain does not increase as fast as it does in other countries. We should be careful to distinguish here, however, between the demand for manufactured goods and the demand for *domestically produced* manufactured goods. It seems that, in the UK, a fair proportion of any increase in demand is satisfied by an increase in imports; that is, the propensity to import in the UK seems quite high, so that any increase in demand does not necessarily create very much demand for domestic manufacturing industry.

The result is that import penetration has been marked. In other words, foreign manufacturers have penetrated the UK market for manufactured goods, ousting domestic producers. This, coupled with a slow growth of UK exports of manufactures, has led to the decline in manufacturing output we have observed.

Although this is a plausible hypothesis, and one which has received widespread popular support, the evidence to back it up is not clear cut. Table 10.7 gives some estimates of the propensity to import manufactured goods. This shows the proportion of the

Table 10.7 Imports of manufactures

	Per cent of domestic demand for manufactures			
	1970	1980	Average annual growth 1970–80 (%)	1983 (est.)
Canada	27.4	31.4	1.4	34
USA	5.6	9.3	5.3	10
Japan	4.7	5.8	2.0	$5\frac{1}{2}$
France	16.2	23.3	3.7	$24\frac{1}{2}$
W. Germany	19.3	31.4	5.0	36
Italy	16.2	32.0	7.0	$33\frac{1}{2}$
Netherlands	51.5	61.7	1.8	68
UK	16.2	28.2	5.7	31

Source: *Economic Progress Report*, June–July 1985.

domestic demand for manufactures which is accounted for by imports. As can be seen, this has risen everywhere in the period 1970–80. Although the rate of growth (of this percentage) was relatively high in the UK, the estimated percentage for 1983 for the UK was not particularly high when compared to other countries. Specifically it is estimated that 31 per cent of manufactured goods bought in the UK in 1983 were imported, a somewhat lower percentage than in West Germany or Italy or the Netherlands.

One should bear in mind, however, that import propensities – for manufactured goods and goods generally – are inversely related to country size. Large countries such as the United States have a smaller propensity to import since they are more self sufficient. This helps explain why, in Table 10.7, small countries such as the Netherlands have such a large propensity to import manufactures.

Import propensities for manufactures can only present a partial picture of course. The performance of *exports* of manufactures is also relevant. In short, one should look at the manufacturing *trade balance*. Allegedly it is here that we find the most convincing evidence that deindustrialization in the UK has proceeded at a pace faster than that in other countries. The data shows that the manufacturing trade balance which historically has always shown a surplus has been slipping inexorably into deficit. The first deficit was recorded in 1983.

The fact that the UK's receipts from exports of manufactures is no longer sufficient to pay for our imports of manufactures does indeed seem a disturbing trend. We should put this in context however. As Table 10.8 shows, countries which have a deficit on manufactured trade – such as the UK, Canada and Norway – tend to have a surplus of approximately the same order of magnitude in trade in other goods and services. Similarly the large surpluses on manufactured trade in Japan, West Germany and Italy have to be seen in the context of the large deficits which these countries have in trade in other goods and services.

It should be noted also that, with the exception of the United States, the countries shown in Table 10.8 which have a deficit on manufactured trade – namely Canada, Norway, the Netherlands and the UK – are all energy producers. There may well be some causal relationship at work here, whereby oil exports displace an equivalent amount of non-oil exports. The causal mechanism which allegedly brings this about can be sketched as follows. Firstly, assume that for the country in question the balance on capital account is zero. With no net capital flows it follows that the balance of trade will tend towards equilibrium given a floating exchange rate and a few more assumptions.[5] A deficit on one sector of the trade account must therefore be offset by an

Table 10.8 Trade balances as a percentage of total imports

		1973–79 average	1980	1981	1982	1983
Canada	Manufacturing trade balance	−19.6	−13.9	−16.0	−8.0	−11.0
	Balance on other goods & services	+20.0	+21.0	+20.6	+26.0	+25.6
	Overall balance on goods & services	**+ 0.4**	**+ 7.1**	**+ 4.6**	**+ 18.0**	**+ 14.6**
USA	Manufacturing trade balance	+ 4.7	+ 7.0	+ 4.2	− 1.8	−10.3
	Balance on other goods & services	−10.3	−14.2	−11.6	− 8.2	− 8.0
	Overall balance on goods & services	**− 5.6**	**− 7.2**	**− 7.4**	**− 10.0**	**− 18.3**
Japan	Manufacturing trade balance	+67.5	+61.0	+69.7	+68.7	+78.4
	Balance on other goods & services	−63.6	−67.1	−64.0	−63.2	−62.4
	Overall balance on goods & services	**+ 3.9**	**− 6.1**	**+ 5.7**	**+ 5.5**	**+ 16.0**
France	Manufacturing trade balance	+ 9.1	+ 4.5	+ 6.2	+ 2.2	+ 5.5
	Balance on other goods & services	− 9.2	−11.8	−12.1	−11.2	− 8.0
	Overall balance on goods & services	**− 0.1**	**− 7.3**	**− 5.9**	**− 9.0**	**− 2.5**

W. Germany					
Manufacturing trade balance	+39.7	+27.5	+31.3	+35.6	+32.4
Balance on other goods & services	−28.3	−29.3	−28.5	−27.0	−25.0
Overall balance on goods & services	**+ 11.4**	**− 1.8**	**+ 2.8**	**+ 8.6**	**+ 7.4**
Italy					
Manufacturing trade balance	+24.5	+15.6	+22.7	+23.7	+28.0
Balance on other goods & services	−26.1	−25.9	−29.3	−27.2	−25.6
Overall balance on goods & services	**− 1.6**	**− 10.3**	**− 6.6**	**− 3.5**	**+ 2.4**
Netherlands					
Manufacturing trade balance	− 3.9	− 4.5	− 1.0	− 0.4	− 0.5
Balance on other goods & services	+ 8.0	+ 3.5	+ 5.4	+ 7.5	+ 6.4
Overall balance on goods & services	**+ 4.1**	**− 1.0**	**+ 6.4**	**+ 7.9**	**+ 6.9**
Norway					
Manufacturing trade balance	−16.5	−16.3	−18.2	−21.3	−17.4
Balance on other goods & services	+ 8.4	+31.1	+38.0	+35.4	+38.8
Overall balance on goods & services	**− 8.4**	**− 14.8**	**+ 19.8**	**+ 14.1**	**+ 21.4**
UK					
Manufacturing trade balance	+ 9.9	+ 6.4	+ 5.1	+ 0.9	− 6.3
Balance on other goods & services	−13.2	+ 3.4	+ 7.1	+ 8.2	+10.7
Overall balance on goods & services	**− 3.3**	**+ 9.8**	**+ 12.2**	**+ 9.1**	**+ 4.4**

Source: *Economic Progress Report*, June–July 1935.

equivalent surplus on the rest of the trade account if the balance of trade is to be in overall equilibrium. Although, roughly speaking, this tends to be borne out by the data in Table 10.8, the precise nature of the forces which cause this to happen is uncertain. Induced movements in the exchange rate are partly responsible, as are deflationary or reflationary actions taken by the government to restore balance of trade equilibrium.

We have not as yet attempted to provide an answer to the final set of questions posed at the beginning of this section. Nor shall we, for the issues involved are too complex for simplistic answers. We shall, however, sketch out the main lines the debate has followed.

On the one hand there are those who argue that the decline in manufacturing in the UK is not a cause for concern. They point quite correctly to the fact that a similar decline has occurred elsewhere. This is a worldwide process of structural readjustment, they argue, the speed of which is dictated not by the policies of national governments but by market forces. The market ensures that countries specialize in producing those goods and services in which they have a *comparative advantage*. The fact that at one time Britain had a comparative advantage in producing, say, textiles does not mean that she will retain that advantage forever. When she loses it the subsequent decline in the UK textile industry cannot be prevented. Protectionism can only serve to slow down a historical inevitability. Thus it is with any activity which is subject to market forces. There is nothing sacrosanct about manufacturing, they argue. If Britain's manufacturing sector declines then the resources thus freed can be more profitably employed in some other activity.

In contrast, there are those who argue that the manufacturing sector, though not sacrosanct, is especially important to the future prosperity of the economy. The manufacturing sector is important not just for the employment it brings but for its contribution to the balance of trade. It is argued that the service sector on its own is not capable of earning the foreign exchange necessary to pay for our manufactured imports. There are three reasons for this. Firstly many services are by their nature not tradeable – that is, they cannot be traded internationally. Some can – such as tourism, insurance, banking and civil aviation and shipping – but things such as retailing and distribution clearly cannot.

Secondly it is argued that the potential for raising productivity is greater in manufacturing than it is in the service sector. Although in some parts of the service sector – for example, in retailing and in financial services – very substantial increases in productivity continue to be made, the scope for raising productivity is limited in those sectors in which the performance of a personal service is an intrinsic part of the activity – health care and education spring immediately to mind.

Finally it is argued that the service sector, though large in terms of domestic employment, is small in terms of its contribution to foreign exchange earnings. Thus it would take a very large expansion of invisible earnings to make up for a further small decline in trade in manufactures. This, it is said, is unlikely to be achieved. When we look at the evidence in support of this view, however, we find, perhaps surprisingly, that a rather dramatic decline in the importance of manufactured exports has been accompanied by an equally dramatic increase in earnings from invisibles.

Figure 10.3 shows the contribution made to our foreign exchange earnings by manufactures, by oil and by the major categories services. As can be seen throughout the 1970s, manufacturing was by far the most important source of foreign exchange, contributing on average over 45 per cent of total credits on the balance of payments current account. Between 1978 and 1981, however, the importance of manufactured exports declined dramatically, then stabilized at about 32 per cent of total foreign exchange earnings. It was the category of invisible exports known as interest, profits and dividends (IPD) which expanded to fill the gap left by the decline in manufactures. Other invisibles such as shipping and tourism declined slightly in importance. As can be seen in Fig. 10.3, the increase in importance of IPD almost exactly mirrors the decline in manufactures. IPD is now a more important source of foreign exchange than manufactures are. The growth in IPD results primarily from increased overseas lending by UK banks. In 1984 70 per cent of IPD came from external lending by UK banks, mostly in foreign currency.

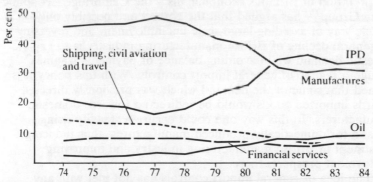

Fig. 10.3 Sources of foreign exchange 1974–84 (percentage of total credits on balance of payments current account)

Source: *UK Balance of Payments Pink Book 1985*, Tables 1.3 and 2.3

It is difficult to appraise the significance of this. There is, however, a widely held view that it is complacent to assume that a further expansion of such banking activity as a source of foreign exchange is possible or desirable. Many writers do not relish the prospect of the British economy becoming so heavily dependent on invisible earnings such as these.

When one also considers the decline in the production of North Sea oil, which is expected to be well under way by 1990, the prospect for the British economy, in this pessimistic analysis, seems bleak. Unless the performance of the manufacturing sector can be improved, and the trade deficit on manufactures eliminated, a scenario is envisaged in which the British economy once again becomes balance-of-payments constrained. Domestic demand will have to be held tightly in check in order to restrain the growth of manufactured imports.

In such a scenario there are two possible strategies that could be employed to extricate the economy from the vicious circle in which it is once again trapped. One is protectionism which is the subject of the next section. The second is to force the exchange rate down to improve competitiveness – an option discussed in section 8.5.

10.8.1 Import controls as a solution to the problem of deindustrialization: 'fortress Britain'

We have seen how, according to one interpretation, the decline of the manufacturing sector and the consequent loss of jobs that this entails has been brought about by unwise demand management policies, which have failed to ensure the sustained fast expansion of domestic markets. One school of thought which supports this interpretation of Britain's economic ills – the Cambridge Economic Policy Group[5] – has argued that the correct and possibly only feasible way of avoiding large-scale unemployment and reversing the general decline of British manufacturing industry is to expand domestic demand while avoiding balance of payments traumas through a regime of general import controls. With this policy it is claimed that some of the demand which was previously directed towards imported goods would be redirected towards domestic manufacturers. In this way one could ensure a steadily rising demand for domestically produced manufactures, thus inducing investment in British manufacturing industry and improving employment prospects there.

The idea of general import controls has not met with any official favour. As a member of the European Common Market and as a signatory to the General Agreement on Tariffs and Trade (GATT) it is claimed that Britain has obligations which prohibit such controls on imports, though such an argument, if it is believed, appears to display a naivety about the realities of international politics. Moreover, it is argued, if import controls were introduced this would invite retaliation from our trading partners.

For their part, the Cambridge Economic Policy Group argue that the British economy already practises a regime of general import controls – but that the policy takes the form of a general domestic deflation. They argue that total imports need not necessarily be any less under a regime of genuine import controls than they are at present under a regime where spending on imports is controlled by a general dampening of domestic demand. If demand is allowed to expand behind a protective wall of tariffs industry will be encouraged to invest, enabling a larger volume of output to be produced, both for the home market and for export, which will thus allow a larger volume of imports to be purchased without creating a trade deficit. Thus, they argue, there is no reason why total imports should be any lower than under the alternative policy of deflation. Since other countries would be no worse off, there would be no reason why they should impose retaliatory import controls. Moreover, since the revenue from tariffs could be used to finance indirect tax cuts, the effect on inflation would be neutral.

10.9 Growth in the 1980s

With a title such as 'growth in the 1980s' this is necessarily a short section for, in the first half of the 1980s at least, the growth of the British economy was negligible. As can be seen from Table 10.9, the economy peaked in 1979. There then followed three years of deep recession. It was not until 1983 that the economy regained the level of output achieved in 1979. On a provisional estimate by the third quarter of 1985 GNP was a mere 3.3 per cent higher than it had been at the end of 1979.

Throughout this period of course unemployment rose at a very rapid rate (as we saw in Table 9.4), the rise only being checked when the economy started expanding again in 1984–85. The

Table 10.9 GNP at constant market prices – average measure. Index 1980=100

75	76	77	78	79	80	81	82	83	84
92.4	95.3	96.6	100.5	103.2	100	98.8	100.8	104.4	107.4

Source: *UK National Accounts Blue Book,* 1985 Table 1.15.

recession in the British economy, and the consequent rise in unemployment, was of course part of a world wide phenomenon. It was, however, more severe in the UK than elsewhere. The relatively poor performance of the British economy in comparison to other countries can be ascribed to two sets of factors. The first is those factors we have identified in sections 10.1–10.9 of this chapter. The second set of factors relates to the policies which were pursued by the government in the UK at the time. It is difficult to quantify the relative contribution of these two sets of factors to Britain's poor performance – or at least it is not possible to do so in a way that all economists would agree with. Using the sorts of models described in Chapter 13, however, it is possible to give a very approximate estimate. One such study, conducted by the National Institute for Economic and Social Research in 1985[7] concluded that about half of the output gap – that is, the difference between what could have been produced and what was produced in the 1980s – was attributable to the world recession with the other half being attributable to government policies. These policies, particularly those on public spending, are discussed in chapter 11.

10.10 The limits to growth

As we mentioned in the introduction to this chapter, the idea that economic growth could unequivocally be regarded as beneficial was a belief which was held almost universally in the period which followed the Second World War. More recently, however, increasing numbers of people have begun to question the validity of such a belief. There are essentially two aspects to such a debate: first, is continued economic growth possible given the physical constraints of our planet?; and second, is economic growth desirable in the sense that the benefits that it provides clearly outweigh the costs?

The question of whether continued economic growth was possible came to the forefront with the publication of the Meadows[8] study, *The Limits to Growth*, in 1972. The question they were concerned with was as follows: given the finite nature of the earth's resources and its capacity for absorbing waste, what would be the effect of continued exponential economic growth? Now, of course, if one poses the question in this form, the answer is immediately obvious. Whether growth is proceeding exponentially at 1 per cent a year or 10 per cent a year, the absolute increase in output gets bigger every year. Given the finite nature of resources, there must therefore come a time when all those resources are used up and economic growth comes to a halt. Indeed, not only economic growth would cease but our whole way of life, built on the profligate use of non-renewable resources, would cease to be possible. One notable feature of exponentially growing systems is the suddenness with which catastrophic changes occur. Consider the well-known example of a pond in which there grows a lily doubling in size every seven days. (Mathematicians will know that this is equal to an exponential growth of 10 per cent per day.) Suppose that after one year the lily completely covers the pond. How long did it take for the pond to be half covered? The answer is, of course, 51 weeks. Now if one considers the finite limits of the pond to be the analogue of the finite resources of the planet earth, one can appreciate the suddeness with which the catastrophe occurs. Moreover, even when the danger of exhaustion of natural resources becomes apparent, society may be unable to amend its resource-using behaviour in time to prevent catastrophe.

The forecasts presented by Meadows suggest that, within the next century, mankind faces a threefold dilemma. First, there is the problem caused by the impending exhaustion of the world's non-renewable natural resources. Second, they predict, the pollution problem will become so acute that the capacity of the physical environment for self-cleaning and re-generation will be exhausted. Third, the worldwide population explosion will reach a point where the human species will destroy itself through sheer weight of numbers. As these various trends interact there then follows a decline in world population because of pollution and the shortage of food and natural resources. The physical and psychological stress caused by crowding will cause further population collapse from war, disease and social strife. Those few who remain will be able to enjoy only a very meagre existence as they pick over the detritus of the former industrial age.

Such models have, of course, been criticized for being unnecessarily alarmist. Predictions of impending disaster following the exhaustion of natural resources are not exclusively a twentieth century phenomenon; the Industrial Revolution in England in fact provoked a similar response from some people, who predicted then that the world coal reserves were rapidly approaching exhaustion. Moreover, the critics of the Doomsday models claim that these predictions fail to take account of the workings of the price system as a device by which impending exhaustion of resources tends to reduce their usage slowly and in advance.

Let us examine briefly the role of the price mechanism in limiting the usage of scarce natural resources. As resources become scarce their price tends to rise relative to those resources which remain in plentiful supply. This causes both consumers and producers to reduce their usage of the scarce resource.

Suppose, for example, that world supplies of aluminium were

approaching exhaustion. The price of aluminium would therefore rise and goods containing this metal would also rise in price. Consumers would therefore amend their consumption behaviour and buy less of those products with a high aluminium content. This in itself would tend to reduce the demand for aluminium, but such substitution in consumption, as it is called, would be reinforced by substitution in production. Those manufacturers who were producing goods with high aluminium content would find that their sales would be reduced as a result of the high prices they found it necessary to charge for their goods. Producers would therefore search for substitute materials which would do the task formerly performed by the aluminium component. Substitutes such as stainless steel, copper, plastics or wood might be suitable, depending upon circumstances. Manufacturers would therefore reduce their demand for aluminium. The more scarce aluminium became, the more it would increase in price and the greater would be the incentive to economize on its use through substitution in consumption and production. It is important to note, moreover, that this economizing on the use of a scarce raw material takes place automatically through the workings of the price mechanism, without the need for any governmental or supra-national intervention.

It is, however, possible to criticize this line of argument. The readjustment in the rates of depletion of the various resources is brought about by a change in relative prices. But it is essentially a readjustment rather than an overall reduction which occurs, since the reduction in the rate of usage of aluminium brings about an increase in the rate of usage of aluminium substitutes – stainless steel, copper and so on. Thus, their prices will rise as they, in turn, become scarce, and a general increase in the price of raw materials thus ensues, as general shortages develop. A cost-push inflation thus results. Because of the high price of raw materials it becomes economic to exploit the more marginal oilfields, to mine the poorer quality coal lying deeper in the ground and to farm the more marginal land. Improvements in technology may enable the higher real costs of production to be more than offset – the record so far shows that, by and large, this has occurred – but if this ceases to happen then increased production costs will result in a reduction in the amount of goods that consumers can afford to purchase; that is, the standard of living generally will decline. The age of plenty gives way to the age of scarcity.

It should be noted that the price mechanism does effectively limit the demand for a scarce commodity, through a change in relative prices, provided only a few commodities are in short supply. But, if there are widespread shortages, a rise in the price *level* (or inflation) occurs rather than a change in relative prices.

This does not necessarily limit demand, since demand itself can be manipulated by governmental forces.

Thus, it could be surmised that the inflation of the 1970s is, in part, the result of resource shortages. The spectre of an international struggle for resources, forecast in the Doomsday models, may already be upon us, and this signals the end of the era of rapid and continued increases in living standards which seemed, since the beginning of the Industrial Revolution, to be the natural order of things.

10.11 The social limits to growth[9]

10.11.1 Is economic growth synonymous with increased welfare?

The idea that economic growth improves living standards underlies the first part of this chapter; economic growth is desirable since it is synonymous with an increase in welfare. In section 9.9, however, we asked whether there might not be some physical limits to the extent to which the industrial society can actually continue to increase the welfare of its citizens. We now turn to a more fundamental appraisal of the nature of economic growth and ask whether, in fact, an increase in a country's GNP, conventionally defined, really is synonymous with an improvement in its citizens' standard of life

On a fairly simple level this is equivalent to asking whether the increased output of goods and services that constitutes economic growth has not been of an unbalanced nature, producing primarily an increase in those goods and services which, though they may give short-term pleasure, do not produce long-term satisfaction. On a more fundamental level, however, we should ask whether the idea of increasing human happiness through economic growth may not prove self-defeating.

10.11.2 Social scarcity

As societies develop they pass through the stage of being able to supply all the biological necessities for existence. When consumption rises beyond this level, then consumption takes on an increasingly social as well as an individual aspect; that is, the satisfaction that individuals derive from consumption depends not just on their own consumption levels, but on the consumption levels of others as well. For example, the satisfaction to be derived from owning a car depends to a large extent on the number of other people that own cars and therefore the level of congestion that they create. The level of other people's consumption may be a more important determinant of the satisfaction to be derived from car ownership than the purely private characteristics of the car – its speed, its comfort and so on. What the individual enjoys consuming is not the car itself but the personal transportation services it offers – and the quality of these services will have a social aspect as well as the purely technical one. Even if the value which the individual attaches to his car derives not from its value in use but from its value as a status symbol, a means of displaying his affluence, then this too will have a social aspect since the degree of status which the car conveys depends not on its size, speed or cost in absolute terms, but on its size, speed or cost relative to his neighbour's car. It follows, therefore, that economic growth, even if it enables every household to own a better car or to become a two-, three- or even four-car household, does not necessarily increase the wellbeing of the individual, since this is dependent not just on his own consumption but on the consumption levels of others as well.

The self-defeating nature of economic growth does not spring simply from the congestion problem cited above, but is derived from the fundamental observation that economic growth, though it may be able to reduce the amount of physical scarcity, cannot reduce the amount of *social scarcity*. Certain goods and facilities from which individuals derive satisfaction are subject to absolute limitations in supply. The availability of these so-called *positional goods* is not increased by economic growth, no matter how rapid. Thus, even though physical congestion can be reduced (by building more roads), social congestion cannot be reduced. For example, satisfaction is derived from employment in a high status job. The greater the responsibility involved, the higher the status and the more benefit the individual derives from it. But the individual can only increase his status in society if he moves up the ladder – in other words, if he moves nearer the top of the heap. It is not possible for all individuals simultaneously to improve their status, since status depends upon their relative position in the hierarchy. Employment prospects, in other words, are subject to social scarcity.

There are many other examples of positional goods whose availability is fixed, either because of physical scarcity or social scarcity. Country cottages in quiet rural surroundings are clearly positional goods, access to which is determined by one's position in the income distribution. The supply of such commodities is not merely fixed but shrinking, in the sense that the increased demand for the available supply of cottages reduces the quality of the 'quiet rural surroundings' of those that do exist, thereby further reducing the availability and increasing the price of cottages in 'unspoilt' surroundings.

Foreign travel is another example of a positional good; a

service which, at one time, was only available to the rich, but is now so cheap that it is available to all. But the increased availability of travel, made possible by technical progress and economic growth, has at the same time reduced the value of it. When travel was only available to the rich it was 'worth doing'. Now our attitude to it can be summed up by '...it's not worth going there. Everybody goes there...'

Air travel in particular, which has resulted in the mass migration of individuals across the globe, has had a two-fold effect. First, people are no longer going to the place they thought they were going to, but a place which has changed simply because they are there; and second, the influx of people to the more remote corners of the world has had a corrupting influence on the host society, reducing everything to the lowest common denominator of the Coke can and the digital wristwatch. The multinational mentality is one of increasing sameness.

10.11.3 Positional and material goods

The value of positional goods derives from the element of social scarcity embodied in them. They are in fixed supply and the access which any individual has to these positional goods depends on his position in the distribution of income. The value of so-called *material* goods, on the other hand, is not dependent on their scarcity – thus, to a starving man, food has an absolute value which is unaffected by other considerations. The supply of material goods is not fixed but will increase in line with output per head (assuming that raw material shortages can be overcome by improvements in technology). If we assume that individual preferences for positional *vis-à-vis* material output remain constant as income rises, then the fixity of supply of positional goods means that their price will rise relative to the price of material goods; that is, the more that economic growth provides an increasing supply of material goods, the less highly will these goods be valued. Positional goods become more highly valued, but their supply cannot be increased. The things that are valued most are precisely those goods that economic growth cannot provide.

10.11.4 Public goods, private goods and externalities

The concepts of public goods and externalities will extend the reader's appreciation of the foregoing analysis. Public goods, in the sense in which the term is being used here, need not be produced in the public sector. In fact, they may not be produced at all. For example, a river or the air in a city comes within the economist's definition of a public good. The distinguishing characteristic of public goods is that they are *non-excludable* and *non-rival*. A pure private good is excludable in the sense that the seller can determine who shall enjoy the benefits of the good or service being offered. This means that he can exclude those people who do not pay from consuming the good or service. In this sense, defence-of-the-realm is a pure public good since an individual who cheats by not paying his taxes cannot be excluded from enjoying the benefits of being defended.

Defence is also non-rival in the sense that the benefits which an individual derives from it do not detract from the benefits which his neighbour derives from it. On the other hand, a pure private good such as a glass of beer is a rival good – if I drink it then no one else can drink it. Fig. 10.4 may clarify the point.

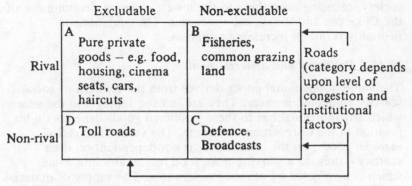

Fig. 10.4

Pure private goods are both rival and excludable. They include food, houses, cinema seats, cars and haircuts. Pure public goods, which are both non-rival and non-excludable, include defence and radio and TV broadcasts. It is interesting to note, however, that although TV broadcasts are, by their nature, non-excludable (in the sense that anyone with a TV set can enjoy the benefits of them) attempts are often made to use the legal system to make them excludable – to receive broadcasts without first purchasing a licence is illegal. Because of the nature of the good, however, such laws are difficult to enforce.

A great many goods are, however, neither pure public goods nor pure private goods in the sense that the extent to which they possess the elements of rivalness or non-excludability depends upon the conditions of use. Roads, for example, become a rival good when the level of use reaches the stage where journey times are increased by congestion. They are typically non-excludable, but there are also instances where they are excludable; for example, toll roads. Public parks may be excludable (for example, Woburn

Safari Park) or non-excludable (for example, the Lake District National Park). Like roads, they become rival goods only when they become so crowded that the presence or the activities of one group of people detract from the enjoyment that other people derive from them. This may be at quite a low level of use if people go to national parks in search of seclusion and solitude. When the activities of one person or group affect the enjoyment or benefit which another person or group can derive from a given situation, then *externalities* are said to exist. For example, suppose that one group of people enjoys water-skiing. The noise of the power boats annoys other people who come to the area in search of peace and quiet. It therefore reduces their enjoyment. In this instance, the water-skiers are said to impose external costs or externalities on the other holiday-makers. They impose costs on the environment for which they do not have to pay.

In this instance, the national park is a public good in as much as it is non-excludable. As is the case with many public goods, the extent to which any one individual has rights is ill-defined by the law. In order to limit the use made by individuals of the public good, the State (or, in this case, the National Park Authority) has to use the legal system to define more exactly what activities will be permitted in the park (in other words, what the property rights of the individual extend to).

10.11.5 The reluctant collectivism

We have seen how the satisfaction which an individual derives from the consumption of a public good is often affected by the activities of others. Individuals, by their behaviour, impose externalities on others. Now the existence of externalities was at one time treated by economists as a special case. It is now clear, however, how externalities affect the vast majority of consumption and production activities. Modern man, living in an industrial, urban society, affects his fellow man in almost everything he does. Many of these externalities are trivial, some are beneficial or positive (such as the enjoyment you may derive from contemplating your neighbour's well-kept flower garden). But many are negative externalities – the smoke from your neighbour's bonfire or the unpleasant habits of his dog, the noise of passing traffic or aircraft, the smoke from a chimney or the litter that adorns your favourite beauty spot. All of these things affect the individual's standard of living in a negative way. Moreover, it is clear that economic growth which increases everyone's income does not reduce the extent of these negative externalities. Only if the individual's income grows faster than that of his fellow men (in other words, if he moves up the income distribution) is he able to avoid these externalities by moving to a more expensive house where he is further away from his neighbour's bonfire and dog, and from the noise of traffic.

Given the pervasiveness of externalities it is difficult for economic growth to increase the standard of living of the average citizen since so many of the goods from which he derives utility are positional goods, which are in fixed supply. If the individual moves up the income distribution he can improve his access to these positional goods but, by definition, it is impossible for the average citizen to move up the income distribution.

The only conceivable way of increasing average living standards is to attempt to limit the amount of externalities. In other words, to limit the freedom of the individual by imposing restrictions on his right to pollute the environment with noise or smoke, and by imposing heavy penalties on those who are guilty of creating such externalities. Thus, the freedom of the individual is constrained and the role of the State is increased. Societies move reluctantly towards increasing State intervention.

Summary

In this section we have seen how the ability of a market economy to bring about real and sustained improvements in the welfare of its citizens is constrained by social scarcity, the need for public goods and the existence of externalities. Goods which by their nature are public goods cannot be produced efficiently by the market. As societies become more urbanized and industrialized so the demand for such goods increases and so therefore does the role of the State. This same urbanization makes the problem of externalities more acute and, again, the logical response of a democratic society is, however reluctantly, to increase government controls. Thus, we see that the rationale for State intervention is based not on political dogma, but on necessity.

There is an opposing view, however, which deprecates the rapid expansion of State activity which has taken place in the postwar era. The public sector, according to this view, has grown too large. In the following chapter, after a discussion of some technical matters, we consider this view.

Notes

1. **Denison E. F.** (1967) *Why Growth Rates Differ*, Brookings Institution.
2. **Kindleberger C. P.** (1967) *Europe's Postwar Growth: the Role of Labour Supply*, Harvard University Press.

3. **Kaldor N.** (1968) *Causes of the Slow Rate of Economic Growth of the United Kingdom*, Cambridge University Press.
4. **Bacon R. and Eltis W.** (1975) *Britain's Economic Problem: Too Few Producers*, Macmillan.
5. Some rather crucial – and controversial – assumptions are in fact required, which the reader may care to try to work out for him or her self, as an exercise. One could start by thinking about elasticities.
6. This is a recurrent theme in the *Cambridge Economic Policy Review* from the mid-1970s onwards.
7. This was an unpublished simulation exercise conducted with the NIESR model.
8. **Meadows D. et al.** (1972) *The Limits to Growth*, Earth Island.
9. The title is taken from **Hirsch F.** (1977) *The Social Limits to Growth* Routledge, Kegan & Paul, on which this section is based.

Questions

1. The term 'economic growth' refers to an increase in

   (a) GNP;
   (b) GDP per capita;
   (c) GDP per person employed;
   (d) GNP per unit of capital employed;
   (e) GNP or GDP depending on how you look at it.

2. Which of the following statements are correct?

   (a) A high rate of growth of output increases expenditure on new plant and machinery to meet the anticipated future rise in demand.
   (b) A high level of investment spending (on fixed capital formation) leads to an increase in output. It is a sufficient condition for economic growth.
   (c) Investment is a necessary condition for economic growth.

3. 'If interest rates in the United Kingdom rise, direct investment will fall but portfolio investment will increase.' Explain this paradox (i.e. explain the difference between *direct* investment and *portfolio* investment).

4. 'If they suffer an unexpected fall in sales, manufacturers are forced to invest in stocks and cut other investment.' Explain this paradox. Useful concepts: inventory investment, fixed capital formation.

5. 'A reflationary policy will increase demand. This may not, however, increase output because:

   (a) things might be too expensive for people to buy;
   (b) the increased demand may be dissipated in higher prices;
   (c) people's wants may already be satisfied;
   (d) the increased demand may all go overseas resulting in increased import penetration.

6. Explain what you understand by the following:

    (a) intervention currency;
    (b) seignorage;
    (c) stop-go policy.

7. Is the distinction between marketed and non-marketed output the same as that between tradable and non-tradable goods?

8. Give examples of goods or services which are:

    (a) marketable and tradable;
    (b) non-marketable and non-tradable;
    (c) marketable and non-tradable;
    (d) non-marketable and tradable.

The last one is very difficult.

9. Can you give examples of goods or services which are:

    (a) Produced in the public sector but are marketable.
    (b) Produced in the private sector but are non-marketable.

10. What does crowding-out imply about the magnitude of the government spending multiplier?

11. Referring to Table 10.5, on p.191 state which year since 1970 saw the largest decline in manufacturing employment in Britain. Can you suggest reasons for this?

12. Fig. 10.5 is based on the data from Tables 10.5 and 10.6. Note that both axes are drawn to the same scale so that the 45° line is of some significance. Explain what the diagram is saying, commenting on why you think some countries are to the right and others to the left of the 45° line. What do the UK, Canada, Norway and the Netherlands have in common?

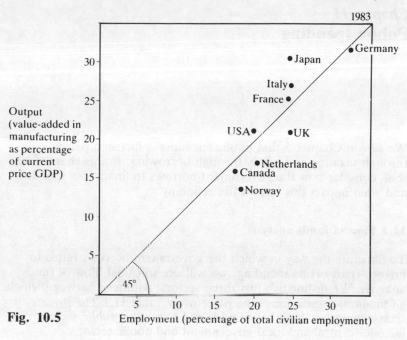

Fig. 10.5

1983

Output (value-added in manufacturing as percentage of current price GDP)

Employment (percentage of total civilian employment)

215

Chapter 11
Public spending

We saw in Chapter 5 that public spending is financed partly through taxation and partly through borrowing. In this chapter we shall consider how the government borrows to finance its spending and what impact this has on the economy.

11.1 Flow of funds analysis

To illustrate the way in which the government borrows funds to finance (part of) its spending, we will use so-called 'flow of funds' analysis. We distinguish just three sectors, within or between which all financial transactions take place as in Table 11.1 The *private* sector comprises both households and firms; the *public* sector includes central and local government and public sector corporations; and the *overseas* sector comprises all non-resident persons, companies and institutions. Each sector has both income and expenditure, and if expenditure exceeds income that sector is said to have a financial deficit, which means that it is accumulating debts with one or both of the other sectors. This indebtedness takes the form of currency, bonds, loans, etc., depending upon the sectors involved. If the sector has a financial surplus, income exceeding expenditure, then the sector as a whole is acquiring financial assets which constitute claims on other sectors.

A sector with a financial surplus is said to have a positive *net acquisition of financial assets* (NAFA). A negative NAFA on the other hand corresponds to a financial deficit. To summarize, for each sector:

Income minus expenditure = financial deficit/surplus = NAFA

For the three sectors taken together, deficits should exactly cancel out surpluses so that (apart from a residual error) the overall NAFA is equal to zero. Table 11.1 incorporates some illustrative figures for 1984. The public sector in 1984 had a deficit of approximately £12.5 bn. One can think of this as being financed by selling financial assets to the private sector which had a surplus of £19 bn. The overseas sector had a deficit of £1 bn. – in other words there was a balance of payments surplus of this amount. The

Table 11.1 Flow of funds analysis

Sector	Income	Expenditure	£ bn. NAFA (1984)	Types of asset involved
Private (i.e. households plus companies)	Households' incomes plus corporate income	Spending by households; current and capital expenditure by firms	+19	Individuals hold National Savings certificates, local authority bonds and currency. Financial institutions and companies hold Treasury Bills and other government securities
Public (i.e. central and local government plus nationalized industries)	Income from taxation (income tax, VAT, rates) plus public corporations' income from sales to public	Total spending on defence NHS, etc., current and capital spending by public corporations	+12.5	Central government sells Treasury Bills, other government securities and National Savings certificates. Local authorities and public corporations issue bonds, Bank of England issues notes and coin
Overseas (i.e. non-resident persons and companies and institutions)	Income received by foreign companies exporting to Britain, etc.	Expenditure by foreigners on buying British exports, etc.	−1	Sales of government securities overseas; also some local authority and public corporation debt. Change in reserves of foreign currency
Residual error			−5.5	

217

residual error in 1984 was quite large – £5.5 bn. Since the error term represents net errors and omissions in recording transactions between the sectors, its size gives a very rough indication of the reliability of the statistics. Finally it should be emphasized that this analysis illustrates *net* flows of funds between the three sectors – the total or gross amount of borrowing and lending between the three sectors is, of course, much larger than this.

Table 11.2 gives a more detailed breakdown. Here, seven sectors are distinguished. The private sector is disaggregated into the personal, corporate and banking sectors, and the public sector is broken down into central government, local authorities and public corporations. Note that each sector has a NAFA which is determined, as before, by the difference between its income and its expenditure. In Table 11.2, however, this is shown to be equal to the difference between the sector's current saving (i.e. the excess of income over current expenditure) and its *investment* expenditure. To summarize:

income minus current expenditure = 'saving'
'saving' minus investment spending = financial deficit/surplus
= NAFA

A number of features should be noted from Table 11.2. In 1979 and 1984 the personal sector had large positive savings. After investment expenditure had been completed (and most of this investment was in fixed capital formation) there still remained a substantial surplus which constituted a positive NAFA. In the non-bank corporate sector in 1984 there was also a substantial surplus. In 1979, however, even though there were large positive savings these were insufficient to finance investment in fixed capital and in stocks – principally because of the large amount of unintended inventory investment. The result therefore was that the corporate sector had an overall deficit in 1979. The picture is similar for industries in the public sector. Even though there was a substantial excess of income over current expenditure, the resulting saving (or 'profit' or 'trading surplus') was insufficient to finance the investment expenditures which the public corporations undertook. Thus the public corporations borrowed from other sectors.

The financial surpluses or deficits of the three sectors are summarised at the bottom of Table 11.2. The general picture which emerges is one in which a substantial public sector deficit is financed more or less by a private sector surplus. Unfortunately an interpretation is often put on this picture which is quite unwarranted. This interpretation is that surpluses are in some sense 'good' and deficits in some sense 'bad'. Therefore, so the erroneous argument runs, the private sector surplus is 'healthy' and the public sector deficit is cause for concern since it represents the

Table 11.2 Financial surplus or deficit: analysis by sector

	£ m.	
	1979	**1984**
Private sector		
1. Personal sector		
Saving	18 669	27 371
less investment	−9 185	−16 387
financial surplus	9 484	10 984
2. Industrial and commercial companies		
Saving	21 778	30 804
less fixed capital formation	−14 113	−18 858
less inventory investment	−9 268	−4 736
financial surplus or deficit	−1 603	7 210
3. Financial companies and institutions		
Saving	4 048	7 310
less investment	−3 881	−6 646
financial surplus	167	664
Public sector		
4. Public corporations		
Saving	4 101	7 029
less investment	−6 255	−7 323
financial deficit	−2 154	−294
5. Central government		
Saving	−2 927	−7 517
less investment	−1 528	−2 623
financial deficit	−4 455	−10 140
6. Local authorities		
Saving	1 641	1 579
less investment	3 617	3 732
financial deficit	−1 976	−2 153
7. Overseas sector		
financial surplus or deficit	736	−935
Financial surplus or deficit:		
Private sector	8 048	18 858
Public sector	−8 585	−12 587
Overseas sector	736	−935
Residual error	−199	−5 336

Source: *National Accounts Blue Book 1985*, Table 13.1.

burden which the public sector imposes on the rest of the economy. As we shall argue later, this interpretation is wrong. A sector deficit or surplus is neither a good thing nor a bad thing. It would be equally logical to argue that the company sector should display a deficit as to argue it should display a surplus. Surpluses merely reflect low levels of investment spending it could be said. Looked at in this way the deficits of the public corporations reflect their high levels of investment spending relative to net income (saving). If it is praiseworthy for companies in the private sector to borrow in order to finance investment in fixed capital formation, similar actions on the part of companies in the public sector cannot be deprecated. By extension the same also applies to the other parts of the public sector. Borrowing from other sectors in order to finance fixed capital formation in infrastructure is not, in itself, a bad thing.

Note finally that what we have said about the merits or otherwise of sector deficits does not necessarily apply to the overseas sector deficit or surplus since other considerations apply here. In 1984 the overseas sector had a deficit of almost £1 bn. This is equal (with the sign changed) to net investment abroad. In other words there was a net outflow of investment spending from the UK of this amount.

11.2 The Public Sector Borrowing Requirement

The financial deficit of the public sector is financed by borrowing from various sources. The total borrowing of the public sector, the so-called Public Sector Borrowing Requirement (PSBR) depends upon the public sector financial deficit (PSFD) but it should be noted that the two are not equal. Table 11.3 shows that there were three main reasons why the PSBR differed from the PSFD in 1984. Firstly there were 'transactions concerning certain public sector pension schemes' which tended to reduce the PSBR below what it would otherwise have been. Secondly there is an item called 'accruals adjustment' which tends to increase the PSBR. This adjustment has to be made to make the financial account accounts balance when, for example, payments fall due but are not in fact paid. Suppose, for example, that a company or individual owes the government tax but withholds payment. Since the government has not yet received the funds, it will have to borrow funds to finance the expenditure to which it is committed. Bearing this in mind, it is easier to appreciate the distinction between the PSBR and the PSFD. They measure two different things. The PSBR shows the total requirement for loanable funds – that is, it is the *borrowing*

Table 11.3 Relationship between the public sector financial deficit and borrowing requirement (1984)

	£m
Public sector financial deficit	12 587
Lending to private sector and overseas (net)	84
Transactions concerning public sector pension schemes and other financial transactions	−795
Accruals adjustment (net)	527
Sales of assets	−2 673
Balancing item	511
Public sector borrowing requirement	10 241
Made up of Central Government Borrowing Requirement (CGBR)	10 186
Local Authority Borrowing Requirement (LABR)	−470
Public Corporations' Borrowing Requirement (PCBR)	525

Source: derived from *UK National Accounts 1985*

requirement, whereas the financial deficit shows the excess of expenditure over revenue.

As can be seen from Table 11.3, however, the single most important reason why the PSBR was less than the PSFD in 1984 was because of sales of shares in former nationalized industries such as British Telecom. In Table 11.3 these are shown as sales of assets (£2.6 bn.) though in the national accounts these are euphemistically shown as 'cash expenditure on company securities' (a negative amount of £2.6 bn.).

11.3 Is the PSBR too high?

With the upsurge of monetarist thinking in the 1970s, it became fashionable to concentrate attention on the PSBR as a key statistic in macroeconomic management, despite the fact that many economists were unhappy about its use as such. The concern with the size of the PSBR echoed an earlier preoccupation of economists and politicians with the size of the national debt. As we saw earlier, the national debt is made up of debt accumulated by governments in the past. Other things being equal, a PSBR of £10 bn. thus adds £10 bn. to the national debt. It was argued that an increase in the national debt (= a positive PSBR) was a bad thing

221

because it represented the extent to which the country or the government was 'living beyond its means'. Future generations, it was argued, were being put in hock. The government was imposing a burden on the nation by failing to keep its expenditure in line with its income.

As is so often the case in economics, things which have been shown to be completely false reappear a few years later. Things which have been learnt are forgotten and have to be discovered and learnt again. In a classic work in 1944, Abba Lerner had written[1]:

> The size of the national debt (when held by citizens of the country) is a matter of almost no significance beside the importance of maintaining full employment. The national debt is not a burden on posterity because if posterity pays the debt it will be paying it to the same posterity that will be alive at the time when the payment is made. The national debt is not a burden on the nation because every cent in interest or repayment that is collected from the citizens as taxpayers to meet the debt service is received by the citizens as government bondholders. The national debt is not a sign of national poverty any more than the certificates of ownership of government bonds are a sign of national wealth – the two amounts exactly cancel out in any measure of the national wealth. Just as increasing the national debt does not make the nation poorer, so repaying the national debt does not make the nation richer. It is not true that the national debt "must be repaid sometime" any more than it is true that all the banks must call in all their debts and repay their depositors on some catastrophic day or that all firms and corporations will have to be dissolved someday to repay the obligations to the individuals who invested in them. Every individual buyer of government bonds must be able to get his money when it is due, but another lender can take his place when this happens (if the individual should not wish to renew his loan) and the national debt can continue – just as the forest can go on forever even though every tree in it must ultimately fall.

Note, however, that this only applies if the debt is held by the citizens of the country. If it is held externally (that is, by non-residents) then this does represent a burden for future generations in the sense that redeeming this debt or paying interest charges on it will constitute a drain on the balance of payments. However, apart from a small percentage held overseas (about 8.5 per cent in 1985) Britain's national debt is, in fact, held internally. Table 11.4 shows the distribution of the national debt in 1985.

Note, also, that for Lerner in 1944 the significance of the national debt was its importance in maintaining full employment.

Table 11.4 Distribution of the sterling national debt: end of March 1985

	Per cent	£ bn.
Market holdings		
Public corporations and local authorities	0.6	1.0
monetary sector	5.1	8.0
Other financial institutions:		
Insurance companies and pension funds	37.0	57.5
Other	8.9	13.8
Overseas residents	8.5	13.2
Individuals and private trusts	22.3	34.7
Other (including residual)	10.0	15.6
Official holdings	7.5	11.6
Total Debt	100.0	155.4

Source: *Bank of England Quarterly Bulletin*, December 1985.

In a recession, government tax revenue falls as fewer people are employed and company profits are lower. Government expenditure, on the other hand, tends to rise as expenditure on unemployment benefit and social security increases. The gap between government receipts and payments therefore widens, leading to a corresponding rise in its borrowing requirement. The effect of the budget deficit is to increase the overall level of demand, above what it would otherwise have been. This helps to offset the effects of the recession, since it helps to maintain the level of demand thus preventing demand-deficient unemployment. The Keynesians, of course, would go further than this. In a recession, they would argue, not only should the government allow the PSBR to increase but it should actively engineer such an increase by increasing public spending and reducing taxes, thereby boosting demand. To try to reduce the PSBR in a recession is the opposite of what is required.

Given that public sector borrowing is not in itself a bad thing, how therefore can one explain the current preoccupation with the size of the PSBR? There are three possible explanations. The first of these is the totally irrational view that 'the government of a country must keep to the fiscal principles appropriate to a grocery store'.[3] In other words, they should follow Mr Micawber's philosophy of keeping their expenditure within their income since living beyond one's means would lead to bankruptcy and ruin. Although this view is quite clearly incorrect – for the government at least, and arguably for individuals and companies as well – it is deeply ingrained within our consciousness. Children learn that they cannot spend more than they are given in pocket money. Since their income consists of the cash they are given at the beginning of the week, they soon come to understand the benefits of thrift and financial responsibility and the seemingly absolute necessity of keeping expenditure within the limits of income. If companies accepted this maxim, however, they would find it very difficult to expand. Since they could not borrow to finance their investment, they would be limited to whatever funds they could generate internally. If individuals accepted this view they would never take out bank loans or mortgages and they would never buy on credit. In short, they would never *borrow*. Neither, therefore, would anyone lend, since for every borrower there has to be a corresponding lender. No one's consumption would exceed their income. Usury would not exist.

Leaving aside the question of whether people would feel more righteous as a result of this, they would certainly feel, and be, very much poorer since the economy would collapse. Any economic activity beyond subsistence agriculture would come to a halt.

Although the prejudice against public sector borrowing is mostly irrational and can be explained in terms of the ethical position mentioned above, there are two more reasons for it, which have more substance. The first is connected with the view that government spending financed by borrowing can lead to an undesirable increase in the money supply. The second is that public sector borrowing displaces or 'crowds out' the private sector investment that would otherwise have taken place. We shall deal with each of these in turn.

11.4 The impact on the money supply

We saw earlier that the impact on the money supply of the sale of public sector debt depended crucially upon whether the debt was being sold to the banking sector or to the non-bank private sector. Certain types of public sector debt (e.g. Treasury Bills) were regarded by the banks as assets which were sufficiently liquid so as to be a very good substitute for cash. If the banks bought Treasury Bills, therefore, the amount of liquid assets they held would remain unchanged (since they would now have less cash but more Treasury Bills), so that they would not have to curtail their lending. In fact, they could *increase* their lending, since the public spending, which was being undertaken by the funds so generated, would *increase* their holdings of liquid assets. Thus, the net effect of public spending financed by sales of Treasury Bills to banks was to increase the money supply. The same effect would not occur if public sector debt was sold to the non-bank private sector since, in this case, banks would suffer a reduction in their holdings of liquid assets when purchasers of Treasury Bills drew cheques on their bank accounts in favour of the Bank of England.

As can be seen from Table 11.5, the bulk of the PSBR has in recent years been financed by selling debt to the non-bank private sector in the UK; that is, it has been sold *internally* and normally in such a way that monetary expansion has not resulted. In certain years, however, notably in 1975, a large PSBR resulted in substantial sales of debt to the banking sector. Other things being equal, this would have resulted in growth of the money supply after a certain time lag – at least in theory. Kaldor[3] has pointed out, however, that empirically there is no statistically significant relationship between changes in the money stock and unfunded public sector borrowing ('unfunded' borrowing is that part which is financed by selling short term debt, such as Treasury Bills, to the banks).

It is sometimes argued, however, that even when the Bank of England seems to have been successful in financing the borrowing requirement by off-loading government debt on the non-bank private sector, often this has only been achieved at the cost of increases in interest rates which have had a discouraging effect on private sector investment. It is to this 'crowding out' hypothesis that we now turn.

Table 11.5 Financing of the PSBR

	£ bn.					
	1975	1980	1981	1982	1983	1984
Non-bank private sector	6.3	9.8	9.3	6.4	12.2	8.4
of which:						
Other financial institutions	4.1	5.9	5.5	4.6	6.5	5.4
Industrial and commercial companies	0.6	0.2	− 2.8	−3.6	1.1	− 2.7
Personal sector	1.6	3.6	6.7	5.4	4.5	5.7
Monetary sector	3.1	1.3	− 0.6	−2.8	− 2.0	0.5
Overseas sector	0.7	0.8	1.9	1.4	1.4	1.4
PSBR	10.1	11.8	10.6	4.9	11.6	10.2

Note: totals may not sum to zero due to rounding errors.

Source: *UK National Accounts 1985,* Table 13.14.

11.5 Crowding out: 'the Treasury view'

In the depression of the 1930s Keynes was advocating budget
deficits to boost demand and thereby raise output and
employment. The conventional wisdom of the time took the
opposite view, that the government should pursue 'sound' financial
policies, which meant balancing the budget. According to this
view, which came to be known as 'the Treasury view',
expansionary fiscal policies would not raise output and employment
because extra public spending would lead to a fall in output in the
private sector as firms became starved of resources. The modern
counterpart of this Treasury view is the crowding out hypothesis –
high levels of public spending result in a large borrowing
requirement. This forces up interest rates, which depresses private
sector investment and hence output falls in the private sector.

11.6 'Crowding out' or 'crowding in'

Imagine a hypothetical closed economy which is currently
operating at full capacity. Suppose that if all the economy's
productive resources were devoted to producing private sector
output, the maximum amount available would be Oy as in
Fig. 11.1. Similarly, if all resources were devoted to public sector
output the amount available would be Ox. The line joining point y
with point x is known as a production possibility frontier. It shows
combinations of private sector and public sector output that are
available with a given state of technology. Output levels beyond
this frontier are not attainable unless the productive potential of
the economy is enhanced, perhaps by an improvement in
technology.

Consider a point such as A on the frontier. Since we are
already on the frontier, public sector output can only be increased
at the expense of private sector output. Increased public spending
will take us to a point such as B, in which case the extra public
spending will have displaced or 'crowded out' a certain amount of
private sector spending. The cost to society of the extra public
sector output has been the forgoing of private sector output.
Economists term this the *opportunity cost* of the extra public sector
output. It is the real cost to society of the extra public sector
output.

In such a situation society should choose the point on the
production possibility curve it deems optimal, choosing more
public sector output and less private sector output or vice versa.
This choice should be expressed through the democratic process,
however imperfect that process may be. On the assumptions that

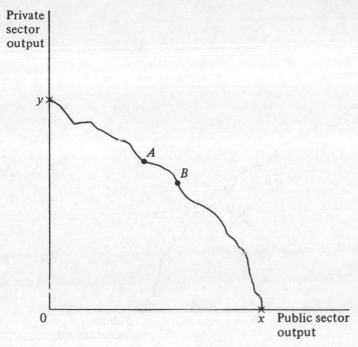

Fig. 11.1

we have made, it follows quite logically that increased public sector output can only be achieved at the expense of less private sector output, that is, a form of 'crowding out' occurs.

It should be noted, however, that although output levels *beyond* the frontier are impossible to attain, output levels *within* the frontier, such as point C in Fig. 10.2, are quite probable. At point C the economy is operating at less than full capacity, that is, there exist unemployed resources of capital and labour in the economy. Suppose we now increase public spending.

There is no *a priori* reason why private sector output should suffer as a result; in fact the reverse seems intuitively more likely, that the increased demand in the economy will induce an increase in output in the private sector. Thus public spending has 'crowded in' rather than 'crowded out' private sector output.

What of the reverse situation, when we start at a point such as *D* and reduce public spending in an attempt to increase private sector output? Will the economy move to a point such as *E* (for Enterprise) or *F* (for Failure)? Consider the two scenarios.

Understanding the economy

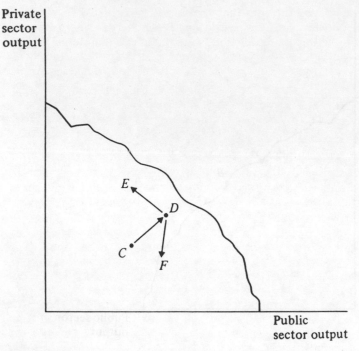

Fig. 11.2

E for enterprise

Because the government is spending less, its borrowing
requirement is reduced. Personal sector savings, which previously
were lent to the government, are now channelled to private sector
firms, who as a result increase their expenditure on fixed capital
formation. Lower public spending enables taxes to be reduced,
resulting in a rise in disposable income and hence a rise in
consumption spending. The private sector responds by increasing
output, which has been made possible by the increased investment
it has undertaken.

F for failure

The cut in public spending will cause some firms, who previously
sold to the public sector, to experience a fall in demand. Some
public sector workers will suffer a fall in income as a result of pay
restraint or redundancy. These groups thus cut their spending.
Since spending and incomes fall, tax revenues fall, leading to an
increase in the borrowing requirement. In an attempt to 'get back
on course' public spending is cut still more, deepening the
recession. The decline is cumulative.

On the face of it both these scenarios seem plausible but, on closer inspection, we see that the first is seriously flawed because it ignores the influence of demand. A reduction in the budget deficit will reduce the overall level of demand. If demand falls, supply is most unlikely to rise; in fact it is likely to fall too because supply or output is basically demand determined. The gap left by the reduced public spending will not necessarily be filled because, although Nature abhors a vacuum and rushes in to fill it up, there is no such general tendency in the economies of complex industrial societies.

We should note, however, that this view – that the level of output is demand determined – is not universally accepted. The so-called 'supply siders' of the monetarist school argue that much greater attention should be paid to the factors which shape the decisions of individual workers and firms as regards what they produce and sell. One such influence would be the rewards available from work, and here they argue that a cut in tax rates will encourage greater effort and enterprise and thus boost output. We examine the views of the supply siders in the next chapter.

Before we do so, however, it is worth looking at what happened in the British economy in the period after 1979 when the authorities attempted to restrain public spending in the belief that by doing so the private sector would be encouraged to expand. As Fig. 11.3 shows, the timing of this strategy was unfortunate, since it happened to coincide with a period in which the world economy was experiencing a recession of considerable severity. The deflationary policies pursued in the UK in 1979 and the early 1980s coupled with this recession appear to have created a gap which was not filled. Indeed it was not until 1985 that the level of industrial production regained the level achieved in 1979.

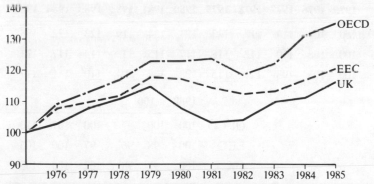

Fig. 11.3 Industrial production index (1975 = 100)
Source: *OECD Main Economic Indicators*

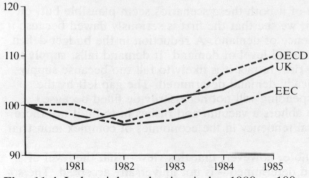

Fig. 11.4 Industrial production index 1980 = 100

Source: *OECD Main Economic Indicators*

Finally, as an aside, and to see how easy it is to mislead with statistics, compare Fig. 11.3 with Fig. 11.4. Both figures show the same thing, namely indexes of industrial production. The only difference is that Fig. 11.4 has 1980 = 100 as its base year whereas Fig. 11.3 has 1975 = 100 as its base year. Both figures are correct – check them with the data shown in Table 11.6 from which they are derived. But note how the two figures present a totally different picture and tell a different story. Figure 11.4 appears to present a relatively rosy picture of industrial production in the United Kingdom, but this is only because the basis of comparison is 1980, which as we can see from Fig. 11.3 was a disastrous year for industrial production in the UK. The picture shown in Fig. 11.4

Table 11.6 Industrial production

	1975 = 100										
	1975	1976	1977	1978	1979	1980	1981	1982	1983	1984	1985
OECD	100	109	113	117	123	123	124	119	123	132	135
EEC	100	108	110	112	118	117	115	113	114	117	121
UK	100	103	108	111	115	108	104	104	110	111	117
					1980 = 100						
				OECD	100	100	97	100	107	110	
				EEC	100	98	96	97	100	103	
				UK	100	97	98	102	103	108	

Source: *OECD Main Economic Indicators* (figures have been founded to nearest 1 per cent).

is unbalanced and misleading – but technically it is correct. As Disraeli said, 'there are lies, damned lies and statistics.'

Notes

1. Abba P. Lerner, *The Economics of Control*, 1944.
2. The phrase is taken from Lerner (1944) (op. cit.). Lerner could not possibly have foreseen that one day a grocer's daughter would control the economic policy of Britain!
3. See Kaldor N. (1982) 'Evidence to Treasury and Civil Service Committee' in *The Scourge of Monetarism* O.U.P.

Questions

1. The following table gives some information on the financial surplus or deficit of the private, public and overseas sectors in 1979, 1980 and 1981 in the United Kingdom (in £ bn.).

	1979	1980	1981
Private sector	8.0	13.9	14.1
Public sector	−8.6	?	−8.3
Overseas sector	0.6	−3.1	?

   (a) What was the size of the public sector's surplus or deficit in 1980?
   (b) What was the overseas sector's surplus or deficit in 1981?
   (c) Does the negative sign for the overseas sector in 1980 indicate that net investment from the United Kingdom was positive or negative? Explain what this means.

2. Which of the following will result from a positive PSBR

   (a) the National Debt will increase;
   (b) interest rates will rise;
   (c) demand will be higher than if there had been no public sector borrowing;
   (d) private sector borrowing will fall;
   (e) the ratio of the PSBR to GDP will rise.

3. Suppose that asset sales (such as British Gas) are expected to raise about £5 bn. in 1986 and 1987. Which of the following are true:

   (a) The PSFD will be £5 bn. less than if there had been no asset sales.
   (b) The PSBR will be £5 bn. less than if there had been no asset sales.
   (c) this allows the Chancellor to cut taxation by £5 bn. and still achieve his target for the PSBR.

4. Refer to Fig. 11.3, Fig. 11.4 and Table 11.6. Which of the following are correct:

 (a) The trough of the world recession was in 1982. The recession in the United Kingdom started earlier and was of greater severity.
 (b) Since 1981 industrial production in the United Kingdom has grown more rapidly than in the EEC.
 (c) Since 1978 industrial production in the United Kingdom has grown less rapidly than in the EEC.
 (d) in 1985 industrial production in the United Kingdom was less than 2 per cent up on production in 1979. For the OECD the corresponding increase was about 10 per cent.

Chapter 12
The real wage debate and supply side economics

12.1 The real wage debate – a historical perspective

There is no new thing under the sun. Or, at least, so it must
appear to those who observe the waxing and waning of economic
ideas. In the depression years of the 1930s Keynes argued that
demand could and should be expanded to reduce unemployment.
The classical economists resisted, arguing in favour of balanced
budgets and action to reduce wages. Neither side can be said to
have won the intellectual argument at the time; rather the reflation
that occurred in the late 1930s resulted from rearmament. In the
post-war era Keynesian economics held sway. It was the
conventional wisdom. Perhaps as a result of Keynesian policies or
perhaps coincidentally the 1950s and 1960s was a period of
unprecedented growth and prosperity. By the mid 1970s, however,
the conventional wisdom was under attack. By 1980 Keynesian
economics was in the wilderness. The Western economies
generally, but Britain in particular, were in deep recession with
unemployment reaching levels which had not been seen since the
1930s, while influential economists, with the ear of the
government, argued that unemployment could not be reduced by
reflation. This view was popularly labelled 'monetarist' though it
was rather different from the old style monetarism of Milton
Friedman with its emphasis on the money supply as a determinant
of aggregate demand. New-style monetarism was the absolute
negation of the Keynesian belief that demand management was
capable of raising output and reducing unemployment. The
government, it argued, was powerless to reduce unemployment.
The wheel had come full circle.

The first part of the attack on Keynesianism came with the so-
called crowding-out hypothesis which we discussed in sections 10.7
and 11.6. The essence of this hypothesis was that the government
was incapable of raising demand because any increase in
government spending would displace an equivalent amount of
private investment-spending. Although it is too simplistic to say
that the crowding-out hypotheses was disproved, it is certainly true
to say that it lost support in the 1980s as a mass of empirical

evidence built up against it. In the meantime, however, a much more sophisticated and damaging critique of Keynesian views was being developed. This critique went under the heading of 'rational expectations'. Thus, in the mid 1980s, the stage was set for a replay of the debate which had taken place in the 1930s. This time it was called the *real wage debate*. It centred around the question of whether unemployment was the result of real wages being too high. Had workers priced themselves out of jobs and would unemployment fall if workers accepted lower real wages? Would an expansion of demand engineered by the government succeed in reducing unemployment or would it merely lead to wage inflation without any impact on employment levels?

12.2 Expectations

An important aspect of the real wage debate was concerned with the way in which expectations (of future price changes) were formed. In the late 1970s and early 1980s a novel – some would say revolutionary – way of modelling expectations was increasingly discussed by economists. This was the so-called Rational Expectations Hypothesis (REH or simply RE). An appreciation of how one might model expectations is essential to an understanding of the debate about labour market dynamics and hence we discuss it here.

Economic agents – that is, firms, consumers, employers, trade union negotiators and so on – necessarily have expectations about certain key economic variables. For example, firms will have some view about their sales revenue next year. Consumers will have some view about what their incomes are likely to be in three years' time, and so on. The most important variable that economic agents form expectations about, however, is the price level. In other words, all economic agents have some view about future inflation rates. These expectations will influence the decisions they take in the present about things such as the level of wage settlements. Those decisions themselves will, in turn, influence future events – for example, the actual rate of increase of wage costs will influence the rate of increase of prices.

Economists have traditionally modelled expectations in a backward-looking way. In other words, an economic agent was assumed to base his expectations of the future on what had happened in the recent past. For example, if the rate of inflation this year is known to be 3 per cent then, in the absence of any information to the contrary, he will expect the rate of inflation next year to be 3 per cent as well. On the face of it this seems sensible. But imagine a situation in which the rate of inflation is falling from, say, 5 per cent two years ago to 4 per cent last year, to 3 per cent this year. If inflation really does continue to fall, but our economic agent still bases his expectations on the most recently experienced actual rate of inflation, he will tend to overpredict the rate of inflation for next year (he will predict 3 per cent, whereas the actual rate next year turns out to be lower). More important, expectations formed in this way cannot pick up turning points – that is, if the rate of inflation in the past has been on a rising trend, but the government and monetary authorities take action to reduce it, our economic agent's expectations of the rate of inflation will be much higher than the rate which actually occurs.

Modelling expectations formation in this way therefore presupposes a degree of irrationality – agents always get it wrong. Let us suppose, the advocates of RE argue, that we make the opposite assumption, namely that economic agents are *rational* in the sense that they get it right, or, at least, that on average they get it right. To be able to do so, of course, economic agents would need to have in their minds some model of the economy which could, on average, correctly forecast inflation (and other key economic variables.) Critics of RE point out that this requirement will not be fulfilled. Not even the best informed group of economic forecasters can correctly predict the future so the man in the street, they argue, cannot possibly hope to do so. In reply the advocates of RE argue that to assume rationality (in the sense used here) on the part of economic agents is no more implausible than to assume the sort of irrationality implied by modelling expectations in a backward-looking way. Moreover, and this is a vital distinction, the Rational Expectations Hypotheses does not assume that economic agents forecast correctly. Rather it assumes that *on average* they forecast correctly, or more exactly that on average the expectations of economic agents will be the same as those generated by a correct model of the economy.

12.3 The implications of RE for policy

On the face of it, the REH seems to be a fairly minor piece of theory – perhaps a little implausible but definitely innocuous. It seems to be policy-neutral in the sense that it does not appear to strengthen or weaken the case for any particular policy stance. It is surprising to find therefore that the REH has provoked so much controversy amongst economists, being heralded by some as the most important theoretical advance in economic theory in the 1980s while others have treated it with disdain and derision.

There are probably two reasons for the popularity – if that is the right word – of RE. The first and least important is a technical one; namely, that for those engaged in producing forecasts from economic models (which we discuss in Chapter 13) RE appears to offer a neat way of producing consistent forecasts. More important, however, when RE is combined with a certain view of the labour market it appears to offer a theoretical justification for the sort of policy stance which right-wing governments like to adopt. That is, RE provides radical right-wing governments (such as that of Mrs Thatcher) with a justification for eschewing any sort of reflationary actions to reduce unemployment since it forms a vital part of an analysis which concludes that such reflationary policies are ineffective and damaging. If the REH is true, and if the labour market works in the way that monetarists believe, then expansionary fiscal and monetary policies cannot alleviate unemployment. Reflation brings inflation without any increase in real output. Demand management, in a Keynesian sense, is dead and the way is open for 'supply-side' policies – 'making markets work better.' Thus RE is the missing link which the opponents of Keynesianism have been seeking. It may, like the missing-link in the evolutionary debate, turn out to be a fraud.

12.4 The dynamics of labour market adjustment

Suppose we accept (as monetarists do) that the labour market can be modelled by the sort of demand and supply analysis illustrated in Fig. 12.1. The monetarist view of the labour market was sketched out in section 9.7.1 and the reader may find it worthwhile to re-read that section before proceeding. It is important to recall also that the demand curve for labour is the marginal revenue product curve (explained in section 9.7.4). Note in Fig. 12.1 that both the demand for labour and the supply of labour depend upon the real wage (W/P). Figure 12.1 illustrates a situation of long-run equilibrium. In equilibrium the market *clears* in the sense that the level of real wages is just sufficient to ensure that the demand for labour and the supply of labour are equal. Thus there is no involuntary unemployment. All those who wish to work can find a job.

A long-run equilibrium situation such as this is not particularly interesting since equilibrium is defined in such a way that the problem we are studying is defined out of existence. The problem we are interested in is that of unemployment. If the labour market is in equilibrium then by definition unemployment cannot exist.

We also noted, in section 9.7.1, an important corollary of this argument, namely that expansionist monetary and fiscal policies could not in the long run move the level of employment away from

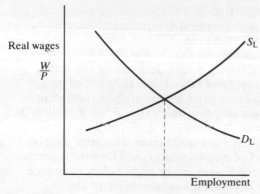

Fig. 12.1

its natural level. Hence the level of unemployment also remained
at its natural level in the long run. In summary, unemployment
could not, in the long run, be reduced by monetary and fiscal
expansion.

As Keynes is said to have remarked, however, in the long run
we are all dead. We live here and now in the short run, in a world
in which markets do not necessarily clear. Is it possible, in this
short run, for expansionist policies to increase employment?

If this question can be answered in the affirmative then the
possibility of reducing unemployment by stimulating demand is
proved. In fairness, to *permanently* reduce unemployment it might
be necessary to keep on applying successive stimuli to demand,
and this might result in accelerating inflation, but the ability of
governments to reduce unemployment if they wish to do so is
demonstrated. It would then become clear that a high level of
unemployment reflected the fact that the government had taken
the conscious decision not to expand demand and thereby reduce
unemployment, since it gave a higher priority to reducing inflation
and avoiding balance of payments difficulties than to reducing
unemployment. This is an intellectually defensible, if somewhat
callous, position but it is not one which is likely to appeal to the
hearts and minds of the electorate. A certain amount of disquiet
and unease might result, even in the minds of the policy makers
themselves, if it were recognized that the well-being of the
employed majority was being purchased at the expense of the
unemployed minority. How much simpler to argue that even in the
short run it was *impossible* to reduce unemployment by stimulating
demand.

This is where rational expectations enters the analysis.
Deviations from the long-run equilibrium depicted in Fig. 12.1 can
only be achieved if there is some divergence between the actual

and the expected real wage. If such divergences are impossible
then deviations away from the natural level of employment are
also impossible, even in the short run.

To illustrate this let us assume that in Fig. 12.2 the demand
for labour is a function of money wages deflated by the actual
price index whereas the supply of labour is a function of money
wages deflated by the expected price index. If the expected price
index is the same as the actual price index (i.e. $P^e = P^a$) then the
market stays in equilibrium. If, however, actual and expected
prices diverge it is possible for disequilibrium situations to arise.
This implies that the level of employment could deviate from its
natural level. The scope for discretionary fiscal policy to reduce
unemployment therefore depends upon the ability of the
authorities to generate such disequilibria.

For example, suppose wages are rising at 10 per cent per
annum and prices are also expected to rise at the same rate.
Expected real wages (W/P^e) thus remain the same so there is no
change in the supply of labour. Suppose, however, that prices
actually rise by 12 per cent; actual real wages thus fall leading to
an increase in the demand for labour. This is illustrated in Fig.
12.2 where a movement down the demand curve for labour results

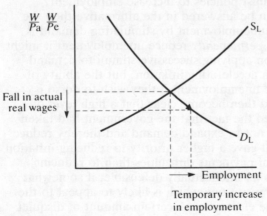

Fig. 12.2

in a temporary increase in employment. Notice, however, that this
will only occur if the authorities generate an actual rate of inflation
which is different from the expected rate of inflation. If the
suppliers of labour form their expectations in a rational way – that
is, if an average

$$P^e = P^a$$

then such deviations away from long-run equilibrium will not occur. This is because the rate of inflation which actually occurs will always be fully – and correctly – anticipated by workers. Thus expected real wages are equal to actual real wages

$$\frac{W}{P^e} \quad \frac{W}{P^a}$$

and deviations from the natural level of employment cannot occur even in the short run.

This analysis of labour market dynamics has very important implications for policy. Firstly, if the analysis is correct it implies that the only way for the government to permanently reduce unemployment is to keep generating surprises, by producing an actual rate of inflation which is higher than the expected rate. After a while it would become more and more difficult to surprise people, since the surprises would become anticipated. The expected rate of inflation would equal the actual rate. Expected and actual real wages would therefore remain unaffected by expansionary fiscal and monetary policies. Such policies would result only in higher and higher rates of inflation, as the authorities strove ineffectually to generate surprises and there would be no effect on employment even in the short run.

In addition to demonstrating that reflationary policies do not reduce unemployment, the REH also implies, of course, that deflationary policies do not increase unemployment. Suppose the government deflates the economy to reduce inflation. If the ensuing fall in the rate of inflation is fully anticipated by all economic agents then expected and actual real wages will remain unchanged. Inflation will be brought down painlessly. The transition from a high rate of inflation to a low rate of inflation is accomplished without the need to go through a high-unemployment period of transition in which economic agents gradually adjust their expectations – and hence their wage demands – to the lower rate of inflation.

12.5 Rational expectations and the Medium Term Financial Strategy

The emphasis which this analysis puts on expectations explains the thinking behind the so-called Medium Term Financial Strategy which the Conservative Government introduced in the early 1980s. The essence of the MTFS was the announcement of a target rate of growth for certain monetary aggregates (M3 or M0 or whatever). Economic agents, it was thought, would take note of the projected fall in the growth of the money supply and would anticipate that a fall in the rate of inflation would result. They would therefore adjust their behaviour accordingly – in particular they would moderate their wage demands. The resulting fall in wage inflation would help reduce price inflation (though the prime mover was the reduction in monetary growth) and this would confirm that agents' expectations had been correct.

It seems incredible now that anyone could ever have believed that economic agents in the real world would behave in the way outlined. In the event the authorities consistently failed to reach their pre-set monetary targets. Even if they had not existed beforehand, expectations were thus generated that the authorities would in future miss their monetary targets, which were thus effectively ignored. Even if the authorities had met their monetary targets it was becoming increasingly apparent by the mid-1980s that the power of the money supply statistics to predict the rate of inflation was very poor. The Medium Term Financial Strategy faded away.

12.6 RE: an assessment

We saw in section 12.3 how a monetarist view of the labour market, when combined with RE, could be used to support the notion that reflation would not reduce unemployment. Such a conclusion was anathema to Keynesian economists who were thus initially highly critical of RE. The Keynesian attack was somewhat misplaced, however, since the critical part of the analysis was not RE itself but rather the monetarist view of the workings of the labour market. Forward looking expectations could in fact form part of a Keynesian model of the economy and by the mid 1980s some Keynesian macro models had indeed incorporated such a feature.

RE is now acknowledged as a significant innovation in economic analysis. It has done little to increase our understanding of macroeconomic behaviour, however, since the propositions of the REH are so difficult to prove – or rather disprove – empirically. On a simplistic level the REH is obviously incorrect. What little evidence there is from surveys (of people's price expectations) shows quite clearly that people do not on average guess the future rate of price inflation correctly. On a more sophisticated level, however, it seems sensible to acknowledge that people do anticipate future changes in economic variables, and that their expectations are based on quite complex models of the causal links within the economy – though these models are implicit rather than explicit.

The real wage debate remains unresolved. If the labour market does indeed function in the way that monetarists believe then it is a logical possibility that reflation could lead to an increase in both prices and wages which would leave real wages and the level of employment essentially unchanged. The crucial question is whether the labour market really can be modelled in the way that monetarists believe.

12.7 Supply-side economics

As we have seen, the rational expectations revolution (so-called) made some governments question whether demand management in a Keynesian sense was sufficient to bring about the goals of low inflation, low unemployment and rapid economic growth. Some time during the 1970s the phrase 'supply-side economics' emerged. The supply-siders argued that demand management at the macro level was relatively ineffective. What was needed was a policy at the micro level to improve the competitive efficiency of markets. In particular, attention was directed towards the labour market. Incentives could be improved, it was argued, both for those in work and those currently out of work.

12.7.1 Taxation and incentives

The supply-siders argued that high rates of income tax represented a disincentive to work effort. If taxes were reduced people would work harder and the economy would become more productive. Unemployment would also be reduced since those who had previously been discouraged from working by high marginal tax rates and had registered as unemployed would now re-enter employment.

To assess the validity of this analysis we need firstly to distinguish between the *marginal* rate of income tax and the *average* rate of income tax. The average tax rate is the proportion of total income paid in tax. The marginal tax rate is the proportion of any additional income paid in tax. For all taxpayers the marginal rate of tax is higher than the average rate of tax because of the presence of initial allowances and also because, for those on higher incomes, marginal tax rates rise as income rises. Marginal tax rates tend to receive more public attention and discussion than average tax rates simply because they are more apparent. Most people know what their marginal tax rate is. Relatively few will know what their average tax rate is.

Two groups of individuals are subject to high marginal tax rates – those on very high incomes and, paradoxically, those on very low incomes. For some people on low incomes it is now officially recognized that the marginal 'tax' rate effectively exceeds 100 per cent. This is because of the withdrawal of certain means-tested cash benefits which results when such people experience a small increase in pre-tax income. For such people a poverty trap exists because attempts to increase their income make them worse off. This is an unintended consequence of the tax and benefit system which is obviously undesirable but is difficult to avoid if a means-tested system of benefits is employed together with a tax system which extends downwards to encompass those on comparatively small incomes.

In contrast, the high marginal tax rate paid by those on high incomes is an intentional feature of any progressive tax system. Taxation is linked to ability to pay. When the Conservative Government took office in 1979 the top rate of income tax was 83 per cent (or 98 per cent if you include the investment income surcharge). In their first budget in June 1979 this was reduced to 60 per cent. This is now widely regarded as a sensible reduction since most of those on high money incomes were able to arrange their affairs so as to avoid such high rates of deduction.

Is there a distinctive effect which results from high taxes and, in particular, from high marginal rates of income tax? One cannot give a definitive answer to this question since the outcome depends on the strength of the so-called *income and substitution effects* which result from the change in relative prices brought about by the imposition of a tax. Taxes change the terms of the trade-off between labour and leisure, reducing the reward for a given amount of labour. Since leisure is pleasant and labour unpleasant it is argued that, at the margin, individuals will opt for more leisure since the opportunity cost of an hour spent in leisure has been reduced by taxation. Thus, the higher the marginal tax rate the greater the disincentive effect. This is known as the substitution effect since individuals substitute leisure for labour at the margin because of the change in relative prices.

One could equally well argue, of course, that taxes on income encourage rather than discourage work effort. Suppose one's objective is to secure a given amount of post-tax income. The higher the tax rate the higher the level of pre-tax income necessary to secure it. Thus the higher the tax rate the greater the incentive effect. This is called the income effect.

It is well known to economists that a change in relative prices (such as that produced by taxes) produces both a substitution effect and an income effect. *A priori*, one cannot say which of the two effects will be the stronger; therefore one cannot say with certainty what the effect of taxation will be on work effort and incentives. What one can say, in criticism of this approach, is that many people do not typically have the option of substituting labour for leisure at the margin since their hours of work are fixed. Moreover, it may not be correct to equate work effort with hours spent working. A more telling point is that pecuniary rewards, either pre-tax or post-tax, are not necessarily closely related to work effort.

Perhaps a more fundamental objection is that although most people are motivated by money to a greater or lesser extent, almost no one would claim that money is the only thing that motivates them in their work. Status, intellectual interest, contributing to the well-being of others, companionship and comradeship, meeting other people or simply 'getting out of the house' are all aspects of working which, for most people, provide an important incentive in addition to the pecuniary one. Moreover, these non-pecuniary incentives are obviously present to a greater degree for highly paid and therefore highly taxed workers like doctors and company executives than they are for low-paid workers on the factory floor.

For several years economists have tried to assess empirically whether taxes on income do have a disincentive effect. In principle there are two ways of finding an answer to this question. Either one can simply put the question to a sample of people in a questionnaire or an interview, or one can make inferences from past behaviour. The first method is open to the objection that people's behaviour and their perception of that behaviour do not necessarily coincide. What people say they do and what they actually do are two different things. More important, the researcher can perhaps unwittingly slant the question he asks in such a way as to elicit the answer he wishes to receive. It is very difficult not to 'lead' the interviewee into a particular response, no matter how objective and unbiased the interviewer tries to be. For example, suppose a group of company executives were asked the following questions:

1. Does the fact that you pay high marginal tax rates discourage you from working longer hours or from taking a more stressful but better paid job?

or

2. Does the fact that you pay high marginal tax rates mean that you don't put as much effort into your job as you could do?

Although the two questions are trying to shed light on the same basic issue, namely whether or not taxes have a disincentive effect, respondants are more likely to reply 'No' to the second question than to the first.

An alternative method is to make inferences from past behaviour by applying statistical techniques to macroeconomic data. Although this method is more 'objective' in the sense that it uses data derived from what people have actually done as opposed to what they say they would do, it suffers from the usual objection that it is difficult to prove or disprove any proposition in the social sciences by statistical means. Statistical studies in this area have often been built around the Laffer curve, a relationship noted by the American economist Art Laffer. In the folklore of economics Laffer is said to have drawn the relationship shown here as Fig. 12.3 on the back of a cigarette packet. He observed that total revenue from income taxes would be zero if the tax rate was zero, but tax revenue would also be zero if tax rates were 100 per cent since in this case there would be no incentive for people to work (for money income) and hence the tax base would be zero. He further pointed out that there must be some relationship joining these two points. Attempts have been made to estimate this relationship since its shape tells us something about the disincentive effect of taxation.

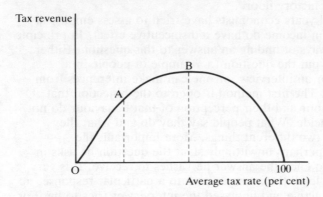

Fig. 12.3

Up to point A in Fig. 12.3 tax revenue increases proportionately with the tax rate. We can interpret this as implying that there is no disincentive effect up to this point. Between point A and point B there is evidence of a disincentive effect since tax revenue increases less than proportionately with the tax rate. Beyond point B further increases in the tax rate succeed only in reducing tax revenue which indicates a very pronounced disincentive effect. In this range the substitution effect dominates the income effect.

Clearly it would not make sense to operate the economy beyond point B. What is perhaps less clear is that the peak of the curve at B is an optimum only if the objective is to maximize tax revenue. Furthermore, it is not necessarily true that the economy should never be operated beyond point A. Indeed one might be prepared to put up with a small disincentive effect and trade this off against the benefits to be derived from higher tax revenue.

The crucial question regarding the Laffer curve, however, is whether the data supports the hypothesis that the relationship between tax revenue and tax rates is similar to the one illustrated in Fig. 12.3. In other words, is the relationship linear (as it is up to point A) or is it non-linear (as it is beyond point A). A linear relationship suggests there is no disincentive effect whereas a non-linear relationship suggests there is. The evidence appears inconclusive. While some researchers[1] claim to have found evidence of non-linearity, the present author found that data for the UK economy for the period 1972–85 was consistent only with a linear relationship between the average tax rate and tax revenue. There was no statistically significant evidence of non-linearity.

12.7.2 Taxation and incentives: policy implications

The policy implications of the above analysis are not as straightforward as might at first have been supposed. In practice, policy makers have a number of objectives, one of which is concerned with the distribution of income (though the Conservative Government in Britain has given this low priority). The tax instrument affects the amount of tax revenue raised and therefore, *ceteris paribus*, affects the amount of public expenditure which can be undertaken. But the way the tax instrument is wielded also affects the distribution of income. It may also, if there are disincentive effects, affect the level of that income and output. It follows therefore that a policy which may produce a small stimulus to output at the cost of a relatively major shift in the distribution of income away from the poorer section of society is not necessarily a preferred policy. There may be a trade-off between the twin objectives of what we might call economic efficiency (maximizing output) and economic equality (the distribution of income.) The hypothesis that such a trade-off exists is, however, based on the notion that taxation in some sense has a deadening effect on incentives and that income and output would be increased if taxation were to be reduced.

We have to be careful to distinguish here between two quite distinct ideas. One is the notion that output would be increased if taxation in general were to be reduced. The other is that output would be increased if the balance of taxation were shifted from direct to indirect taxation. Direct taxes are taxes on earnings, such as income tax and National Insurance contributions. Indirect taxes are taxes on spending, such as value added tax, customs and excise duties and other specific taxes such as car tax. The argument that

Table 12.1 Percentage of total taxation derived from various sources

	1977	1982
Taxes on persons		
Direct taxes	36	30
Social Security contributions	19	17
	55	47
Indirect taxes	38	43
Taxes on companies	6	10

Source: 'International comparisons of taxes and social security
         contributions in 20 OECD countries 1972–1982; *Economic*
         Trends, February 1985, No. 376.

taxation reduces incentives relates of course only to direct taxes.
Taxes on expenditure cannot have a disincentive effect on work
effort and therefore if the burden of taxation is shifted to indirect
taxation this should, it is argued, reduce the overall disincentive
effect of taxation. The Conservative Government which took office
in Britain in 1979 brought about a significant shift in the balance of
personal taxation as Table 12.1 shows. As a result of the 1979
Budget the share of tax revenue obtained from indirect taxes
jumped from about 38 per cent to 43 per cent, since when it has
remained fairly constant.

Unfortunately indirect taxes tend to be regressive in the sense
that people on low incomes pay a larger proportion of their income
in tax than people on high incomes. This results from the fact that
people on low incomes spend proportionately more of their
incomes on highly taxed items such as tobacco. Even before the
balance of taxation shifted towards indirect taxation a number of
studies had shown that the weak progressivity of the direct tax
system is offset almost completely by the regressivity of the
indirect tax system. The net effect of the tax system in the United
Kingdom is to leave the distribution of post-tax incomes more or
less unchanged. It is only the system of cash payments (such as
social security benefit) and income-in-kind (such as free school
meals) which leads to any substantial redistribution of income.
Table 12.2 gives illustrative data for the United Kingdom for 1979
and 1983 which gives some indication of the potential redistributive
effect of direct taxes, indirect taxes, cash benefits and benefits in
kind.

Table 12.2 Taxes and benefits as percentage of household income by quintile group of households

	1979	1983
Income tax and NI contributions as a percent of gross income		
Bottom quintile group	—	—
2nd quintile group	10	9
3rd quintile group	18	18
4th quintile group	19	21
top quintile group	21	23
Indirect taxes as a percent of disposable income		
Bottom quintile group	23	27
2nd quintile group	25	29
3rd quintile group	25	28
4th quintile group	24	25
top quintile group	21	23
Cash benefits as a percent of gross income		
Bottom quintile group	92	96
2nd quintile group	33	47
3rd quintile group	9	14
4th quintile group	5	7
top quintile group	3	3
Benefits in kind as a percent of final income		
Bottom quintile group	35	37
2nd quintile group	27	28
3rd quintile group	23	24
4th quintile group	17	18
top quintile group	12	12

Source: The effect of taxes and benefits on household income, 1983, *Economic Trends*, December 1984.

12.7.3 Incentives for the out-of-work

Although the social security system is the most effective way of redistributing income it is argued that an unfortunate side-effect is to produce disincentives for those currently out of work. In Britain the two major elements of the income-maintenance programme for those of working age (other than the chronically sick and disabled) are unemployment benefit and social security benefit. The objective of these cash payments is to raise the incomes of those out of work to some minimum acceptable level. The advocates of supply-side economics argue, however, that such payments have an undesirable effect on the labour market since they lead people to choose longer spells out of work than would otherwise be the case. Rather than being forced to accept the first low-paid job that comes along the unemployed can be more discerning and can afford to spend longer periods looking for more attractive jobs. As already noted, the fact that those who qualify for social security benefit also qualify for other means-tested benefits (such as free school meals) creates a poverty trap. Those previously unemployed who take a low paid job can find themselves worse off in employment than they were when unemployed. It is argued that a relatively generous income-maintenance programme will lead to higher recorded unemployment levels. In terms of what has been said earlier, the natural level of unemployment will be higher, the higher is the level of social security and unemployment benefits relative to wages. If one's only objective is to reduce recorded unemployment it therefore follows that a policy which makes it less attractive to be unemployed (such as cutting unemployment benefit) will, *ceteris paribus*, reduce recorded unemployment. Such a policy, however, conflicts directly with the purpose of the income maintenance programme, which is to provide a safety-net for those whose incomes would otherwise be unacceptably low. Such a policy may also bring about a reduction in recorded unemployment without bringing any 'real' change in unemployment levels. This takes us back to the point we made in section 9.1 that the official statistics may underestimate the 'true' level of unemployment.

12.7.4 *Making the labour market work better*

In addition to increasing the incentive to work, supply side policies aim to remove the rigidities in the labour market which prevent it operating like the neo-classical model. In this model prices adjust rapidly so as to equate demand and supply. The market clears. There is no stickiness. Economic agents respond to price signals and information is costless.

Whether the labour market could ever operate like the neo-classical model is open to question. What is certain is that supply-siders believe that the existence of trade unions can introduce rigidities which hinder the smooth operation of market forces. They therefore advocate that measures should be taken to curb the power of the trade unions. Advocates of supply side policies also call for further legislation to change the institutional framework within which the labour market operates. For example, various statutes enacted in the past to protect employees from unfair dismissal and to provide compensation for redundancy may now have the effect of discouraging potential employers from taking on new workers because the cost of dismissing such workers, once hired, is so high. The repeal of such statutes, it is argued, would increase the willingness of employers to recruit new workers. Supply-siders also advocate the abolition of Wages Councils which were established to raise wages in the lowest-paid occupations. These Wages Councils, it is argued, keep wages artificially high and therefore reduce the level of employment in such occupations.

Notes

1. See for example: Beenstock M., 'Taxation and incentives in the UK', *Lloyds Bank Review*, October 1979 Number 134. Beenstock, however, used total tax revenue rather than revenue from direct taxes or revenue from direct personal taxes. My estimate, using NIESR data, related revenue from direct personal taxes to the average tax rate. The estimated equations were:

$$REV = 13.1 + 285.3T \quad R^2 = 0.625$$
$$(2.4) \quad (9.2)$$

$$REV = -18.2 + 638.3T - 982.3T^2 \quad R^2 = 0.620$$
$$(-0.3) \quad (1.1) \quad (-0.6)$$

The fact that the coefficient on T^2 is statistically insignificant suggests a linear relationship rather than a non linear one.

Questions

1. Which of the following statements best describes the concept of 'rationality' embodied in rational expectations:

   (a) Economic agents always forecast the future correctly.
   (b) People anticipate future events. On average their expectations are correct.
   (c) Economic agents base their expectations of the future on past events.
   (d) People's expectations of price inflation next year are correct.

2. Suppose it could be shown that the relationship between tax revenue and the average (direct personal) tax rate was non-linear (as it is between points A and B in Fig. 12.3). Which of the following are necessarily true:

   (a) This is evidence that taxes have a disincentive effect.
   (b) If tax rates were lowered tax revenue would rise.
   (c) If tax rates were lowered tax revenue would fall.

3. Classify the following taxes into direct or indirect tax:

    (a) Income tax.
    (b) Capital gains tax.
    (c) Value added tax.
    (d) Vehicle excise duty.
    (e) Local authority rates.

4. Table 12.2 shows the impact on various income groups of indirect taxes, direct taxes, cash benefits and benefits in kind. Which of these four measures is the most regressive and which is the most progressive?

5. Which of the following are valid arguments for not making the tax system more progressive:

    (a) It will encourage the growth of the black economy.
    (b) People have already reached the limit of their taxable capacity.
    (c) It will further encourage evasion.
    (d) People are more aware of income taxes than they are of taxes on spending. Therefore they resent them more.

6. The following measures were all listed under the heading 'Helping markets work better' in the *Economic Progress Report*, December 1985:

    (a) Reduction in National Insurance Contributions for low paid workers.
    (b) Increase in income tax personal allowances (i.e. that part of income which is free of tax).
    (c) Reform/abolition of Wages Councils.
    (d) New trade union laws (e.g. 'secondary picketing' can now be subject to civil action in the courts).
    (e) The Youth Training Scheme.
    (f) Ending of monopoly in certain services (e.g. opticians' supply of spectacles, solicitors' near monopoly of conveyancing).

Explain the rationale for each of these measures and appraise their impact.

Chapter 13
The formulation and implementation of economic policies

13.1 The objectives of macroeconomic policy

In the preceding chapters we have discussed in detail the major objectives of macroeconomic policy. The primary objective of the policy maker must be to ensure a standard of living for all citizens that is as high as possible, both now and in the future. This overriding objective, which is necessarily somewhat vague, can be made more precise and operational by expressing it in the following form:
1. The rate of growth of real output should be as high as possible.
2. The rate of inflation should be as low as possible.
3. The level of unemployment should be as low as possible.
4. Balance of payments deficits should not be allowed to become so large that they make other objectives more difficult to achieve.

Not everyone would agree with the way in which these four objectives have been specified, nor the way in which they have been ranked, but there would be general agreement that, when we are considering inflation for example, less is better than more; and that when we are considering economic growth, more is better than less. To these four major macroeconomic objectives we could add many others: to achieve a reduction in regional disparities in income and employment; to ensure that the standard of the public services – education, health and so on – is as high as possible; to achieve an acceptable distribution of real income amongst the members of society, and so on.

13.2 The balance between public and private spending

To a large extent, however, political opinions colour one's attitudes towards these issues. One of the major areas of disagreement between left and right wing parties is the balance between public and private spending. This is a disagreement both about ends and about the means by which these ends should be achieved.

In as much as a high level of consumption of, for example, health care and education is accepted as a desirable end, the dispute between the parties is about the means by which that high level of consumption should be brought about – should these services be provided publicly or should the individual purchase them for himself. But in as much as the high level of public expenditure determines the degree of influence of the State on the lives of its citizens, the debate over the extent to which the State should provide these services is also a debate about the desirability of increased public expenditure as an end in itself.

The public provision of these services is also an egalitarian measure, however, providing income in kind for all members of society and therefore leading to a more equal distribution of real income. Increased public expenditure on these services will therefore tend to find more support from those who advocate a more equal distribution of income. In this sense increased public expenditure is a means towards the end of a greater equality, and in this case there is disagreement as to the desirability of that end.

13.3 Conflicts in objectives

As we saw earlier, each of the four major objectives mentioned in section 13.1 – economic growth, the control of inflation and employment, and the avoidance of balance of payments deficits – would be more or less universally accepted as desirable when considered separately. The problem is that these four objectives are often in conflict so that an improvement in one of them can only be achieved at the expense of one or more of the others. For example, a reduction in unemployment can normally be achieved by stimulating aggregate demand (for example, by cutting income tax). But this same increase in aggregate demand will also increase the demand for imports and thus may lead to a trade deficit. Moreover, any increase in aggregate demand will increase demand-inflationary pressures and may increase the rate of inflation. Similarly, measures which are taken to remove a trade deficit, such as domestic deflation and high interest rates, may have an adverse long-term effect on economic growth since they discourage investment.

13.4 The instruments of economic policy

Faced with these (often conflicting) objectives, the policy maker has a variety of instruments available. These can be classified as either fiscal or monetary or direct controls. Fiscal policy, which emanates from the Treasury and is normally the subject of the annual Budget, consists of changes in taxation (of all forms) and in all forms of public spending. Monetary policy, which emanates from the Bank of England, which is a separate institution from the Treasury, consists of changes in interest rates and in the growth of the money supply. The term 'direct controls' covers the remaining policy instruments; for example, direct controls on wages or import controls.

13.5 Targets and instruments

Each of the instruments which the policy maker has at his disposal will have an impact on several of the objectives, or target variables as we shall call them. For example, an increase in public spending may reduce unemployment, but at the same time it may increase imports and the rate of inflation. The pressure on the balance of payments can be eased by using a second instrument, such as raising interest rates, to encourage an inflow of short term capital. This, however, may discourage firms from investing, in which case a third instrument, such as a tax-cut, may be required to boost demand for domestic output, and so encourage investment.

Clearly the macroeconomy that we are dealing with is a very complex set of inter-relationships between variables. We could say that ultimately a change in any one of our instrument variables will affect all the other variables in the system. An economic policy can be defined as a set of changes (many of them zero) in all of the instruments that the policy maker has at his disposal. The question is, how should the policy maker go about formulating an economic policy so as to bring about the best possible outcome in the economy of which he has charge?

13.6 Constructing an economic model

There are several stages in the formulation of an economic policy. The first stage, and the essential prerequisite, is to have some idea about the way the economy works. These ideas can be formalized in terms of an economic model which will take the form of a set of equations which describe the inter-relationships between the variables in the system. These interrelationships can be visually represented by means of a flow-chart such as that shown in Fig. 13.1, where the direction of the arrows between the boxes represents the direction of causation between variables. For example, the exchange rate affects import prices, which, in turn, affect the volume of imports. This, in turn, affects the current trade balance. Import prices are also affected by foreign prices and by the overall domestic price index and so on. It may be

FLOW CHART OF THE TREASURY

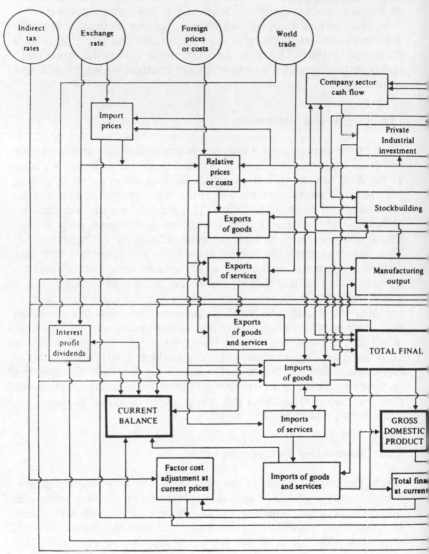

Source: *H.M. Treasury Macroeconomic Model Technical Manual*, 1978

Fig. 13.1 Flow chart of the Treasury macroeconomic model
Source: *HM Treasury Macroeconomic Model Technical Manual*, 1978

MACROECONOMIC MODEL

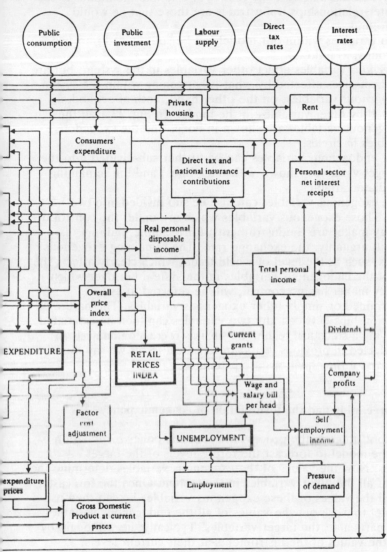

instructive at this stage for the reader to examine the model to see if the inter-relationships it illustrates are those that he would expect to find.

The variables within our model can be sub-divided into two main groups, as follows:

1. *Exogenous* variables affect other variables in the system, but are not themselves affected by what is happening within the system.
2. *Endogenous* variables, on the other hand, both affect and are affected by other variables in the model. In Fig. 13.1 all the endogenous variables are shown in boxes and the exogenous variables in circles.

The endogenous variables can be further sub-divided into the main target variables (shown with thick lines) and the remaining intermediate variables.

The exogenous variables can also be sub-divided into two subsets. Those exogenous variables which are under the control of the policy maker are the instruments; for example, indirect tax rates and, arguably, the exchange rate. The remaining exogenous variables, such as the level of world trade, which clearly affects the values of the endogenous variables in the system but over which the policy maker has no control, will be referred to as predetermined or simply other exogenous variables. The nature of the relationships between any two variables can then be estimated by applying a statistical technique such as regression analysis to data collected in previous years. In technical terms we say that the parameters of the equations are estimated.

13.7 Forecasting and the formulation of economic policy

The second stage in the process of economic policy formulation is to use the model to forecast the future levels of the target variables. Now the values of the exogenous variables determine the values of all the other variables in the system. Once the forecaster has fixed the values of these exogenous variables he can then use the model to work out the values of all the endogenous variables and, in particular, the target variables. Typically, he will begin by setting the values of the instruments at their current levels, (indicating no change in policy). The predetermined or other exogenous variables will have to be forecast separately, or some other forecast of their values used.

The process of policy formulation starts with this initial forecast. The forecast values of the target variables represent the forecaster's best estimate of what is likely to happen in the economy in, say, twelve months' time, if current policies are unchanged. The values of the target variables are inspected and if, as usually happens, they appear unsatisfactory in the sense that, for example, the predicted rate of inflation is higher than we would like it to be, then the model is used to investigate the probable effects of changing one or more of the instruments. For example, the effect of reducing income tax by three pence in the pound can be predicted by setting the tax rate at this new lower level, while leaving all the other exogenous variables unchanged, and using the model to predict the new levels of the target variables. Normally, some of the targets will be better and some worse than previously.

In this way a series of laboratory experiments or simulations can be conducted, whose purpose is to investigate the effects on the targets of changes in our instruments. Since, in the real macroeconomy, experimentation is impractical and controlled experimentation is impossible, these simulations, made possible by advances in statistical techniques, but more importantly by the advent of the computer, fulfil a vital role. To quote from the Treasury itself: *'The Treasury model is used extensively for estimating the effects of possible policy changes: along with forecasting, this is the model's major use.'*[1]

Several different policies can be tried out by conducting several simulation exercises. In this way the policy maker can find out which policies produce an acceptable set of solution values for the target variables. Several acceptable sets will probably present themselves and the policy maker can then pick what he regards as the 'best' solution.

It should be made clear that the simulation exercises themselves cannot tell the policy maker what is the 'best' attainable set of solution values and it therefore cannot tell him what is the 'best' policy to pursue. To see the reason for this, consider the hypothetical forecast outcomes of two policies A and B, where A involves a lower level of public spending than B. The results are shown in Table 13.1.

Clearly one cannot say that A produces a better result than B

Table 13.1

| | State of economy after 12 months – | |
	if policy A followed (lower public spending)	if policy B followed (higher public spending)
Growth	2%	2½%
Inflation	4%	10%
Unemployment	2.8 m.	1 m.
Trade balance (12 month total)	deficit of £1 bn	deficit of £3 bn

or that B produces a better result than A. Only if one specifies the relative importance which one attaches to the various objectives can one begin to talk of one policy being superior to another. For example, if one decided that the overriding objective was to maximize the rate of growth, then B is apparently more effective in achieving this. Things may not be quite as simple as they appear, however, since the effect of B *may* be to produce a lower rate of growth in the long term than A. Suppose, in this hypothetical example, that the forecasted state of the economy after thirty months was as shown in Table 13.2.

Table 13.2

	State of economy after 30 months –	
	if policy A followed (lower public spending)	if policy B followed (higher public spending)
Growth	2.2%	2%
Inflation	4%	8%
Unemployment	2.7 m.	2.1 m.
Trade balance	surplus of £1 bn	deficit of £3 bn

The policy maker then has to choose between a policy which produces relatively rapid growth for a short time but at high cost in terms of inflation and the balance of trade (policy B) and a policy which produces a higher rate of sustained growth but at a high cost in terms of unemployment (policy A). Thus the policy maker not only has to decide on his priorities but also on his time preferences. The policy maker's time horizon may be relatively short, particularly when faced with a general election. Myopia, it is said, is the price we pay for democracy.

13.8 The implementation of economic policy

Let us assume that, for whatever reason, the policy maker has decided upon his best policy. The implementation of this policy then involves setting the values of his instruments at the levels that the simulation indicates are required. This may or may not be straightforward but, in any event, it will take some time to achieve. Particular difficulties may be experienced if a reduction in public spending is called for.

The actual outcome of the chosen policy in the real world will not, of course, be exactly the same as the predicted outcome in the simulation exercises. In other words, the forecasts will be wrong.

Of this the forecaster can be certain. The only thing he is uncertain about is by how much they will be wrong, and in what direction.

There are various reasons why the actual outcome will not be the same as the predicted outcome. Many of these are what we could call errors of technique. For example, the parameters of the model – the numbers in the equations – may have been incorrectly estimated either because of poor statistical technique or because of inaccurate data used in the estimation procedure. Worse still, the structure of the model may be wrong. For example, the model may be constructed around a basically Keynesian paradigm whereas a monetarist paradigm may be more appropriate. Finally, since forecasting is not a completely mechanistic procedure, it involves the exercise of judgement which may, at times, be faulty.

Apart from these errors of technique there remain more fundamental reasons why the actual outcome will not be the same as the predicted outcome. First, the economy of the real world is subject to random shocks which cannot be predicted. Events such as war in the Middle East, a dock strike or an exceptionally hard winter will all affect the target variables, and although it may be possible to assign probabilities to the occurrence of these events, this is of little practical value to the forecaster.

Second, there is a problem which lies at the heart of econometric forecasting – that of structural change. The equations embodied within the model represent a more or less accurate description of the supposed structural relationships which existed in the real world during the period in which we collected our data. There is no reason to suppose, however, that the structural relationships in the real world will continue to hold in that future period to which our forecast relates. Indeed, there is every reason to suppose that the parameters will change over time, sometimes quite rapidly, and this effectively removes the statistical justification from our forecasting procedure. For example, the propensity to save out of income may, for all practical purposes, have remained constant for a long period. Suppose that, during this period, we collected data on savings and income and the constancy of the ratio between the two may have lulled us into a belief that our 'law' of savings behaviour, which we had 'discovered', was true for all time. But, unlike the laws of physics, the relationships between variables in the social world are not immutable, so that the forecasting process which implicitly assumes a constancy in social behaviour is based on shaky foundations.

13.9 The accuracy of economic forecasts

In Britain a number of economic forecasts are published on a regular basis. The Treasury is committed by Act of Parliament to publishing twice-yearly forecasts of all the major components of GDP, together with forecasts of retail prices and public sector borrowing. In addition, it publishes an economic commentary on the recent past and the prospects, as it sees them, for the next eighteen months. The National Institute for Economic and Social Research (NIESR) publishes quarterly forecasts and analyses of a similar nature. The computer model on which the National Institute forecasts are based is described as being in the Keynesian tradition. In contrast, the London Business School model, from which regular forecasts are published, has been described as 'monetarist', though the reader should be aware that these two terms can have a rather wide interpretation. The Treasury model, which at one time could legitimately have been described as Keynesian, has recently followed fashion by attempting to incorporate more directly the influence of monetary variables within its structure.

All of these forecasts are called *short term* because they predict up to eighteen months ahead. Longer-term forecasts are published by the Cambridge Economic Policy Group. Their twice-yearly forecasts predict up to four years ahead. In addition to the above, a number of other organizations publish regular forecasts.

One question which immediately arises is, how accurate are such forecasts? Unfortunately, it is not possible to give a sensible answer to the question posed in this form since all forecasts are based on assumptions, which are rarely correct. The assumption most commonly adopted is that of unchanged policies. If a change does occur – for example, in the rate of income tax in the period to which the forecast relates – then, even if the *model* from which the forecast is derived is completely correct, the forecast will still turn out to be wrong. Rather than enquire into the accuracy of the forecasts themselves, therefore, it is more sensible to use the predictions to gauge the accuracy of the model from which these predictions were derived. An example will make this point clearer.

Imagine that the predicted rate of inflation for a particular year was 15 per cent, based on the assumption of unchanged policies. Suppose that in fact VAT is increased and, if the forecaster had incorporated this change into his simulation, his model would have predicted a rate of inflation of 20 per cent. If the actual rate of inflation turns out to be 15 per cent, what is the size of the error? Clearly there is no difference between forecast and out-turn, but this comparison is invalid because, if the correct assumption had been incorporated into the model, the error would have been 5 per cent, and this therefore is the true error.

Ideally this would be the way in which forecasters assessed the predictive accuracy of their models and this was what was envisaged in the Industry Act, 1975, which laid down guidelines for the Treasury to follow in assessing the accuracy of its predictions. Unfortunately, the Treasury chooses not to use this method. It states:

> *In principle, there are two ways (of assessing the accuracy of forecasting models). The first is to ask what would have been forecast if the correct assumptions on policy had been made: the answer is that nobody knows, because it is not possible to reassemble the people responsible for the original forecast, their technical apparatus and their state of mind at the time.*[2]

This statement seems unconvincing, particularly as, when it was written, the NIESR had already attempted such an exercise, which we shall consider presently. The Treasury continues:

> *The second way is to ask present day forecasters what the outcome would have been if the assumed policies (rather than the actual ones) had been carried out. With the aid of an econometric model, some kind of an answer can be provided.*

There appears to be little justification for this approach, other than the fact that it is easier to carry out than the first method. It is impossible to gauge the predictive accuracy of the Treasury's model, as it stood when the forecast was made, using this hybrid method. It is not clear what the question is to which 'some kind of an answer' is being provided. The interested reader is, however, referred to the Economic Progress Report, June 1981, in which this technique is used to measure forecasting errors in the Treasury.

13.10 Ex ante and ex post forecasts

Before we look at some estimates of the predictive accuracy of one particular econometric model, it will be useful to consider how the equations of such a model are estimated. Suppose, for illustrative purposes, that we wished to estimate an export function of the form:

$$X = a + bW \qquad [13.1]$$

where X is UK exports, W is world trade and a and b are the parameters of the equation – the numbers whose values we wish to estimate. In practice, an export function would be more complicated than this, since other explanatory variables apart from world trade – such as the exchange rate – would affect exports. The advantage of this simplified version, however, is that we can illustrate the relationship on a two-dimensional graph. Moreover, this export function can be treated independently of the rest of the model since here exports are a function of an exogenous variable only. It would not be so straightforward to deal with an import equation such as:

$$M = F(Yd) \qquad [13.2]$$

where M is imports and Yd is disposable income since both these variables are endogenous and hence both have to be forecast together, using the whole model rather than a single equation.

Suppose that we have a series of observations on UK exports and world trade as in Table 13.3 and Fig. 13.2. We have selected the period 1969–78 for expositional convenience. As we noted in Table 8.5, the world recession in 1980 causes world trade to decline and this makes it more difficult to see at a glance how the two variables are related. In fact, as we can see from Fig. 13.2 there is a relationship between the two variables which is approximately linear. Thus we can legitimately represent this relationship by a model of the form

$$X = a + bW \qquad [13.1 \text{ repeated}]$$

where the reader should note that we are using the term 'model' to refer to a single equation. However, we wish to know how good this model is and we will use predictive accuracy as an indicator of this. We can use the model to forecast the level of exports in 1978 and compare the forecasted value with the actual value – which in this example is known already.

We could use all of the data to estimate the relationship. The line which provides the best fit[3] to the set of points for 1969–78 is:

$$X = 5329 + 49.3\ W$$

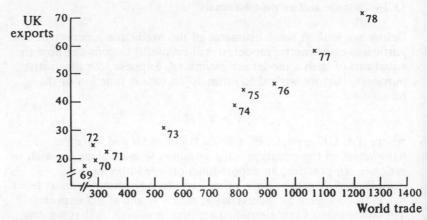

Fig. 13.2

Table 13.3

		X	W
	1969	17 614	257.1
X = UK exports	1970	19 351	294.6
(millions of US dollars)	1971	22 333	329.0
	1972	24 345	284.9
W = world trade	1973	30 659	534.9
(billions of US dollars)	1974	38 881	785.2
	1975	44 523	814.0
	1976	46 696	922.9
	1977	58 205	1 000.3
	1978	71 705	1 229.6

Source: *International Financial Statistics*

Such a model would underpredict the level of exports in 1978. In fact, the predicted or forecast level of exports in 1978 is:

$$5329 + 49.3 \ (1229.6) = 65 \ 948$$

The forecast error is therefore the actual level of exports in 1978 minus the predicted level:

$$71 \ 705 - 65 \ 948 = 5757$$

This is known as an *ex post* forecast error since the forecast was derived from a model, the parameters of which were estimated when the actual level of exports was already known.

By comparison, an *ex ante* forecast is one which predicts into the future using a model estimated from past data. In this example, if we left off the last observation and estimated the parameters using data for the period 1969–77 only, then the line which best fits this set of points is:

$$X = 7468 + 44.5 \ W$$

If we assume that the value of the exogenous variable is known, having been derived independently from some completely accurate forecasting procedure, we can plug this value into the equation and, therefore, the ex ante forecast of exports in 1978 is:

$$7468 + 44.5 \ (1229.6) = 62 \ 185$$

and the ex ante forecast error is:

$$71 \ 705 - 62 \ 185 = 9520$$

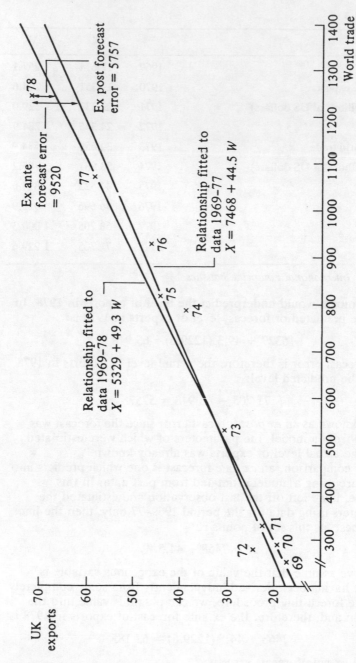

Fig. 13.3

This is illustrated in Fig. 13.3. Note that the inclusion of the observation for 1978 has the effect of rotating the fitted line slightly in an anti-clockwise direction. Note also that, as we would expect, the ex post forecast error is smaller than the ex ante forecast error. Since this is generally true, it is therefore very important, in assessing the accuracy of forecasts, to know whether ex post or ex ante forecasts are being discussed.

Finally, we should note that the ex ante forecast is *conditional* upon the value of the exogenous variable world trade. We assumed that the correct value of this was known. In practice, of course, when ex ante forecasts are made of the future, the exogenous variables themselves have to be forecast first and these forecasts will be subject to error. Thus, an ex ante forecast of exports will contain a total error which can be decomposed into two parts:
  (i) the error which results from the use of an incorrect value for the exogenous variable world trade; and
 (ii) the model error which still remains because the equation is not a perfect explanation of the behaviour of exports.

13.11 NIESR model errors, 1971–79

We have seen how it is possible to decompose total forecasting errors into their constituent parts. Such an exercise has been undertaken by the NIESR on its forecasting model and Table 11.4 gives an analysis of the results. The table relates to the forecast for the next twelve months made in February 1979.

The total forecasting error is broken down into four parts:
1. *Exogenous variable error.* This is explained in the previous section. It is the error which results when the value of a variable exogenous to the system is incorrect. Variables such as world trade and foreign interest rates are exogenous to the system but so too are instruments like tax rates.
2. *Model error.* This too is explained in the previous section.
3. *Residual adjustment.* Although the estimated equations do not fit the data exactly, on average they should neither systematically overpredict nor systematically underpredict. If such a fault develops over time, then the equation should be re-estimated to remove the bias. This may not be possible, however, and in this case a 'residual' is added on to the equation in forecasting to take the systematic error into account. In other words, the forecaster uses his judgement to slightly modify the forecast produced by the model. The residual adjustment shown in Table 13.4 consists of setting all of these judgemental adjustments back to zero.
4. *Data revision.* This takes account of the revisions to the published data on both endogenous and exogenous variables

Understanding the economy

Table 13.4 NIESR Feb. 1979 forecast: decomposition of forecast error

		1	2	3	4	5	6	7
					Composed of effects from			
Variable	Units of measurement	Feb. '79 forecast values	Actual values	Total error	Exogenous variable error	Model error	Residual adjustment	Data revision
GDP (output method)	index 1975 = 100	110.2	110.2	—	-0.6	5.3	-5.6	0.3
GDP (expenditure method)	£ m. 1975 prices	103 482	102 563	-919	-138	220	-1 328	328
Consumers' expenditure	£ m. 1975 prices	68 777	70 816	2 039	805	1 747	-898	384
Gross fixed investment	£ m. 1975 prices	20 835	20 506	-329	-496	-234	186	215
Stockbuilding	£ m. 1975 prices	11 390	11 610	220	94	680	-424	-130
General govt. consumption	£ m. 1975 prices	24 020	24 334	314	314	—	—	—
Exports	£ m. 1975 prices	33 713	32 896	-817	210	726	-1 570	-203
Imports	£ m. 1975 prices	33 430	35 250	1 820	965	1 853	-891	-107
Employment	thousands	22 232	22 269	37	44	36	-115	71
Unemployment	thousands	1 350	1 243	-107	-97	9	86	-105
Consumer prices	1975 = 100	158.0	162.1	4.1	1.9	2.0	-1.4	1.6
Money supply (M$_3$)	£ m.	57 497	59 411	1 914	3 863	42	-1 360	-631
PSFS	£ m.	-7 991	-8 344	-353	-1 322	1 656	-3 650	2 963
Visible balance	£ m.	95	-3 404	-3 499	-2 454	315	-1 189	-171
Effective exchange rate	May 1971 = 100	63.5	68.7	5.2	5.2	—	—	—

Source: National Institute Economic Review, Feb. 1981

which are frequently carried out in the period following the initial publication.

The total error to be explained (col. 3) is the difference between actual values (col. 2) and ex ante forecast values (col. 1). Apart from rounding errors cols. 4, 5, 6, and 7 sum to the total error in col. 3. Table 13.4 contains rather too much information to be easily assimilable, and the primary reason for its inclusion here is to illustrate how the total forecast error can be decomposed. A number of comments can, however, be made about the relationship between these components, the relative importance of which can be gauged by comparing the size of the errors (ignoring signs)in col. 4 to 7.

The exogenous variable error is large for quite a number of variables. Much of this is due to the 'unchanged policies' assumption under which the NIESR normally forecasts. Errors in forecasting the exogenous variables often have a 'knock-on' effect on some of the endogenous variables. For example, the underprediction for the exchange rate is partly responsible for the underprediction of consumption spending and spending on imports. The underprediction of imports in turn is the major cause of the error in the visible balance (the forecast was for a surplus on visible trade of about £0.1 bn, the outturn was a deficit of £3.4 bn).In short, an error in one of the exogenous variables can feed through into the rest of the system.

We now move on to consider just 'model error' and, rather than comment on this particular forecast, we will look at the average model errors over the period 1971–79. These are shown in Table 13.5, which compares actual values of the endogenous variables with values forecast by the model using zero residual adjustments and actual values of the exogenous variables over the forecast period.

The first part of the table gives the model errors for GDP and its components. Columns 1, 2 and 3 show various ways of measuring the size of the average errors. Since errors are calculated as 'actual minus predicted' a negative sign means an overprediction. Thus on average over the period the model overpredicted GDP by some £397 m., equivalent to about 0.3 per cent of GDP. However, in calculating a crude average, large negative errors can be offset by large positive ones, thus giving the impression that the model predicts much better than in fact it does; hence the inclusion of the average absolute error (where the *sign* of the error is ignored) in col. 3. Thus, for GDP the fairly large average absolute error relative to the average error is an indication that quarterly errors change sign fairly frequently, the model oscillating between overprediction and underprediction. By

Table 13.5 Dynamic model errors: 1971–79

Variable	Average error	Average percentage error	Average absolute error
Gross domestic product	− 397	− 0.3	1 579
Consumers' expenditure	+ 426	+ 0.6	820
Gross investment	− 274	− 1.4	347
Stockbuilding	+ 156	—	924
Exports of goods and services	+ 104	+ 0.3	771
Imports of goods and services	− 673	+ 1.9	1 144
Employment (000s)	− 42	− 0.2	142
Unemployment (000s)	+ 41	+ 3.8	133
Consumer price index	−0.3	− 0.1	1.2
Money supply (M3)	−1 484	− 2.9	1 813
Public sector financial surplus	+1 921	−57.3	2 279
Visible balance	+1 069	−60.4	1 614
Effective exchange rate	+4.4	+ 6.5	5.9

Units of measurement as for Table 11.4

Source: *National Institute Economic Review*, Feb. 1981, p. 28.

comparison, investment, which is also overpredicted, tends to be *consistently* overpredicted as evidenced by the rather small average absolute error relative to the average error and this can be considered a fault since it suggests statistical bias.

Exports are predicted reasonably accurately but imports tend to be underpredicted, particularly according to the NIESR, in 1978 and 1979. This explains most of the error in the visible balance which, in percentage terms, has a very large error. The balance of payments has traditionally been the most difficult thing to forecast accurately.

Most surprising is the very large percentage error on the public sector financial surplus, which is consistently overpredicted; that is, the public sector deficit turns out to be not as large as it is forecast to be. This is partly responsible for the overprediction of money supply growth.

13.12 Fine tuning

Our analysis so far has neglected one important aspect of economic policy, namely that the operation of such policies is subject to long and variable time lags. The existence of these lags, which are difficult to judge precisely, could mean that a policy designed to stabilize the level of demand could end up by producing a destabilizing effect on the economy.

Suppose, for illustrative purposes, that demand is subject to fluctuations over time, as in Fig. 13.4. In the real world these cycles in economic activity are irregular in both duration and in severity but, for the purpose of illustration, we have assumed that they are reasonably regular around a rising trend, which indicates the growth path of the economy.

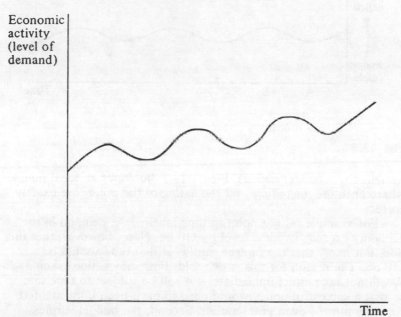

Economic activity (level of demand)

Time

Fig. 13.4

In the absence of any attempt by the authorities at smoothing out the fluctuations the peaks of the cycle will be characterized by the economy 'overheating', leading to shortages of labour and capital and to inflation; and the trough of the cycle will be characterized by rising unemployment, falling profits and falling output. Clearly a successful demand management policy would *reduce* the level of demand during the peaks of the cycle (by engineering a budget surplus) and *increase* demand during the

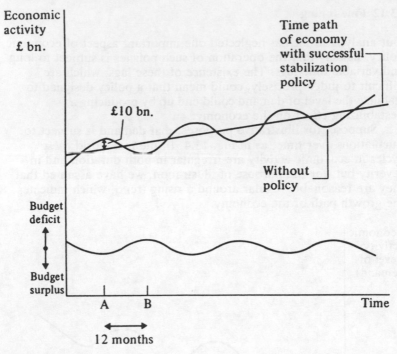

Fig. 13.5

troughs (by a budget deficit). Figure 13.5 illustrates an ideal policy where both the *magnitude* and the *timing* of the policy are exactly correct.

For example, at the point in time labelled A, demand in the economy exceeds its ideal level by £10 bn. Note, however, that this does not imply that the budget surplus at that time should be £10 bn. The reason for this is two-fold. First, any action taken at A will not take effect immediately; it will be subject to time lags, so that a successful policy would need to have been implemented some months or even years earlier. Second, the budget surplus would not have to be exactly £10 bn., because any fiscal policy would be subject to a multiplier effect, the exact size of which may be difficult to estimate. Both these problems emphasize the vital necessity of constructing forecasting models which accurately reflect the way the economy works.

Suppose, however, that the policy is mis-timed even though its magnitude is correct. In the worst possible case, deflationary policies taken at A do not have their full effect on the economy until, say, twelve months later at point B. Here the boom has already passed and the economy is in the trough of a recession, so

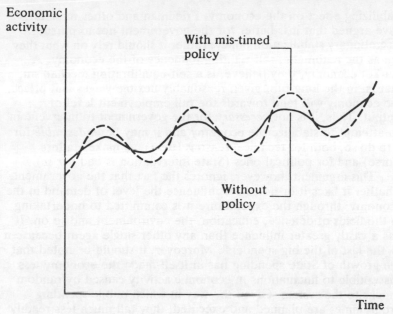

Fig. 13.6

that further deflationary policies just make matters worse. In this extreme case, illustrated in Fig. 13.6, the fluctuations in economic activity are made worse by the ill-timed stabilization policy of the Government.

Because it is, in theory, possible that the existence of these long and variable time lags could make stabilization policy operate in a perverse manner, some economists have argued that the government should not attempt to 'fine tune' the economy. Consider the analogy with a shower. Your objective, when standing in the shower, is to get the water temperature just right. There are two instruments available, a hot tap and a cold tap, both of which are subject to long and variable time lags. If the water is slightly too cold, you may be tempted to turn on the hot tap a little more, but when you do this, at first nothing seems to happen, so you turn it on a lot more. Then suddenly the shower is far too hot, so you turn off the hot tap and turn on the cold tap and this makes it much too cold. Your intervention has made matters worse rather than better because you did not fully appreciate the long and variable time lags involved in your actions.

In short, when the government tries to fine tune the economy, there are difficult technical problems of timing and magnitude which may result in the policy having a destabilizing rather than a stabilizing effect on the economy. Friedman and other monetarists have argued that it is better for the government not to pursue discretionary stabilization policy; rather it should rely on what they see as the automatic, self-righting tendency of the economy. A market economy, they believe, is a self-equilibrating mechanism; that is, in the long run, given reasonably flexible wages and prices, the economy will tend towards the full-employment level of output. Thus, it is not *necessary* for the government to intervene in an attempt to stabilize the economy and it may be *undesirable* for it to do so, both for technical reasons (they may make matters worse) and for political ones (State intervention is bad *per se*).

This argument, however, ignores the fact that the government, whether it likes it or not, *does* influence the level of demand in the economy, through the expenditure it is committed to undertaking in the fields of defence, education, the environment and so on. It has a vastly greater influence than any other single agent because it is 'the last of the big spenders'. Moreover, it should be noted that the growth of State spending has in itself made the economy less susceptible to fluctuations in economic activity caused by random shocks to the system. Given the way in which public spending programmes are planned and executed, they fall much less readily in a recession than, for example, investment spending by private firms. This tends to damp down fluctuations. Some spending may even act in a counter-cyclical way, since social security and unemployment benefits, for example, tend to rise in a recession and fall in a boom, acting as a sort of automatic stabilizer. Britain in the 1980s, an economy with a large public sector, thus tends to be more robust than in the 1920s and 1930s.

However, given that, as we have seen, the government does exert a great influence on the level of economic activity it follows that it is a powerful influence for good or evil. The idea that the economy is self-righting is quite untenable when one-third of economic activity (more or less depending upon how you define it) is controlled directly or indirectly by government. Thus, although one can admit the difficulties of fine tuning and perhaps the undesirability of attempting to do so, ultimately the government cannot abrogate its responsibility for controlling the economy.

13.13 Forecasting and control

In the public imagination economic forecasters used to occupy the same sort of position as weather forecasters. No one believed either of them and their forecasts were treated with a sort of grim amusement. In recent years, however, photographs of weather systems taken by satellites have given meteorologists a perspective on their study which has enormously improved their forecasting and their knowledge about what determines the weather. Sadly, economic forecasters have still to find this perspective, and given the nature of their study it is unlikely that they ever will.

In comparison with weather forecasters, economic forecasters suffer two major drawbacks. First, they are dealing with a *social* system, the laws of which are subject to change, unlike the laws of nature that determine the weather which are immutable. Second, weather forecasts do not in themselves affect the weather. If storms are predicted, this may cause people to take their umbrellas when they go out, but this in itself does not increase the probability of rain. In the economy, however, the outturn is not independent of the forecast, because forecasts affect people's behaviour. Thus, if high rates of inflation are predicted, this may cause individuals to reduce their stocks of money by purchasing goods and other assets, which in turn may affect their price. Similarly, business confidence and hence the level of corporate investment may be affected by the publication of surveys of companies' investment intentions. In short, forecasts can have an impact on events in the economy.

While this may be seen as a disadvantage which the economic forecaster has *vis-à-vis* the meteorologist, it also provides the most important reason for continuing to strive to understand the economy. For if he understands the way the economy works, the economist can *control* it. The meteorologist, no matter how good his understanding, can never affect the weather – he can never make the sun shine nor the rains come. But the economist can, if he is successful, improve employment prospects, reduce inflation and improve living standards. He can, in short, make a better world. Or, if he is misguided or incompetent, a worse one.

Notes

1. Economic Progress Report, June 1981, p. 2.
2. Economic Progress Report, June 1981, p. 3.
3. Using Ordinary Least Squares regression. This technique fits a line such that the sum of the squared differences between the actual export levels and predicted export levels is minimized.

Questions

1. Here is a list of variables which enter into most macroeconomic models. Classify them into:

    Exogenous   – instruments (controlled by policy-makers)
                       – pre-determined (not controlled by policy-makers).
    Endogenous – targets
                       – other endogenous.

But beware: controversy exists as to how certain of these variables should be classified.

(a) indirect tax rates;
(b) revenue from direct taxes;
(c) the exchange rate;
(d) the price index;
(e) import prices;
(f) world trade;
(g) interest rates;
(h) government spending;
(i) the labour supply;
(j) the money supply.

2. Below are listed four macroeconomic variables which are all related. Draw a diagram to show how they are related (similar to Fig. 13.1) with arrows indicating the direction of causation. Hint: you will need four arrows in your diagram.

(a) Exchange rate (sterling/dollar).
(b) Import prices in sterling.
(c) Consumer price index.
(d) Foreign prices and costs in dollars.

3. What are the four sources of forecast error? Explain what each of them means. Use the data in Table 4.3 to illustrate the size of the error that could result from data revision.

Appendix A
The tools of demand and supply

This appendix is designed to provide the reader with an elementary understanding of the microeconomic theory of value, or what is usually known as the laws of demand and supply. These form part, undoubtedly the most basic part, of the economist's analytical apparatus – the 'bag of tools' which he uses to interpret economic events taking place in the real world. Any student who has successfully completed an introductory course in microeconomics will already be familiar with these concepts.

A.1 Demand

We can illustrate the concepts of demand and supply in the context of the market for a particular good or commodity. The 'market' that we are talking about here need not have any physical existence in space or time (although some markets such as the stock market do possess these attributes), but in general the word market refers to the totality of buyers and sellers, both actual and potential, of a particular good or commodity. Thus, we could talk about the housing market, the market for cars, for shoes, for wine and so on. We shall illustrate the concepts of demand and supply in the context of the market for video cassette recorders. Although it is obvious that there are different brands of these machines, some makes being more expensive than others, and there being a variety of different specifications, we will make the not unreasonable assumption that they are all sufficiently similar to be treated as the same commodity. That is, we will assume that they are *homogeneous*.

It seems intrinsically obvious that the demand for video cassette recorders will be inversely related to the price of them – that is, the lower the price the larger the number of people willing to buy, and conversely, the higher the price the more people will be discouraged from buying. Other factors will also affect the demand for video cassette recorders, such as the extent to which they are promoted by advertising, the extent to which finance companies are willing to provide loans for their purchase, and so on. For the moment let us imagine that all these other factors can be held constant – this is the so-called *ceteris paribus* assumption. We can then study the relationship between the demand for video cassette recorders and their price in isolation. Such a relationship, if it were plotted on a graph, might look like that in Fig. A.1. If the selling price were very high, say £900, then few people would be prepared to buy them – so sales would be only 5000 sets per month in our example. But, if the price were to drop to, say, £500, then sales would rise to, say, 20 000 sets; and if the price were to fall further to £300, then sales of 50 000 sets a month would occur.

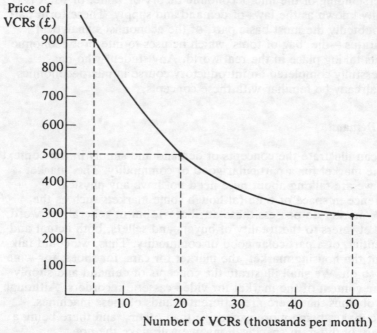

Fig. A.1

The demand curve (or demand schedule) shown in Fig. A.1 is of course, only illustrative, but it demonstrates the fundamental axiom that in the market for any commodity, if all other factors are held constant, then demand will be inversely related to price – the higher the price the less will be the demand and so on.

A.2 Price elasticity of demand

If we continue to assume that all the other factors which affect the demand for video cassette recorders remain fixed, we can then proceed to consider the question 'How sensitive is the demand for video cassette recorders to price changes?' For example, would a fall in the price of video cassette recorders of, say, 10 per cent lead to an increase in the demand for them of 5 per cent, 10 per cent or 20 per cent?

Economists use the term *elasticity* to describe the responsiveness of one variable (in this case demand) to another variable (in this case price). Thus, we can define what we call the price elasticity of demand, whose numerical value describes the degree of responsiveness of demand to changes in price. Price elasticity of demand (E_D) is defined as:

$$E_D = - \frac{\% \text{ change in quantity demanded}}{\% \text{ change in price}}$$

This number will vary between zero and infinity. We can identify three ranges, as follows:—

less than 1   – inelastic. That is, not very responsive to price changes.
         1 – unit elasticity.
greater than 1 – elastic. That is, very responsive to price changes.

For example, if a 10 per cent fall in price leads to a 10 per cent increase in demand, then the demand is said to be of unit elasticity. If a 10 per cent fall in price leads to a rise in demand of only 5 per cent then demand would be described as inelastic ($E_D = 0.5$), that is, demand is not very responsive to price changes. Finally, if a 10 per cent fall in price leads to a rise in demand of, say 30 per cent, then demand would be described as elastic ($E_D = 3$).

There is a relationship between the slope of the demand curve and the elasticity of demand and, as a rough approximation, we can say that the steeper the slope of the demand curve, the more inelastic (insensitive) is demand. Figure A.2 illustrates this. The same fall in price produces a much greater increase in demand when demand is elastic (as in b) than when the demand is inelastic (as in a).

A.3 Shifts in demand

Up to now we have been analysing the demand for video cassette recorders *as if* the non-price factors affecting demand were constant (the *ceteris paribus* assumption). We can now relax this assumption and consider the effect of changes in these other variables. The demand for video cassette recorders can be expected to increase as a result of a successful advertising

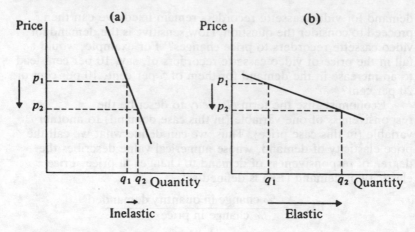

Fig. A.2

campaign by one or more of the manufacturers. We can show the effect of this, in terms of our diagram, by a shift to the right of the demand curve, indicating an increased willingness to purchase video cassette recorders.

In Fig. A.3 the effect of the advertising campaign is to shift the demand curve to D'. Thus, at a price of £500 demand increases from 20 000 units per month before the campaign to 25 000 units per month after the campaign. Another way of expressing the same idea is that, in order to sell 20 000 units, it was necessary before the campaign to sell at a price no higher than £500, whereas after the campaign it is possible to sell 20 000 units at the much higher price of £650.

To develop this point a little further, we can see in Fig. A.3 how an increase in demand from 15 000 to 20 000 units per month could have been caused by one of two factors, viz:

(a) In the absence of any advertising campaign, price falls from £650 to £500 per unit. This causes a movement along the demand curve D. In this case, the non-price factors affecting demand remain constant (*ceteris paribus*) and the amount demanded increases as a result of the fall in price.

(b) With price remaining fixed at £650, the demand curve shifts from D to D', again causing the amount demanded to increase from 15 000 to 20 000 units.

Thus, the expression 'an increase in demand' may either mean a movement along a given demand curve (case a) or a shift of the demand curve (case b) and it is important to distinguish between the two.

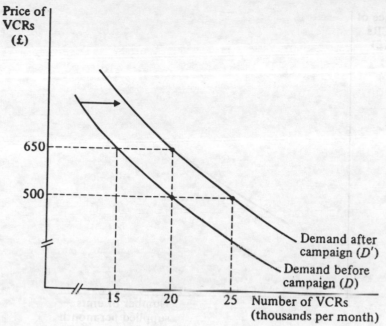

Fig. A.3

A.4 Supply

We now turn to a consideration of those factors which influence the supply of a good. In the example we have chosen, the market for video cassette recorders, the actual supply of these machines obviously emanates from a relatively small number of manufacturers, though there is probably a somewhat larger number of potential manufacturers, and therefore sellers, of these items. We could argue, in fact, that if the demand for these items were very great, so that people were prepared to buy even though prices were very high, more and more electrical firms would find the production and sale of video cassette recorders a profitable business. Hence we could say that the higher the price at which these machines could be sold in the shops, the greater will be the supply of them. Thus, we could imagine a sort of market supply curve – in many ways the analogue of the market demand curve – such as that depicted in Fig. A.4. This market supply curve is drawn under the same *ceteris paribus* assumptions that we applied earlier to the demand curve – that is, all non-price factors which affect the supply of video cassette recorders are assumed to be

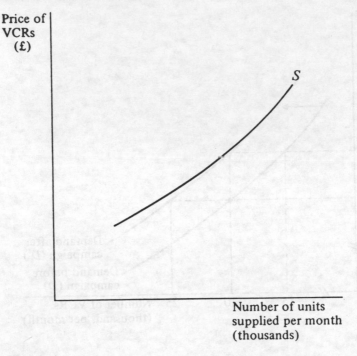

Fig. A.4

held constant. Figure A.4 thus shows the relationship between the number of machines which manufacturers are willing to supply and the price at which they can be sold, *ceteris paribus*. The positive slope of the supply curve illustrates the axiom that an increase in market price is associated with an increase in supply, and vice versa.

A.5 The elasticity of supply

In the same way that we talked in section A.2 about the responsiveness of demand to price changes being measured by the elasticity of demand, so we can talk here about the responsiveness of supply to price changes being measured by the elasticity of supply. The price elasticity of supply (E_S) is defined as:

$$E_S = \frac{\% \text{ change in quantity supplied}}{\% \text{ change in price}}$$

This too will vary between 0 and infinity, a value near zero indicating that supply does not respond very readily to price changes, and a value substantially greater than one indicating that it requires only a small increase in price to bring forth a greatly increased supply. As before, the steepness of the slope of the supply curve gives a rough indication of elasticity of supply, a steep slope indicating inelastic supply and vice versa, as in Fig. A.5. In diagram (a), where supply is elastic, the rise in price results in a much greater increase in supply than that in (b) where supply is inelastic.

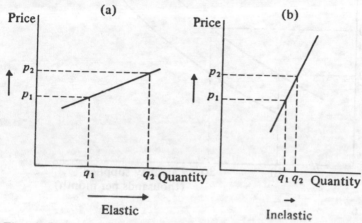

Fig. A.5

A.6 Shifts in the supply curve

Moreover, in the same way that we talked in section A.3 about changes in non-price factors causing shifts in the demand curve, so when we look at the supply curve it is clear that, if we relax the *ceteris paribus* assumption, then changes in certain non-price factors which affect supply will result in a shift to the right or to the left of our supply schedule. For example, a technological advance which allows an important component of a video cassette recorder to be produced much more cheaply will mean that manufacturers will be willing to supply more machines at every price than they were willing to do previously. This is illustrated in Fig. A.6. At a price of £500 per unit, manufacturers are willing to increase their output from 20 000 to 30 000 units per month, since their production costs have fallen. To express the same idea in a different way, we could say that, with the old technology, a monthly output of 30 000 units would only be forthcoming if the price were £650. With the new technology, a price per unit of £500 is sufficient to ensure that level of monthly output.

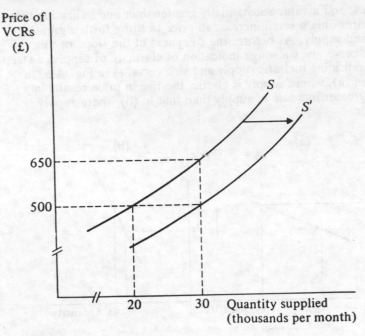

Fig. A.6

A.7 Short run and long run supply

It is tempting to think of the supply curve as a sort of mirror image of the demand curve, and indeed that is the way in which it has been presented here. Although this interpretation is permissible, it is something of an over simplification. The level of monthly output of video cassette recorders which a manufacturer is prepared to produce is obviously limited in the short run by the available manufacturing capacity. When all production lines are fully utilized this sets an upper limit to the amount that can be produced. Generally, the more fully utilized the production line becomes, the more unit costs tend to rise as bottlenecks develop in some stages of the production process; that is, the fixity of certain factors of production results in rising unit costs in the *short run*. This results in an upward sloping unit cost curve (or average cost curve) such as that shown in Fig. A.7.

Moreover, in a somewhat curious way, the short run is *defined* by economists to be that period of time during which at least some factors of production are fixed. Hence the curve in Fig. A.7 would be called a short run average cost curve and its upward slope is due to the fixity of certain factors of production. *In the long run*, that is,

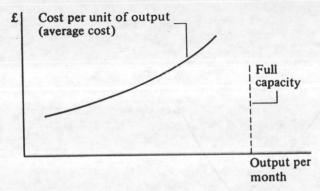

Fig. A.7

in a situation where all factors of production can be varied, there is
no prior reason for supposing that the average cost curve should be
upward sloping. Indeed, a horizontal curve (implying that unit costs
stay constant) or a downward sloping curve (implying that
economies of scale result in lower unit costs as output increases)
would seem to be more likely.

Now, the market supply curve is derived in a rather
complicated way from the addition of the individual cost curves of
the firms within the industry[1]. Thus, we can distinguish between
short run supply curves and long run supply curves depending
upon whether we are thinking of a situation in which there are
some fixed factors (short run) or a situation in which all factors are
variable (long run). The short run supply curve is likely to be
much steeper (that is, more inelastic) than the long run supply
curve since, in the short run, firms will be less able to respond to
increased prices by increasing their output if they are held back by
limited production capacity. In the long run supply will be much
more elastic, since firms can increase their production capacity.

A.8 The interaction of demand and supply: the determination of market price

Having discussed the nature and the determinants of both demand
and supply, we can now proceed to show how the price at which
goods are sold is determined by the interaction of the two. In Fig.
A.8 we put both curves together on the same diagram. At a price
of £500 per unit, total market demand will be 20 000 units per
month. Provided they receive £500 per unit for their product,
manufacturers as a group are willing to supply 20 000 units. Thus
£500 represents an *equilibrium* price, a price at which the demand
is equated with the supply.

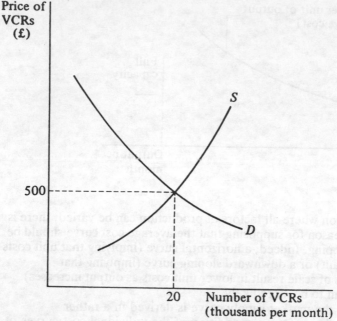

Fig. A.8

To emphasize this point, let us see what would happen at a price of £600 (Fig. A.9). This is a disequilibrium situation because the increase in price from £500 to £600 chokes off some of the demand, which falls back from 20 000 units to 18 000 units per month. Because of the higher sales price, however, manufacturers will be persuaded to increase their output of video cassette recorders to 21 000 units per month. Demand at 18 000 units per month thus falls short of supply at 21 000 units per month. This results in unsold stock in the shops and in the manufacturers' warehouses. Production is cut back in order to avoid an excessive build up of unsold stock and consumers and dealers are offered video cassette recorders at 'discount' prices in an attempt to increase sales. As long as there is an excess supply this process will continue. Prices will fall until we reach the equilibrium price, at which point consumers are prepared to purchase all the output being produced.

It should be stressed that a market – whether it be the market for video cassette recorders or any other market – is a self-equilibriating mechanism. No outside intervention is required in order to ensure that the equilibrium price and equilibrium quantity will eventually be arrived at since there are forces which arise

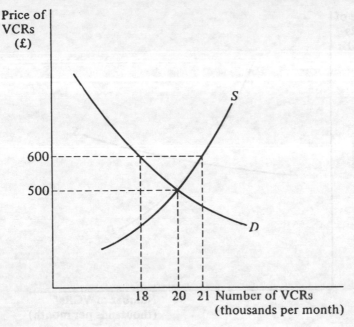

Fig. A.9

automatically, which tend to push the market towards its equilibrium point. Thus, although the market may be out of equilibrium temporarily – and this disequilibrium situation may sometimes be rather prolonged – eventually producers and consumers will respond to the price signals which the market emits, and the amount supplied and demanded will come into equality.

We have chosen to illustrate the economist's conception of the workings of a market in the context of the market for video cassette recorders. This may have seemed a rather unwise choice since, at first sight, it appears as though the price at which video cassette recorders sell in the shops is determined much more by production costs than by the pressure of demand – that is, supply pressures seem to be the dominant influence on price. Although there is an element of truth in this, it is rather like arguing that one blade of a pair of scissors is more important in the cutting process than the other. Both are clearly indispensable, and in the same way price must always be determined by both supply and demand. However, the element of truth is as follows: in the long run, as we argued in section A.7, the supply curve is likely to be fairly elastic, such as that depicted in Fig. A.10. Market price

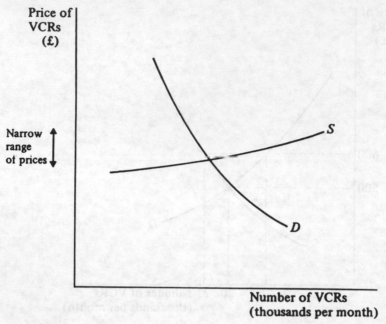

Fig. A.10

therefore will only vary withing a fairly narrow range, and in such a situation we can justifiably talk about price being determined primarily by supply (or cost) factors. The equilibrium quantity is then primarily demand determined.

Note

1. The reader is referred to any microeconomic textbook for a fuller explanation. The market supply curve is (approximately) equal to the horizontal summation of the individual firm's marginal cost curves, assuming each firm is a profit maximizer. Marginal cost is the addition to total cost which results from the production of an additional unit of output, hence it is the first derivative of the total cost function.

Index

absorbtion 66
accelerator 58
accounts, national income 65–9
accuracy of forecasts 259
accuracy of statistics 69–70
accruals adjustment 221
active, economically 149–52
activity rates 161–2
appreciation (of currency) 14
arbitrage, international price 130
asset sales (privatization) 221
asset substitution 88
automatic stabilisers 272
axioms 71

Bacon R. and Eltis W. 185
balance of payments, current
    account 12, 26
balance of payments, capital
    account 13, 26
balance of taxation 245–6
balance of trade 13
balancing item 27
banks, commercial 78
Bank of England 14, 78
barter 1
bilateral exchange rate 134, 139
Bills, Treasury 76, 82, 224
black economy 82
Blue Book 65
Bonds, Treasury 76
bonds, yield of 90
borrowing, impact on money supply
    224
borrowing requirement, public
    sector 220
budget deficit, surplus 50, 76

building society 77–8

capital-output ratio 58
cartel 37, 130
capital account of balance of
    payments 13, 26
cash base 77, 80
cash economy 70, 82
cash ratio 80
CEPG 202, 260
ceteris paribus assumption 276
circular flow of income 5
classical economists 19, 51 3
closed economy 33
commercial banks 77–8
commodity prices 122
comparative advantage 200
comparative statics 62
competitiveness 140
composite commodity 34
consensus on differentials 100
constant price estimates 68
consumption function 54, 61
convertible currency 21
correlation and causation 85
credit money 77
crowding out 82, 226, 233
currency 78
current price estimates 68
cycles 269

debt, national 76, 91, 221
deflation 21, 39
deflator, price 68
de-industrialization 187
demand inflation 47
Dennison E. F. 178